EDUCATION, POLITICS, AND PUBLIC LIFE

Series Editors:
Henry A. Giroux, McMaster University
Susan Searls Giroux, McMaster University

Within the last three decades, education as a political, moral, and ideological practice has become central to rethinking not only the role of public and higher education, but also the emergence of pedagogical sites outside of the schools—which include but are not limited to the Internet, television, film, magazines, and the media of print culture. Education as both a form of schooling and public pedagogy reaches into every aspect of political, economic, and social life. What is particularly important in this highly interdisciplinary and politically nuanced view of education are a number of issues that now connect learning to social change, the operations of democratic public life, and the formation of critically engaged individual and social agents. At the center of this series will be questions regarding what young people, adults, academics, artists, and cultural workers need to know to be able to live in an inclusive and just democracy and what it would mean to develop institutional capacities to reintroduce politics and public commitment into everyday life. Books in this series aim to play a vital role in rethinking the entire project of the related themes of politics, democratic struggles, and critical education within the global public sphere.

SERIES EDITORS:

HENRY A. GIROUX holds the Global TV Network Chair in English and Cultural Studies at McMaster University in Canada. He is on the editorial and advisory boards of numerous national and international scholarly journals.

Professor Giroux was selected as a Kappa Delta Pi Laureate in 1998 and was the recipient of a Getty Research Institute Visiting Scholar Award in 1999. He was the recipient of the Hooker Distinguished Professor Award for 2001. He received an Honorary Doctorate of Letters from Memorial University of Newfoundland in 2005. His most recent books include Take Back Higher Education (coauthored with Susan Searls Giroux, 2006), America on the Edge (2006), Beyond the Spectacle of Terrorism (2006), Stormy Weather: Katrina and the Politics of Disposability (2006), The University in Chains: Confronting the Military-Industrial-Academic Complex (2007), and Against the Terror of Neoliberalism: Politics Beyond the Age of Greed (2008).

SUSAN SEARLS GIROUX is associate professor of English and Cultural Studies at McMaster University. Her most recent books include The Theory Toolbox (coauthored with Jeff Nealon, 2004), Take Back Higher Education (coauthored with Henry A. Giroux, 2006), and Between Race and Reason: Violence, Intellectual Responsibility, and the University to Come (2010).

Professor Giroux is also the managing editor of The Review of Education, Pedagogy, and Cultural Studies.

Critical Pedagogy in Uncertain Times: Hope and Possibilities
Edited by Sheila L. Macrine

The Gift of Education: Public Education and Venture Philanthropy
Kenneth J. Saltman

Feminist Theory in Pursuit of the Public: Women and the "Re-Privatization" of Labor
Robin Truth Goodman

Hollywood's Exploited: Public Pedagogy, Corporate Movies, and Cultural Crisis
Edited by Benjamin Frymer, Tony Kashani, Anthony J. Nocella, II, and Richard Van Heertum; Foreword by Lawrence Grossberg

Education Out of Bounds: Reimagining Cultural Studies for a Posthuman Age
Tyson E. Lewis and Richard Kahn

Academic Freedom in the Post-9/11 Era
Edited by Edward J. Carvalho and David B. Downing

Educating Youth for a World beyond Violence: A Pedagogy for Peace
H. Svi Shapiro

Rituals and Student Identity in Education: Ritual Critique for a New Pedagogy
Richard A. Quantz with Terry O'Connor and Peter Magolda

Citizen Youth: Culture, Activism, and Agency in a Neoliberal Era
Jacqueline Kennelly

Conflicts in Curriculum Theory: Challenging Hegemonic Epistemologies
João M. Paraskeva; Foreword by Donaldo Macedo

Sport, Spectacle, and NASCAR Nation: Consumption and the Cultural Politics of Neoliberalism
Joshua I. Newman and Michael D. Giardina

America According to Colbert: Satire as Public Pedagogy
Sophia A. McClennen

Immigration and the Challenge of Education: A Social Drama Analysis in South Central Los Angeles
Nathalia E. Jaramillo

Education as Civic Engagement: Toward a More Democratic Society
Edited by Gary A. Olson and Lynn Worsham

Why Higher Education Should Have a Leftist Bias
Donald Lazere

WHY HIGHER EDUCATION SHOULD HAVE A LEFTIST BIAS

By Donald Lazere

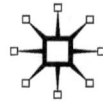

WHY HIGHER EDUCATION SHOULD HAVE A LEFTIST BIAS
Copyright © Donald Lazere, 2013.

All rights reserved.

First published in 2013 by
PALGRAVE MACMILLAN®
in the United States—a division of St. Martin's Press LLC,
175 Fifth Avenue, New York, NY 10010.

Where this book is distributed in the UK, Europe and the rest of the world, this is by Palgrave Macmillan, a division of Macmillan Publishers Limited, registered in England, company number 785998, of Houndmills, Basingstoke, Hampshire RG21 6XS.

Palgrave Macmillan is the global academic imprint of the above companies and has companies and representatives throughout the world.

Palgrave® and Macmillan® are registered trademarks in the United States, the United Kingdom, Europe and other countries.

ISBN: 978–1–137–34964–4

Library of Congress Cataloging-in-Publication Data

Lazere, Donald.
    Why higher education should have a leftist bias / Donald Lazere.
      pages cm.—(Education, politics, and public life)
    Includes bibliographical references and index.
    ISBN 978–1–137–34964–4 (hardback)
     1. Education, Higher—Political aspects—United States. I. Title.

LC173.L39 2013
379.73—dc23   2013023456

A catalogue record of the book is available from the British Library.

Design by Newgen Knowledge Works (P) Ltd., Chennai, India.

First edition: December 2013

10 9 8 7 6 5 4 3 2 1

Contents

Preface — vii

Postscript — xix

Introduction The Dilemma of Culture-Wars Polemics: Distinguishing Valuable Originals from Gross Parodies — 1

Part I Countering the Bias of Business as Usual

1 Conservatism as the Unmarked Norm — 15
2 Restricted-Code Conservatism — 35
3 Socialism as a Cognitive Alternative — 55

Part II Countering the Conservative Counter-Establishment

4 The Conservative Attack Machine: "Admit Nothing, Deny Everything, Launch Counterattack" — 75
5 Right-Wing Deconstruction: Mimicry and False Equivalencies — 95
6 From *Partisan Review* to *Fox News*: Neoconservatives as Defenders of Intellectual Standards — 119
7 Conservative Scholarship: Seeing the Object as It Really Isn't — 143

Part III Responsible Leftist Teaching

8 Balancing Commitment and Openness in Teaching: Giving Conservatives Their Best Shot — 171
9 A Case Study: Leftist versus Conservative Arguments on College Costs — 187

10	The Radical Humanistic Canon	209
Conclusion	An Appeal to Conservative Readers	233

Notes   237
Works Cited   245
Index   261

Preface

In this book, I argue that conservatives' case against leftist bias in education, as well as in media and politics itself, turns reality upside down: Critical pedagogy and left media have a legitimate responsibility to provide minimal balance against the far more powerful forms of conservative bias in American society. I identify two sources of these forms of conservative bias, tacit and calculated. The calculated forms are, at any given time, more newsworthy, egregious, and directly influential on society; thus they might be expected to dominate the opening sections of the book. In my design, however, I defer discussing them until part II, giving priority in part I to the tacit forms because it is only by foregrounding the all-pervasive forms of conservative bias that are generally not even perceived as such but only as business as usual, the "unmarked" norm of neutrality, that the disproportion in the arguments advanced in the calculated forms becomes fully apparent.

Part I, then, begins with the conventions of semantic framing in American public discourse, which may be established partly by conservatives' design but become habitual assumptions in politics, media, education, and general consciousness. Thus our discourse is confined to a narrow spectrum whose leftward limit is the Democratic-Party version of governance by relatively liberal, wealthy corporate and military executives—so that supposed liberals like President Obama must constantly profess their faith in economic free enterprise, American exceptionalism, and military superiority. Meanwhile democratic socialist and even social-democratic viewpoints, even (or especially?) when propounded by distinguished scholars and intellectual journalists, are labeled "loony left," as far off the charts of acceptable discourse as the Ku Klux Klan or American Nazis. This skewing of the public agenda to the right enables conservative polemicists to grossly exaggerate the extent of leftist bias in mainstream discourse. In 2012, future senator Ted Cruz of Texas claimed in a campaign speech that in the early nineties when he and Barack Obama were students at Harvard Law

School, "'There were fewer declared Republicans in the faculty when we were there than Communists! There was one Republican. But there were twelve who would say they were Marxists who believed in the Communists overthrowing the United States government'" (quoted in Mayer, "Is Senator Ted Cruz Our New McCarthy?").

A further tacit, semantic convention is equivocations on the meanings of "conservatism," which play up the more idealistic, theoretical versions while downplaying the more tawdry forms of "actual, existing conservatism," including the multiple realms of corporate power, the unscrupulous pursuit of wealth, and the limited stage of cognitive development in the conservative "base" susceptible to demagogic appeals to religion, patriotism, xenophobia, and every ethnocentric prejudice. One more form of tacit bias is what I call the politics of no politics, an avoidance of thinking about politics at all, which pervades American society and contributes by default to maintaining the conservative status quo, preeminently through erasing public consciousness of the power of corporations in politics. This avoidance results in public attention being directed to issues of political bias only in overt, ad hoc, and sensational instances, say, of left political correctness, while political correctness in business's business as usual goes unremarked.

The calculated forms of conservative bias, surveyed in part II, include periodic offensives launched from the 1970s to the present by an array of organizations, mostly aligned with the Republican Party, that have attempted to control public perceptions of bias in politics, economics, media, and education. As a grizzled veteran of nearly half a century of the culture wars, I review in chapters 6 and 7 the history of neoconservative intellectuals and of conservative academic organizations—including some of my favorite golden-oldie episodes—with the aim of confirming their integral connection, despite their leaders' repeated denials, to the more lowbrow operations of the Republican attack apparatus. I trace the steps by which these intellectual movements have gradually degenerated to the present point where they have merged indistinguishably with the know-nothing right wing of Fox News, the Tea Party, and Sarah Palin (who has been lauded by erstwhile defenders of intellectual standards like Norman Podhoretz and William Kristol).

My introduction and chapter 5 address the dilemmas posed by one tactic in these conservative polemics—to obstruct reasoned public debate by mimicking any and all evidence or arguments favoring leftists, to turn them against leftists. The introduction concludes with my suggested model for a meta-polemical approach to studying this tactic, which becomes a point of reference through the rest of the book.

The three chapters in part III apply the previous themes to my models for responsible teaching practices by leftist college faculties. Chapter 8 describes an argumentative writing course I have taught that embodies my method of facilitating fair-minded study of conservative versus liberal or left sources and arguments, and chapter 9 applies that method to studying the issue of the escalating cost of college education, with detailed attention to the work of conservative economist Richard Vedder on this subject. Chapter 10 challenges both conservative defenses of the humanistic canon and leftist rejections of it, by affirming the elements of rebellion, skepticism, and ribaldry within that canon, as legitimate subject matter for liberal arts courses.

I frame all these issues and arguments within a disciplinary framework of critical thinking, argumentative rhetoric, general semantics, developmental psychology, and sociolinguistics, which was fully developed in *Reading and Writing for Civic Literacy*. And I immodestly put forward this framework, not only as a possible model for the entire enterprise of liberal education, but for American political and media discourse in general. However, I am all too aware that our major political parties and media are generally impervious to such challenges from scholars to their modes of business as usual, and that even within the internal, departmental balkanization of today's academic world and publishing industry, this kind of conceptual framework is just likely to be consigned to one or another obscure disciplinary corner of specialization; indeed, this is one of the many ways I survey in which all potential forces for leftism in America are narrowly confined.

To what audience is this book addressed, then? Aye, there's the rub. In today's balkanized American politics, media, and scholarship, it is extremely difficult to communicate with anyone outside one's own ideological camp. It is similarly difficult for intellectuals and academics to communicate with the broader audience addressed by mass media because of the anti-intellectual, antiacademic, sound-bite bias of mainstream politics, journalism, and entertainment media. This dilemma is compounded by the grim reality that much of the American left has been reduced to scholars or intellectual journalists, so that the anti-intellectualism of mainstream discourse also amounts to an anti-leftist bias. For example, in July 2011, Thomas Frank, a University of Chicago PhD and presently one of the leading leftist intellectual journalists, was allowed a rare appearance on a CNN panel, about the debt-ceiling crisis in Congress. He tried to frame this issue in terms of his book *The Wrecking Crew: How Conservatives Rule*, which describes a self-fulfilling prophecy whereby American conservatives denounce government inefficiency, then when they gain control over government, do their utmost to make sure it is inefficient, while deflecting public anger toward pro-government liberals, in this case President Obama. But Frank was interrupted in mid-sentence about a minute into his extended explanation by the moderator calling time, ignoring what he said, and turning to other panelists who changed the subject. Conservative intellectuals and academics are in somewhat the same dilemma, although conservative think tanks have outdone liberal or leftist ones in using public relations agents to produce press releases, op-eds, and TV and radio appearances for which writers and speakers are prepped in sound bites.

So it is sadly predictable that a book like mine defending the academic left will only be published by a press specializing in that niche market and mainly be read by fellow academic leftists. Nevertheless, I have perhaps wistfully conceived the intended readership for this book as conservative academics and intellectuals and even some mainstream journalists, politicians, and general readers who share some of my concerns and may be open to dialogue on others. At the least, I can hope that such readers will be prompted to engage me in debate on the reasoned, civil level that I call for here as an alternative to polarized culture-wars invective, and I invite them to hold me accountable for lapses in my own reasoning and civility level. On several previous occasions I have tried to establish such a dialogue with conservative intellectuals, in a few cases successfully, in others not so much. I have lengthy email files of such efforts with David Horowitz and the leaders of the National Association of Scholars, which are available to readers on request, at dlazere@igc.org. I have also invited some conservatives I am on good terms with to write a response to be published in the book, without any takers, but I encourage others to respond after publication.

Does the qualified case I make for teachers and scholars advocating a leftist viewpoint mean that I endorse political correctness? To begin with, perhaps that infamous phrase should be in quotation marks, to indicate its reference to the term as a fabrication, by the conservative attack apparatus whose workings over the past four decades I will delineate here, and by the mainstream media that have lazily parroted that attack, generally without bothering to verify the accuracy of its allegations. However, I am not in denial that there is any such reality as political correctness. "Political correctness exists, even if Lynne Cheney and the National Association of Scholars say it does," was a byword of Teachers for a Democratic Culture (TDC), an organization I was active in that thrived in the 1990s, started by English professors Gerald Graff and Gregory Jay, which had a plague-on-both-your-houses position toward both the real thing and unscrupulous conservative exploitation of it. (TDC's position was best supported in two books by John K. Wilson, *The Myth of Political Correctness* and *Patriotic Correctness*.) I have long done scholarly battle with many truly obnoxious leftists and what I call "diverseologues" in academia and elsewhere. (See Lazere, *The Retreat from Political Literacy in Rhetcomp Studies*.)

Nevertheless, in virtually every case, the scale and influence of leftists' misdeeds has been miniscule in proportion to those of countless malefactors on the right whom leftists expose to scrutiny, but about whom conservative critics tend to get far less indignant. I hold no brief for Ward Churchill, but at his worst, after all, how great a public menace was he, compared to Ken Lay, Jack Abramoff, and Bernard Madoff, the bankers who contrived the predatory lending and subprime-mortgage disasters in the late 2000s, or the multitude of corrupt wheeler-dealers in the military-industrial complex? Incidentally, here is a small sampling of the dozens of obscene bigoted, emails Churchill's department at Boulder received after the controversy over Churchill's "little Eichmanns" gaffe (Perez):

From: David Bland
To: Chancellor Phil DiStefano
CC: Ward Churchill

I am writing this letter...to voice my distaste and gross disappointment in your dubious judgment in hiring and retaining such a repugnant and repulsive human being as Ward Churchill....I suppose for a pathetic American Indian like himself, he sees this as some sort of payback to the United States for what he sees as injustices to the American Indian 150 years ago....I implore you not to be intimidated by this pathetic excuse for a man and a human being. Fire his sorry *ass!...It's too bad that he is one Indian that got away!

****

From: Rob Ebright
To: Ethnic Studies
Subject: Ward Churchill is a d*ckhead

I must laugh at your so called college department. Tell Ward, my ancestors killed a lot of Indians and I'm proud of it.

Compare the extent of public attention and indignation toward Churchill's foolishness with that afforded this kind of ignorance and bigotry on the right, which is far more widespread than acknowledged by conservative polemicists, especially those who wallow in self-pity over the abuse they receive from intolerant liberals, such as in a similar display of hate mail received by the American Council of Trustees and Alumni in response to their criticism of unpatriotic academics after 9/11 (Martin and Neal). What annoys me most about irresponsible leftists like Churchill is their ingenuousness in playing into the hands of Republican operatives like the late Andrew Breitbart, who manufactured highly publicized, selectively edited sting videos defaming the Association of Community Organizations for Reform Now (ACORN, US Department of Agriculture official Shirley Sherrod (who sued him), and two pro-labor teachers at the University of Missouri, Kansas City (see http://labornotes.org/2011/04/right-wing-hoaxster-smears-labor-educators).

What kind of leftist am I and what kind of leftism do I advocate teaching? It is a pretty broad, eclectic kind in both cases. My politics lie between democratic socialist and social-democratic, and are on an intellectual level rather than that of militant action by workers, although I am centrally concerned with how intellectuals can act in concert with workers and the undiminished numbers of the wretched of the earth. Anyone in America criticizing free enterprise and saying a word in favor of socialism will be smeared as a commissar seeking to suppress democracy and freedom of enterprise and thought, but I submit that it is the present degeneration of free enterprise that has suppressed a full range of viewpoints, and the essence of my "radicalism" is seeking means of expanding free discourse in politics, media, and education. So I do not advocate dogmatic imposition of socialist views, but only their being allowed a place at the table of American public discourse, evaluated in every instance against the strongest arguments for capitalism or the free market. A voice for socialists is justified more than ever in the atmosphere of the 2010s when our two capitalist-party system and corporate media may be terminally incapable of coping with the economic and environmental problems they have done much to create. Who knows? Maybe the final crisis of capitalism may really be upon us, long after most Marxists consigned it to the realm of fundamentalist End-Times predictions.

Am I a Marxist, then? No, not in the sense of being an authority on Marxism, viewing it as the measure of all things, believing that the working class will be the agent of socialist revolution, or endorsing any government or movement in the world just because it calls itself

Marxist. However, I do find a great deal of validity in anticommunistic Marxist concepts and critical works, especially concerning power relations in political economy and social class, along with the myriad gaps, evasions, and mystifications to be found in public discourse and cultural works that ignore or dismiss those concepts. (I discuss a few examples from cultural criticism in chapter 3.) In that respect, I again simply argue against the red-baiting exclusion of Marxist views (both communistic and anticommunistic) in our public discourse, and I lament the retreat from academic Marxism in recent decades, after its productive peak in the sixties and seventies. Publishers of academic Marxist works like Routledge, Verso, Bergin & Garvey,, Boynton-Cook, Westview, and South End Press have either gone out of business, retreated from left politics, or been engulfed and devoured by corporate conglomerates. (Terry Eagleton, professor emeritus at Oxford, made a brave, nuanced attempt to reaffirm Marxist history and economics in *Why Marx Was Right* in 2011—Eagleton's international eminence as a literary theorist enabled the book to be published by Yale—but it has mostly been ignored in both mainstream and academic media.)

The preface and introduction to my *American Media and Mass Culture: Left Perspectives* in 1987 surveyed the range of Marxist and other (anticommunistic) leftist thought in the emerging, interdisciplinary field of cultural studies; the collection mainly emphasized continuations of Frankfurt School critical theory, which I also attempt to reaffirm in this book, against its facile rejection by postmodernists and other current cultural studies theorists. No conservative critics to my knowledge have ever discussed *American Media* or the responsible level of democratic-left scholarship like that of its 30-some contributors; they prefer to dig up every wilder expression of communism, postmodernism, and cultural studies that can be easily derided. Right-wing demagogues can gain publicity with charges that there is "a Marxist network" of "13,000 faculty members" in American universities (*Conservative Digest*, Jan. 1983), without bothering to document how such figures are calculated, to define Marxism and distinguish communistic from anticommunistic Marxists (or some shades in-between), between self-styled Marxist governments or parties and Marxist intellectual thought, or to acknowledge that there is wide diversity among Marxist scholars, who have about the same range of intelligence and integrity within their ranks as any other academic school, so that the work of each must be evaluated on its own merits. The power of Marxist cultural critique at its best is periodically reconfirmed by works like Henry Giroux's 2013 *Youth in*

Revolt, which draws from Frankfurt School critical theory to launch a devastating assault on the utter surrender by contemporary capitalism of any moral or aesthetic opposition to the debasement of American society by profit-motivated violence in both the proliferation of weaponry and the blood-drenched mass culture, especially as it bombards children and adolescents. (Conflict of Interest Watch: As acknowledged in the front matter, Henry and Susan Giroux are advisory editors for the Palgrave-Macmillan series in which this book was published.)

Nor was I born and bred as a leftist. After growing up in a conservative, completely unintellectual family of shopkeepers and salespeople in Des Moines, I was a scholarship student at Brown and Northwestern. My undergraduate and graduate degrees were in English and French, with emphasis on the intersections between language, literature, and politics, which I have continued to pursue through my subsequent career. In a five-year hiatus after college, I studied for an MA part-time at Columbia while working in a succession of jobs on Madison Avenue in advertising, public relations, and celebrity journalism. That experience exposed me to the more tawdry aspects of the upper circles of power and wealth in America and to the contempt that many of the conservative elitists in those circles privately express toward the masses they claim to champion. I also concluded that the liberal arts are among the few educational or occupational sites in America not subservient to conservative interests, so I moved to Berkeley for doctoral study in English at the height of campus protest in the mid-sixties, which was for me an inspirational challenge to the whole social order epitomized by Madison Avenue. I wrote my dissertation, later published as *The Unique Creation of Albert Camus*, about Camus's integration of literature, language, and politics, as both a writer of fiction and drama and as a political journalist and public intellectual. It also dealt with his importance for American readers, including his influence on the New Left as an advocate of pacifism, nonviolent resistance, and left-communitarianism.

However, the strongest influence in my political formation was my membership in Berkeley, during the years following the Free Speech Movement, in the Independent Socialist Club, whose mentors were Hal Draper, a University of California librarian, veteran of the New York anti-Stalinist left and brilliant independent scholar of Marxism, and his wife Anne, a labor activist. The position of ISC, (later to merge with the International Socialist Organization), was that capitalism and communism were in many ways mirror images (despite capitalism's far less totalitarian modes of rule), whose rival elites perpetrate endless wars (actual or cold) to terrorize, subjugate, and impoverish their own peoples, in the manner of the rulers of the three superpowers in Orwell's *1984*: "So long as they remain in conflict, they prop one another up like three sheaves of corn" (162)—to avert democratic, worker-controlled socialism. This position has been continued in little magazines like *New Politics, Against the Current,* and *International Socialist Review.* ISC's alumni from that period, many of them leaders in the Free Speech Movement, became prominent activists for labor like Michael Parker and Kim Moody, for human rights like Joanne Landy, and for environmentalism like Jack Weinberg (famous in FSM as the arrested protestor in a police car immobilized by a sit-in), along with labor-oriented social scientists Nelson Lichtenstein and James Petras, and political journalist and playwright Barbara Garson, author of several great studies of American working class life like *All the Livelong Day: The Meaning and Demeaning of Routine Work* and *Down the Up Escalator: How the 99 Percent Live in the Great Recession.* My experience there again belies conservatives' unscrupulous lumping together of the communist and anticommunist left.

My second important political affinity group, also going back to New Left activism in the 1960s, has been the Radical Caucus in the Modern Language Association (MLA). Its orientation is toward studies in democratic socialism, American working-class culture, feminism, antiracism, and antimilitarism, embodied in the journal *Radical Teacher,* which since 1975 has maintained a level of scholarly quality that gives the lie to conservative derision of these fields of study. (Radical Caucus has also been more oriented toward Marxist political economy than the Marxist Literary Group in MLA, focused on European philosophical theory.) From the beginning, its most eminent, indefatigable leaders have been Richard Ohmann, Louis Kampf, Paul Lauter, and Susan O'Malley, who have produced an exemplary body of leftist criticism free from dogma or theoretical jargon.[1] They are high among the tenured radicals at prestige colleges whom conservatives love to hate, refusing to grant the respect their accomplishments have earned, Dick at Wesleyan and Paul at Trinity having attained endowed professorships and administrative positions and Louis (now retired, as is Dick) at MIT—where he used to teach a course with Noam Chomsky— having been elected president of the MLA for a year that was quite unrevolutionary, despite the apocalyptic alarms of conservative culture warriors. Susan, longtime activist for labor and feminism, is professor of English at Kingsborough Community College and at City University of New York (Graduate

Center, where she has been chair of the Faculty Senate and Faculty Trustee on the CUNY Board of Trustees. Notwithstanding their comfortable academic positions, all four have donated an incredible amount of their time and energy, without a penny in payment, for over 35 years to the Radical Caucus and *Radical Teacher*, with circulation of a couple thousand. The *RT* financial statement posted in June 2012 indicated a bank balance of $5938.67, and noted, "We are facing three bills for printing and mailing this year. The total should be in the neighborhood of $7,000-$7500. We also have to pay about $500 to subscribers whose subs extend into next year as well as some mailing costs that UIP incurs on our behalf. Dick has indicated that older board members might be counted on for $5000-$6000 in donations." George Soros, please call *RT*!

That is the kind of evidence I adduce against conservative polemicists who grotesquely exaggerate power on the left but who, in some cases, appear to be projecting their own, vastly greater level of power and wealth onto such leftists. In her 1995 book *Telling the Truth*, Lynne Cheney singled out Ohmann (without any indication that she had read more than a few snippets of his work), *RT*, and even me (see chapter 7) as powerful, subversive forces, at the time when her husband had recently been secretary of defense and was then-CEO of Halliburton Industries, with net worth of some $100 million. (*Telling* 96, 100, 111).

My teaching career also contributed strongly to my viewpoint here. Following graduate school and several years of unemployment and part-time teaching in the suddenly depressed job market of the seventies, I was hired in 1977 as a professor at Cal Poly, San Luis Obispo, where for over 20 years my main duties were teaching lower-division general education requirements in composition and literary surveys for students in technological majors. I have also put in stretches as a visiting professor or adjunct at Hayward State, San Jose State, St. Mary's College (in Moraga, California), Loyola College of Maryland, the University of Iowa, and most recently, as an emeritus lecturer, the University of Tennessee at Knoxville, where I now live. The student bodies in most of these schools were predominantly Middle American whites, like I was, from provincial or suburban backgrounds, fresh out of high school, limited in their political views to the conservative commonplaces they had heard from their parents and peers, and single-mindedly motivated toward occupational education—often to the point of resenting any general education requirements at all. Few had ever been exposed to explicitly leftist ideas in their education or exposure to mass media, so it was my years of experiences in trying to introduce them to such ideas that led me to the positions I espouse in this book. Faculty leftists were so rare there that I was regarded by colleagues, administrators, and students as an exotic curiosity, and I got along well with nearly all. Thus my life has cycled between settings that are conservative and liberal, provincial and cosmopolitan, academic and nonacademic, Ivy League and state college—the whole "red state" and "blue state" spectrum. That is why I am amused when conservative critics pigeonhole me as a typical tenured radical disdaining the masses and spouting dogmatic theories from an elitist academic sinecure.

One can understand that as conservative scholars see it, they are outnumbered, outspent, and discriminated against in the humanities and social sciences, and so, as detailed in subsequent chapters, they have turned to corporate foundations and the Republican Party as their only recourse. Nothing should prevent them from doing this, but neither would anything prevent these acolytes of free market competition and overcoming adversity through individual spunk from independently gaining a foothold in academia and expanding it purely through the value of their ideas and scholarship, as leftists like those of us in the Radical Caucus have done over five decades, against a great deal of intimidation, including many of us having lost jobs protesting the Vietnam War and being afraid to list *RT* on our vitas. For every story conservatives produce about discrimination against conservative faculty and students, we can counter with one about the reverse. (See Wilson, *The Myth* and *Patriotic Correctness* and Schrecker, *The Lost Soul of Higher Education*.)

In application to teaching practice, my version of critical pedagogy aims to raise students' level of cognitive development beyond that of the uninformed conservatism of many if not most entering college students at the kind of Middle American colleges where I have taught; that is, I argue here and in other works that the restricted cognitive patterns dominating American socialization in most social classes (with the largest exceptions at the bottom and the top) and in most public discourse also, sometimes inadvertently, induce predominantly conservative attitudes, not in the sense of a reasoned conservative ideology, but in the sense of uncritical conformity that reinforces the social status quo and precludes oppositional consciousness. On this level, liberal education by definition has the mandate of broadening students' perspectives beyond those of their upbringing and fostering more mature, complex modes of reasoning. In other words, our goal should be to raise our students to the level of debate between informed conservatives, liberals, and leftists. My point here is certain to be misrepresented, so although I will be expanding on it throughout the book, I need to qualify it as clearly as possible at the outset. Obviously, conservative positions may be defensible on a more complex cognitive or intellectual level. Indeed, some of my own positions can be interpreted as conservative on that level, and I appeal here to conservative educators to make common cause with liberal and left counterparts in elevating the quality of American civic education to that of reasoned debate in both postsecondary and secondary schooling, as well as in the discourse of politics and media themselves.

Postscript

I formulated many of my positions in this book before Barack Obama's election as president in 2008, and am completing this shortly after his 2012 reelection. His two terms (extending the string of Democratic presidencies to 16 out of the last 24 years), Democratic control of the Senate, the broader leftward movement accompanying them, and the disintegration of the Republican Party's coalition might have somewhat changed the scenario I present. It is also possible, though, that this period might be a blip in the long-term conservative reign and will be erased by backlash against it, partly fueled by worldwide economic decline. At the most optimistic, it is obvious by now that Obama's administration and the Democratic Congress were tightly restrained by the permanent military-industrial-financial complex's control of government and media, and that whatever progressive gains Democrats might have made (e.g., in health care, progressive taxes, environmental issues, and corporate regulation) were likely to be very limited and slow in coming. Barring economic, environmental, or other catastrophes, it would probably take decades of gradual movement to the left in public consciousness, and perhaps an end to the two-capitalist-party monopoly, for significant change in the direction I am advocating here. So my case stands for a role in higher education for leftist viewpoints outside the mainstream of American public discourse. It is conceivable, though unlikely, that the locus of American politics could eventually shift far enough to the left that it would become the "conservative" norm, and higher-level conservatism would become the necessary opposition needing to be promoted by teachers.

Introduction

THE DILEMMA OF CULTURE-WARS POLEMICS: DISTINGUISHING VALUABLE ORIGINALS FROM GROSS PARODIES

> Everything spiritual and valuable has a gross, revolting parody, which looks exactly like it. Only unremitting judgment can distinguish between them.
> (William Empson, paraphrasing Jonathan Swift, *Some 58.*)

My argument in this book is that the ceaseless assault in recent decades by conservative polemicists against political correctness among academic leftists (along with the parallel assault on "the liberal media") has in large part been calculated as a red herring to distract public attention from far more pervasive misdeeds by political and corporate conservatives. Although this assault may in some cases have some validity, in many other cases it does not, and I submit that conservative propagandists have widely subordinated scrupulous efforts to distinguish valid from invalid cases to the greater goal of scapegoating the American left for every socioeconomic or cultural ill. So it is necessary to place the conservative assault on leftist political correctness in the context of a continuous series of political and cultural offensives since the 1970s by what has variously been termed "the right-wing propaganda machine" (Conason), "the Republican noise machine" (Brock), "the conservative counter-establishment" (Blumenthal), or "the conservative echo-chamber" (Alterman). Subsequent chapters will describe in detail the origins, components, and political and rhetorical strategies of this apparatus.

Foremost among those strategies, I suggest, is conservatives' deliberate cooption of any and every piece of evidence or line of argument in support of the left, through initiating pseudo-research purporting to refute all opposing evidence, and through designing "scripts" and "talking points," disseminated throughout the apparatus, to overwhelm all opposing arguments, regardless of their actual merits, through sheer force of volume and repetition. The language of these arguments often is designed precisely to replicate or mimic the vocabulary, reasoning, and ethos of leftists. Thus David Horowitz writes, "I encourage [fellow Republicans] to use the language that the left has deployed so effectively on behalf of its agendas. Radical professors have created a 'hostile learning environment' for conservative students. There is a lack of 'intellectual diversity' on college faculties and in academic classrooms. The conservative viewpoint is 'underrepresented' in the curriculum and on the reading lists. The university should be an 'inclusive' and intellectually 'diverse' community" (Horowitz, "Campus Blacklist"). Conservatives similarly ridicule phrases like "right-wing propaganda machine" as exactly the same kind of loony conspiracy theory that the left claims to find on the right. They further mimic each of the epithets liberals apply to conservatives, turning them into the "left-wing propaganda machine," "the Democratic noise machine," and so on.

But there is a complex dilemma here. It may be that, as in the example of Horowitz, his intention is deceit and obfuscation, but it is also possible that he fully believes it is leftists who are deceitful in their use of such phrases and that conservatives can lay more legitimate claim to them. There are several logical possibilities in such situations. The left allegations against conservatives may be more accurate; conservatives' against the left may be; or both may be partially accurate, with some contradictory views attributable to good faith misunderstandings and subjective interpretations. We all need to guard against ethnocentric assumptions of rectitude on our side. Absent a confession of deviousness by conservatives in any given situation (such as David Brock made in *Blinded by the Right* about his journalistic "hit pieces" against Anita Hill and her supporters against Clarence Thomas), conscientious leftists have no choice but to consider conservatives' assertions at face value and engage them in debate with scholarly support, rhetorical integrity, and "unremitting judgment."

And yet, and yet. The greatest danger made possible by the refinement of the kind of mimicry above is that it can make it virtually impossible for anyone—especially anyone in the general public without leisure time, not attuned to the facts at issue or to critical study of rhetoric—to distinguish a valuable original from a gross parody. Those with the intent to deceive—whoever they may be—will predictably resort to high-minded calls for open-mindedness and a fair hearing for all sides, even as they lie through their teeth and try to stifle their opponents. Their ultimate aim will be to jam the airwaves of public opinion and create political paralysis, leaving the power structure of the status quo unchallenged. A secondary aim will be to keep opponents constantly on the defense, forced to exhaust their energies refuting spurious claims.

Obviously I believe, on the basis of several decades in the trenches of the culture wars, that American conservatives have in fact perpetrated these devious rhetorical strategies, and this book applies unremitting judgment to support that belief. But I also know that conservatives will try to turn the tables on every argument that I and others on the left make. So my case needs to be made in awareness of the general principle that arguments that do not just preach to the converted need to be framed within a rhetorical stance that does not begin from foregone conclusions, that subjects each of us to scrutinize our own subjective or partisan biases, that anticipates counterarguments at every point, and that applies the same critical standards to our own side's arguments to our opponents', leading to comprehensive weighing of arguments and evidence on both sides—ideally in a collaborative effort between opponents.

The rhetorical and pedagogical method I have devised for dealing with these dilemmas strives for a meta-polemical perspective that begins with identifying—in an account acceptable to those on all sides involved—the major realms of power at issue and the interest groups seeking to dominate them. The identification of these realms and interest groups, to the agreement of those on the opposing sides, can become a neutral starting point for analysis of the relative quality of the opposing bodies of evidence and lines of argument—allowing value judgments finally to be made on balance, always subject to contradiction, refinement, and further dialogue. This process can lead, at the very least, toward agreement between opponents on what they disagree about and reduction of their talking past each other with differing definitions, slanted language, and stacking the deck through selectivity in subjects. Any such endeavor obviously depends on willingness by those on both sides to engage in good faith dialogue. If those on one side are unwilling, that would seem to be smoking-gun evidence discrediting their position.

The following is a tentative list of the major forms of political power in contemporary America nationally (and with some adjustments, at the state and local level), and of the kind of interest groups competing for power. The list is randomly ordered, to avoid stacking the deck by rank-ordering them by implied importance of their power. The issue for debate then becomes the balance of power between those that support conservative, libertarian, liberal, or leftist causes, the Republican versus the Democratic Party (or other parties), in terms of the amount of money each has and spends, and of other demonstrable exercises of power. This debate would then be based on the empirical evidence that those on opposing sides are able to produce and the validity of the rhetorical uses of that evidence.

Realms of Power:
- Power of employers (to hire, fire, control wages and working conditions) versus the power of employees (to form unions, strike, resign, and so on)
- Administration, teaching, and scholarship in K-12, college, and university education
- Representation in executive, legislative, judicial, and military branches of government
- Political party organizations
- Lobbies
- Political action committees and campaign contributions
- Control of media
- Public relations, advertising, and political consultancy
- Foundations and research institutes (think tanks)
- Professions

Conservative versus Liberal-to-Leftist Power Groups:
- In government and military agencies, nationally and locally
- In the Democratic, Republican, and other parties
- Labor unions and associations of public employees, teachers, and so on.
- K-12 teachers, college and university faculties, administrators, trustees, school boards (each considered separately)
- Corporations (such as the Fortune 500), for-profit professions, and their collective associations
- Wealthy individuals (such as the Forbes 400) versus those in the middle class and poor
- Media owners and executives, advertisers, journalists, performers, and other employed personnel (each considered separately)
- Lobbies and advocacy organizations: political, religious, civil rights, consumer, professional, environmentalist, educational (administrators, teachers, students, advocates of privatization and corporations seeking to invest in it)

I have never been in an institutional situation that enabled me to conduct a research project encompassing these realms of power, so I am just proposing this to other scholars as the basis, say, for a college course along the lines of "Power and Rhetoric in Contemporary Politics," or to university research centers, foundations, and think tanks as a worthy project to fund, through, for example, creating a yearlong dialogue bringing together scholars on the left and right, perhaps in the form of a refereed "truth and reconciliation commission."

Beyond the battle of statistical and other empirical evidence in these various realms of power, a methodical approach is needed for comparative analysis of partisan arguments about them. I have embodied such a method in three sets of guidelines, or schemas, for students in my argumentative writing courses, with the aim of providing them with tools both for identifying the biases of opposing sources whom they study, and for scrutinizing their own biases in reading and writing about those sources. So the following versions, adapted from my textbook *Reading and Writing for Civic Literacy*, are worded for student use; however, with minimal changes in wording, they are equally applicable to all of us who engage in polemics, and I use them as a point of reference throughout this book in monitoring the rhetoric of those I criticize as well as my own rhetoric on the particular issues addressed here. Once again, I invite readers to catch me in not practicing what I preach.

A Semantic Calculator for Bias in Rhetoric

This guide (inspired by Hugh Rank's "Intensify-Downplay Schema" in *Persuasion Analysis* 134–35) can be applied to writing papers about sources, in application to both those sources' biases and to your own as a writer.

1. What is the author's vantage point, in terms of social class, wealth, occupation, gender, ethnic group, political ideology, educational level, age, and so on? Is that vantage point apt to color her/his attitudes on the issue under discussion? Does she/he have anything personally to gain from the position she/he is arguing for, any conflicts of interest or other reasons for special pleading?
2. What organized financial, political, ethnic, or other interests are backing the advocated position? What groups, or special interests, stand to profit financially, politically, or otherwise from it? In the Latin phrase, cui bono?
3. Once you have determined the author's vantage point and/or the special interests being favored, look for signs of ethnocentrism, rationalization or wishful thinking, sentimentality, one-sidedness, selective vision, or a double standard.

4. Look for the following forms of setting the agenda and stacking the deck reflecting the biases in No. 3:
   a. Playing up:
      (i) arguments favorable to one's own side.
      (ii) arguments unfavorable to the other side
      (iii) the other side's power, wealth, extremism, misdeeds ("A widespread pattern of abuses"), and unity ("A vast conspiracy," "A tightly-coordinated machine")
   b. Downplaying (or suppressing altogether):
      (i) arguments unfavorable to one's own side
      (ii) arguments favorable to the other side
      (iii) one's own side's power, wealth, extremism, misdeeds ("A small number of isolated instances," "A few rotten apples"), and unity ("An uncoordinated collection of diverse, grass-roots groups")
   c. Applying "clean" words (ones with positive connotations) to one's own side, without support. Applying "dirty" words (ones with negative connotations) to the other, without support
   d. Assuming that the representatives of one's own side are trustworthy, truthful, and have no selfish motives, while assuming the opposite of the other side
   e. Giving credit to one's own side for positive events, without support. Blaming the other side for negative events, without support

This calculator indicates the ways in which we all are inclined, intentionally or unintentionally, to react—often with anger and exaggeration—to our opponents' perceived faults and exercises of power, while not seeing our own side's comparable ones. Of course, emphasizing our side's "good" and the other side's "bad" is a perfectly legitimate part of argumentation, so long as it is done honestly, accurately, with sufficient support, and a sense of proportion. But good faith efforts at doing so need to be distinguished from the bad-faith ones of propagandists who stack the deck by deliberately, dishonestly using these techniques to present a simplistic opposition between "good guys" and "bad guys," or of sincere but closed-minded ideologues who resort to the techniques in a knee-jerk conditioned reaction to every public event. In any given case, differential semantic descriptions might serve to make an accurate, supportable judgment on the relative merits of opposing camps—or they might not; it's for you to judge.

So if you don't find blatant signs of the above biases, and if you judge that the emotional language is supported by adequate evidence, that's a good indication that the writer is a credible one. If there are many such signs, that's a good sign that the writer is not a credible source. However, finding signs of the above biases does not in itself prove that the writer's arguments are fallacious. Don't fall into the ad hominem ("to the man") fallacy—evading the issue by attacking the character or motives of the writer or speaker without refuting the substance of the argument itself. What the writer says may or may not be factual, regardless of the semantic biases. The point is not to let yourself be swayed by emotive words alone, especially when you are inclined to wishful thinking on one side of the subject yourself. When you find these biases in other writers, *or in yourself,* that is a sign that you need to be extra careful to check the facts out with a variety of other sources and to find out what the arguments are on the other side of the issue.

Predictable Patterns of Political Rhetoric

The following list of predictable patterns, like the "Semantic Calculator for Bias in Rhetoric," is intended mainly to enable you to recognize

Leftists will play up:	*Rightists will play up:*
Right-wing bias in media and education; power of business interests and administrators	Left-wing bias in media and education; power of employees and unions
Crimes and fraud by the rich; luxury, waste, selfish interests and control of government by private industry and the military	Crimes and fraud by the poor; luxury and waste by government bureaucrats; selfish interests and control over government by labor unions, teachers, civil rights and environmentalist organizations
Conservative ethnocentrism and sentimentality toward the middle and upper classes and American foreign interventions	Leftist "negative thinking," "sour grapes," anti-Americanism, and sentimentality toward the lower classes and America's foreign enemies
U.S. military strengths, right-wing "hawks'" scare tactics about foreign adversaries' strengths and menace	Foreign adversaries' strengths, menace, and manipulation of left-wing "doves"; left-wing scare tactics about negative consequences of American military actions
Conservative rationalization of right-wing extremism and foreign dictatorships allied with the United states	Liberal rationalization of left-wing extremism and left-wing dictatorships, guerillas, and terrorists

a particular line of argument when you see it, not automatically to dismiss it as biased. It is a necessary and perfectly legitimate part of argumentation to make the strongest case you can for your own cause and to point out the faults in opponents' positions. Once you recognize these patterns, the more important task is to evaluate whether the points being played up and downplayed are well-reasoned and supported, or whether they are just appealing one-sidedly to knee-jerk emotional response.

Ground Rules for Polemicists

Do unto your own as you do unto others. Apply the same standards to yourself and your allies that you do to your opponents, in all of the following ways:

1. Identify your own ideological viewpoint and how it might bias your arguments. Having done so, show that you approach opponents' actions and writings with an open mind, not with malice aforethought. Concede the other side's valid arguments—preferably toward the beginning of your critique, not tacked on grudgingly at the end or in inconspicuous subordinate clauses. Acknowledge points on which you agree at least partially and might be able to cooperate.
2. Summarize the other side's case fully and fairly, in an account that they would accept, prior to refuting it. Present it through its most reputable spokespeople and strongest formulations (not through the most outlandish statements of its lunatic fringe), using direct quotes and footnoted sources, not your own, undocumented paraphrases. Allow the most generous interpretation of their statements rather than putting the worst light on them; help them make their arguments stronger when possible.
3. When quoting selected phrases from the other side's texts, accurately summarize the context and tone of the longer passages and full texts in which they appear.
4. When you are repeating a secondhand account of events, say so—do not leave the implication that you were there and are certain of its accuracy. Cite your source and take account of its author's possible biases, especially if the author is your ally.
5. In any account that you use to illustrate the opponents' misbehavior, grant that there may be another side to the story and take pains to find out what it is. If opponents claim they have been misrepresented, give them their say and the benefit of the doubt.

6. Be willing to acknowledge misconduct, errors, and fallacious arguments by your own allies, and try scrupulously to establish an accurate proportion and sense of reciprocity between them and those you criticize in your opponents. Do not play up the other side's forms of power while denying or downplaying your own side's. Do not weigh an ideal, theoretical model of your side's beliefs against the most corrupt actual practices on the other side.
7. Respond forthrightly to opponents' criticisms of your own or your side's previous arguments, without evading key points. Admit it when they make criticisms you cannot refute.
8. Do not substitute ridicule or name-calling for reasoned argument and substantive evidence.

Here is a classic recent example for study in this perspective, as reported by Fairness and Accuracy in Media (FAIR). On 13 Oct. 2011, Reuters ran a wire service story under the headline, "Who's Behind the Wall Street Protests?" Reporters Mark Egan and Michelle Nichols suggested that the Occupy Wall Street (OWS) protests "may have benefited indirectly from the largesse of one of the world's richest men—George Soros. Soros and the protesters deny any connection. But Reuters did find indirect financial links between Soros and Adbusters, an anti-capitalist group in Canada which started the protests." The article continued, "According to disclosure documents from 2007–2009, Soros' Open Society gave grants of $3.5 million to the Tides Center, a San Francisco-based group that acts almost like a clearing house for other donors, directing their contributions to liberal non-profit groups. Among others the Tides Center has partnered with are the Ford Foundation and the Gates Foundation.... Disclosure documents also show Tides, which declined comment, gave Adbusters grants of $185,000 from 2001–2010, including nearly $26,000 between 2007–2009."

On the basis of grants amounting to a yearly average of $18,500 over ten years to an organization, Adbusters, twice removed from Soros, conservative media jumped on the story, with Rush Limbaugh crowing, "George Soros money is behind this." Fox News carried this exchange about OWS between Bill O'Reilly and Margaret Hoover:

> *O'Reilly*: I think these guys were organized by the George Soros-funded MoveOn operations. Reuters, by the way, has an article

on that today that you have to read, Hoover, linking in the Soros money to these agitators.

Hoover: And what that article actually said is that Soros money had funded the original group Adbusters.

O'Reilly: That's right.

Hoover: But the last time Soros directly funded it was seven years ago. Although a lot of Soros money—and this is the thing about Soros money, is that because it is...

O'Reilly: It's everywhere.

Hoover: It's everywhere.

O'Reilly: It's everywhere.

Hoover: And small amounts to all these progressive groups that are progressive groups. There's no way...

O'Reilly: You know what Soros money—did you see "Invasion of the Body Snatchers," where if you went to sleep you became an alien? That's like Soros money. You go to sleep and they come.

In fact, Reuters had quickly changed its headline to "Soros Money Not Behind Wall Street Protests," and several Reuters journalists publicly denounced the story, as in a blog by Felix Salmon: "Reuters cannot—must not—get a reputation as a right-wing media outlet. We have to report the news as impartially as we can. In this case, there was no story, and nothing to report. Inventing a tenuous and intellectually-dishonest link between Soros and OWS might get us traffic from Matt Drudge—but that's traffic which, frankly, we don't particularly value or care for. Much more importantly, it serves to undermine the heart of what Reuters stands for. And we can never afford to do that." (Source: Hart "Is Glenn Beck.")

Although Limbaugh and O'Reilly did not say so in as many words, what was clearly going on here was a preemptive reaction strike against liberal charges that the Tea Party movement was heavily funded by Charles and David Koch through Americans for Prosperity and Richard Armey's FreedomWorks. So we teachers and our students (or media investigative reporters) might begin by researching the sources for, and comparative amounts of, funding for OWS and the Tea Party, the degree of control over them exerted by Soros (or Adbusters) versus the Kochs, and applying the Semantic Calculator to the opposing sides, for example, "What groups or special interests stand to profit financially, politically, or otherwise from [the advocated position]?" Exactly what did Soros and Adbusters have to gain (financially and politically) from OWS, and the Kochs, from the Tea Party? How did the rhetorical tactics of the various sources match up with the facts? I will return to pursue these questions in chapter 5.

As indicated in the Soros-Koch syndrome and my schemas above, the central problem in all polemics is the almost innate tendency of those on all sides consciously or unconsciously to apply a double standard to their own side versus the other. In enumerating examples throughout the book, I use several formulas: "Heads I win, tail you lose," Orwell's "Four legs good, two legs bad," and my own, "the ESBYODS Principle" (short for the inelegant but profound folk saying, "Everyone shits, but your own doesn't stink"). My piling on of criticisms of conservatives displaying these double standards, without my attempting systematically to accord "equal time" to liberals or leftists doing the same, is intended only to demonstrate the very absence of proportion or balance in conservative campaigns against political correctness in education and media. I am not so foolish as to think my own arguments are free from similar blind spots, or that anyone can be free from them. The only remedy is unremitting self-awareness and willingness to engage in dialogue with opponents to provide correctives. From beginning to end, then, this book is framed as an invitation to conservatives to engage in such dialogue in any and every conceivable arena.

Part I

Countering the Bias of Business as Usual

1

CONSERVATISM AS THE UNMARKED NORM

For many years I have been making the case that the ceaseless conservative attack against bias and political correctness among leftists in both education and media disingenuously stands the truth on its head: The far greater bias pervading American society is conservative, but it is not widely perceived as a bias—just as the normative, natural order of things. It is only leftists' attempts to provide minimal counterbalance to the bias of business as usual in media and education, through critical pedagogy in the latter—that is publicly "marked" as biased. These public perceptions of where bias in education or media lies are largely controlled by conservative propagandists through semantic framing and rhetorical agenda-setting, which serve to limit attention to issues of political bias only to overt, ad hoc, and sensational instances of political correctness—the Ward Churchill Syndrome—while the constant biases of business as usual are not considered worthy of notice or subject to criticism. Likewise, most of the recent criticisms of liberal or left bias in higher education have fixated on the humanities and social sciences, whose influence is blown out of proportion to that of every other aspect of both secondary and higher education that serves the interests of corporate society's business as usual. In a 1989 column in the *Chronicle of Higher Education* titled "Conservatives Have a Distorted View of What Constitutes Bias in Academe," I asked, "If conservatives are sincerely committed to academic balance, shouldn't they advocate more of a voice for alternative views such as those of Marx and Nader in business administration courses, of the United Farm Workers in agricultural management courses, of proponents of socialized medicine in medical schools, of nuclear-freeze advocates in weapons laboratories, and of atheists in schools of theology?" I further asked about conservatives who attack academic leftists for debasing academic standards, "When have they ever protested the debasement of academic standards by special admissions policies for athletes and the children of rich donors; by education and research for purely commercial ends, or by semi-professional intercollegiate sports and dionysian Greek social life?" I have never received an answer to my numerous variations on these questions, beyond claims that they are facetious (see National Association of Scholars' president Herbert London's response to my article along similar lines in MLA's *Profession 89*). I certainly did not intend them as such, and to dismiss them that way amounts to a tautological reiteration (whether through opacity or evasion) of blindness to the bias of business as usual.

Even to catalogue the full array of forces for conservatism in America, as I sketchily do in this and subsequent chapters, will provoke accusations that it is me who is stacking the deck in downplaying liberal or left counterforces. Any such full catalogue is also bound to be dismissed by conservatives as "boring," "tiresome," "old news"—another instance of the imperviousness of a status quo that prevails through force of custom without need of the painstaking, and admittedly fatiguing, articulation that challenges to it require. I emphasize, then, that I do not deny the existence of counterforces on the left; I just assert that their relative power can only be accurately assessed in proportion to a full accounting of conservative forces. So I urge conservative readers, and any others who may find my catalogue of conservative forces one-sided, in each instance and at the end of it, to offer substantive counterarguments. On all these points, my intention is not to pronounce the last word, but only the first one toward dialogue at a more sophisticated ideological level than that of present American public discourse.

In historical perspective, I suggest in several following passages that the left turn in college education in the sixties occurred as a filling of the vacuum left by the unprecedented depoliticizing of American culture and scholarship after World War II; the left turn might be said to amount, not to politicization, but to de-depoliticization. Thus I contend that the "leftist bias" in critical pedagogy, and its allied movement cultural studies, can be defended on the grounds that academic studies are one of the few remaining areas of American society since World War II that are, or have the potential to be, a counterforce to society-wide domination by conservative corporate, political, and military influences. Conservatives ridicule sixties radicals for turning to academia as the only avenue hospitable to them anymore; the implication is that conservatives will only be content when no forums remain open to the left.

My case here can be made in terms of the Marxian-Gramscian theory of ideological hegemony or Marcusean one-dimensional language, but no theory is really needed to observe the countless daily manifestations of the conservatism that saturates American culture and education. My position here is also a reaffirmation of the tradition of Marxist humanism, a variety of leftism that is, I believe, more faithful to the essential Marx—the contemporary of Mathew Arnold, Ralph Waldo Emerson, John Ruskin, and other nineteenth-century philosophers of a coherent, organic worldview—than the structuralist and poststructuralist Marxism or the postmodernist pluralism that have attempted to discredit humanism and organicism on the left and have failed to stand against the tide of social incoherence and atomization.

A leftist vision can further apply a classical sense of measure and critical discrimination to the rhetorical excesses and debasement of taste in contemporary society. Thus my principal charge against conservative polemicists is that they fail to exercise Aristotelian *decorum*, in the sense of discerning accurate proportion or what is appropriate to any given situation, especially in application to relative culpability on the American left and right. Consider the claims of those American conservatives who branded Barack Obama a socialist or communist (or even a fascist), or who claimed he was born in Kenya and was a stealth jihadist or Third World revolutionary—even that his "fist bump" with Mrs. Obama on worldwide TV in his election celebration was a secret terrorist signal. While this grotesque distortion of reality was not explicitly endorsed by most responsible conservatives, neither did most of them denounce it as vociferously as they do, say, cases of political correctness among academic and media liberals.[1] Indeed, I suggest that, rather than trying to judge the sins of the Republican right and the PC left in accurate proportion, conservative polemicists have tended to fixate exclusively on the sins of the left as a red herring to distract public attention away from far greater ones on the right.

In this perspective, humanistic education has a mandate to be the "adversary culture" neoconservatives abhor, to combat demagogic irrationality, ideological incoherence, and atomized thought and discourse in America with a comprehensive, coherent—but not doctrinaire—vision. In this respect, those of us committed to the political left and critical pedagogy ought not to accept the label, tendentiously pinned on us by conservatives (abetted, to be sure, by the excesses of progressive postmodernism), as the adversaries of the Arnoldian holistic, disinterested vision of the humanities, but should lay claim to being its legitimate successors. I do not think it is doublethink to regard left commitment as compatible with disinterested scholarship, because in this sense, being on the left does not mean pushing a dogmatic political line, but rather maintaining a critical viewpoint outside the ideological mainstream and striving for an integrative epistemology in opposition to the atomizing and interest-controlled dominant culture.

Controlling the Semantic Agenda

Conservatives have been able to control the public agenda on the issue of bias in American politics, education, and media through constant repetition of claims of liberal or leftist bias that grossly exaggerate the extent of leftism in mainstream American discourse. Most of that discourse is confined to a narrow spectrum whose leftward limit is the Democratic-Party version of governance by relatively liberal multimillionaire corporate, financial, and military executives, most recently incarnated in the Obama administration—albeit with a multicultural spin. In recent elections, Democratic candidates have even refused to label their positions as liberal, while Republican candidates compete to declare themselves the most conservative. Conservative polemicists play up the power of liberal, and even socialist, forces in America, but I ask them: Why, then, has not just socialism but liberalism become the ideology that dare not speak its name?

The more that American politics has shifted toward the right since the sixties, the more outlandish have conservative scare tactics against the left become, like Ted Cruz's 2010 red-baiting of Obama and the Harvard Law School discussed in my preface. In 2012, congressman Allen West declared at a conservative conference, "I believe there's about 78 to 81 members of the Democrat Party who are members of the Communist Party. It's called the Congressional Progressive Caucus" (*Huffington Post*, 11 Apr. 2012). Few Republican colleagues took issue with West or Cruz, though West lost reelection in 2012. When a Norwegian right-winger went on a killing rampage at a Labor Party youth camp in 2011, Glenn Beck compared the camp to the Hitler Youth. Of course, in Beck's political vocabulary, Nazis are defined as socialists, a definition that is half true but that suppresses all the conservative elements of fascism that set it in opposition to Norwegian-style social democracy or to democratic socialism. (Labeling fascism as leftist is one of the semantic ploys conservatives use to distract attention from the realities of right-wing dictatorships and extremism.[2]) Those like Cruz, West, and Beck may be an embarrassment for more responsible American conservatives, but few of the latter have had the integrity to dissociate themselves from their kind or to correct their irresponsible claims—except when a Beck or Patrick Buchanan is perceived by neoconservative champions of Israel to cross the line into antisemitism.

Another key example of semantic agenda-setting that favors conservatives is the ambiguity in American public usage of the very terms *liberalism* and *conservatism*. These terms of course have multiple meanings, so the issue here is the frequent equivocation by conservatives between different meanings. Conservative spokespersons claim to champion definitions of conservatism that have positive ideological substance—accompanied by high-minded evocations of Adam Smith, Edmund Burke, Friedrich Hayek, and Leo Strauss—but they tend to evade the gross contradictions between those definitions and other, far more salient manifestations of "actual, existing conservatism." This is an instance of the fallacy warned against in #6 of my "Ground Rules for Polemicists": "Do not weigh an ideal, theoretical model of your side's beliefs against the most corrupt actual practices on the other side." So conservative intellectuals play up conservatism as social stability, self-restraint, long-term concerns, and Judeo-Christian or classical moral values. They downplay the get-rich-quick-and-ignore-the-long-term variety, the mentality of those who devised the subprime-mortgage bubble and who chanted "Drill, Baby, Drill" before they were silenced by the British Petroleum oil spill that despoiled the solidly Republican Gulf Coast (at which point, of course, Republicans were first in line begging for help from the despised federal government).

Probably the most significantly unacknowledged fact about actual, existing conservatism is that the restricted cognitive codes dominating American socialization and communication in most social classes, with the largest exceptions at the top and bottom, also induce conservative attitudes—not in the sense of a principled conservative ideology, but the sense of mass conformity, philistine anti-intellectualism, and the reasoning characteristics of people fixed in an early developmental stage, basically that of children. My basis for saying this is not intellectual snobbery, but my own socialization in Iowa and later immersion in rural and small-town, "red state" communities. This point is developed in chapter 2.

CORPORATIONS? CORPORATIONS? NOBODY HERE BUT US CHICKENS

A further manifestation of actual, existing conservatism, largely—and quite deliberately—kept off the agenda of American public consciousness, is the power of corporations. A key fact downplayed by conservative theorists of the invisible hand of the free market is that a quite visible hand is considered necessary to manipulate the selling of the conservative agenda, through billions of dollars spent every year by corporations and corporate-wealthy individuals on political lobbying and campaign contributions, public relations (PR) agents and party consultants (AKA operatives and spin-doctors), advertising, law firms, foundations, think tanks, and above all news and entertainment media controlled directly or indirectly by ownership and advertising.

For more than a century, corporate public relations agents and lobbyists have propagated an image of large corporations that renders them invisible as economic special interests and wielders of partisan or—bipartisan—political influence. This PR image depicts corporations as champions of a myriad of mom-and-pop businesses, so that any legislation aimed at curbing big business and the corporate wealthy is deflected by selfless claims that it will harm small business. This image further equates corporations with individual citizens, deserving the same constitutional rights as individuals—an assertion whose ultimate vindication came in the 2009 Supreme Court Citizens United case. (For historical perspective on corporate legal and PR strategies here, see Hartmann; Aune; Fones-Wolf; Stauber and Rampton.) The clearest sign of the triumph of this unrelenting campaign is that when college students and writers of letters to the editor complain about excessive power or corruption in America, its source is almost always identified as "the government," almost never "the corporations." Few of my students over the years have had any awareness of corporate lobbies and PR as influences on public opinion. Thus national debate over President Obama's proposed health care reform became framed (largely through health care industry PR) in terms of the dangers of a government monopoly depriving individuals of free choice—a false dilemma that excluded attention to the financial restrictions on individual free choice under the present system of corporate oligopoly in health care, insurance, and pharmaceuticals, or to the immense profits and executive incomes of those corporations. This same pattern is visible in nearly every other conservative campaign, for example, privatizing

Social Security, Medicare, and public education, where conservative arguments always play up "individual choice," not the potential multibillion-dollar profits for the corporate privatizers behind these campaigns. Likewise with debates over gun control, nearly always framed in terms of individual rights, rarely in terms of the profits of gun manufacturers and sellers, nationally and internationally, or their lobbying power at the federal and state level.

Perhaps the least-scrutinized key fact of American political and civic life is that our major institutions of mass communication are themselves corporations driven by the profit motive; it is almost tautological to say that they are the least-likely source to count on for finding intensive criticism of corporate society in general or of their own biases stemming from ownership and commercial sponsorship by conglomerate megacorporations that are involved in a multitude of cross-promotions and conflicts of interest. The blindness of most news media to the impending financial collapse in 2008, caused by runaway speculation and executive income on Wall Street, must have been partly attributable to their top executives and journalists themselves having profited from the boom to jump into the top percentiles of wealth. Or consider the debasement of American politics by the absurd increase in the length of political campaigns, as presidential candidates begin virtually on one election day to run for the next one four years later, while the primary season drags out for a year before the general election. The prime beneficiary here is parties and individuals who can raise the most money to outlast rivals, and who have constantly increased the stakes in campaign financing, mainly from corporate-wealthy patrons. However, the news media are equally complicit, through the billions of profits they now generate from both campaign advertising and the bump in general advertising for coverage of these protracted campaigns. Further beneficiaries of the boom in campaign advertising are the star TV reporters, commentators (whether conservative or liberal), and debate moderators making millions and glorying in their self-importance; or the Barbi and Ken dolls (now at least including some multicultural ones) who have replaced journalists in "infotainment" newscasts, being fed sound bites through their earbuds or teleprompters, while they flash big smiles and joke uproariously between accounts of bloody world conflicts and natural tragedies. So is it surprising that there is virtually no self-scrutiny aired on national or local TV of the corporate concentration of wealth biasing the ideological perspective of mass media? Corporations? What corporations?

Or consider the saturation point in the media's commercialization and financial corruption of college and professional sports reached in recent decades, when every game has become an orgy of corporate promotions—for example, in the branding of stadiums like Petco Park or GEO Stadium at Florida Atlantic University, sponsored by a private prison corporation, and of golf tournaments like, I kid you not, the Waste Management Open. The funneling of wealth to the corporate elite throughout society is reflected in the increasingly oligarchic major media's compounding of advertising revenue through sports and with commensurate revenue hikes for colleges and pro teams from the broadcasters, enabling hundred-million-dollar income for athletes, who in earlier periods typically were low-paid, blue-collar workers chawing tobacco instead of bubble gum. (Not that I advocate a return to that period when players were slaves to owners—it is again a matter of proportion, with team owners and broadcast media making far more than players.) How often are these issues even discussed on TV sports broadcasts?

The myriad forms of corporations' power—all disappeared from the agenda of public debate—also include their prerogatives as employers, the consequent subservience of students and workers to corporate bosses, the extortion from national and local governments of favoritism under the threat of moving elsewhere, and the willingness of legions to be a good team player, to lie, swindle, and despoil in the pursuit of corporate riches. Most social science scholarship on authoritarianism has focused on authoritarian submission to government rule or militarism, but the most dominant form in contemporary America is obviously to corporations and the corporate wealthy. What explains why so many Americans, including our college students, blank out on placing blame on the wealthy for socioeconomic problems, even as the gap in wealth and political power between the wealthy and everyone else widens exponentially? Most likely a combination of indoctrination into the faith that anyone has a chance to become rich (a faith constantly expressed by my lower-middle-class students at state colleges) and reluctance to bite the hand that feeds you or is likely to in the future. Thus follow all manner of doublethink rationalizations of submission to power that Orwell summed up as loving Big Brother.

To be sure, not all corporate behavior is blameworthy, but isn't the extent of opportunities for—and actual instances of—corporate malfeasance, and the number of humans who will do anything for enough money, sufficient to discredit conservatives' idealized model of free enterprise? Several of my aggressively conservative students have flaunted their ambition to get on the gravy train of Republican-aligned political consultants, media, foundations and think tanks. I recall no instance of liberal students saying they sought riches through labor unions, teaching, civil rights, feminist, and environmental groups, ACORN, or Habitat for Humanity. This is not to deny that some in those circles find ways to cash in through them, but only to suggest that most young people who seek careers in them do not claim this motivation, in the brazen manner of many young conservatives.

Although the Republicans have long been labeled the party of big business, the increasing dominance of big business and the corporate wealthy over the Democrats (and likewise over labor and social-democratic parties in Europe) has rendered meaningless the endless conservative attacks on Democrats' putative liberalism or "socialism." Conservative polemicists love to deride the hypocrisy of Democratic "limousine liberals." I believe it is admirable for liberals who become wealthy to maintain a principled sense of social justice against their own class interests (despite the undeniable ethical dilemmas their retention of wealth poses), but I also argue that a major factor undermining progressive politics is that accession to affluence and power is a conservatizing force that has been irresistible for countless liberals or leftists in every walk of life—including not only politics but also unions, journalism, advocacy organizations, higher education and scholarship, and the arts; in every field their iconoclasm predictably diminishes as they become more established. With dismal frequency, those liberals who have reached the upper levels of their occupations—intoxicated by the sweet smell of success—change into advocates for the status quo of capitalism, producing rationalizations in the mode of Norman Podhoretz's *Making It* and *Breaking Ranks* for the moral virtues of wealth and the free market.

In what might be viewed as a symbolic event in the history of the American culture wars, in *Making It*, Podhoretz recounted the shock to his shabby-genteel, liberal-intellectual consciousness resulting from going on an all-expenses-paid junket to the Bahamas in the early 1960s for an international conference of artists and intellectuals sponsored by billionaire Huntington Hartford (the A&P heir who, Podhoretz failed to note, was a Republican bankroller and notorious playboy in New York nightlife when I was a celebrity journalist there). Podhoretz sighs, "This is what it meant to be rich: to sleep in a huge bright room with a terrace overlooking an incredibly translucent green sea, to stretch one's arms out idly by the side of a swimming pool and have two white-coated servants vie for the privilege of depositing a Bloody Mary into one's hand...without giving money a second thought" (334). (In the Bahamas, these obsequious servants would have almost certainly been black, and the omission of this detail was significant for the author of "My Negro Problem, and Ours.") His point was that "the dirty little secret" of liberal intellectuals was that they were not immune to the lure of wealth and power. Although *Making It* was written before Podhoretz became a neoconservative, after he did so, he continued to fixate on such hypocrisies on the left, without ever acknowledging that personal wealth and power have been more readily available in recent decades to conservative intellectuals, and more often a motivator, underlying their professions of disinterested belief in the virtues of free enterprise. Nor has he ever acknowledged this as a possible motivation in his own latter-day conservatism or that of his many family members and friends, as surveyed in chapter 6 below.

Striking evidence for precisely this motivation in general is found in Jacob Heilbrunn's 2008 insider study of the neoconservatives, *They Knew They Were Right*: "Allan Bloom was close to Irving Kristol, but not until he had become a millionaire. (When I visited Bloom at the University of Chicago shortly before his death, he said that his relationship with Kristol had become 'easier' once he, like Kristol, was wealthy") (96). The very fact that Kristol became wealthy as a conservative propagandist has been suppressed in neoconservative circles, and the details remain to be revealed. Unfortunately, no biographies of either Bloom or Kristol have been written to this date. The implicit moral of this story is precisely that voiced by none other than Bloom in *The Closing of the American Mind*, describing "the intellectual, who attempts to influence and ends up in the power of the would-be influenced. He enhances their power and adapts his thought to their ends" (278). (Chapter 6 recounts the ironic reiteration of this process in Bloom's own career following the success of *The Closing*.)

Undoubtedly, it is very hard to hold out against the conservatizing blandishments of the world of the wealthy. In similar fashion, foreign dictators lavishing money in American public relations have been able to turn the heads of liberal American journalists and scholars, as in the embarrassing case of Moammar Qaddafi with Benjamin Barber and Joseph Nye (see Wiener, "Professors Paid by Qaddafi"). My point is that the co-opting force of access to corporate wealth and power is another subject erased from the agenda of American public discourse, and that an agenda more open to socialist views would include consideration of possible ways of limiting acquisition, by any individual or institution, of excessive wealth and power.

The best smoking-gun evidence I know of for the rhetorical trickery used to disguise the operations of corporate special interests is found in the transcript in a *60 Minutes* interview in March 1995 by Leslie Stahl with tobacco lobbyist Victor Crawford shortly before he died of throat cancer from smoking.

> *Stahl*: You yourself said it wasn't addictive when you were smoking and knew it was addictive.
> *Crawford*: Sure, it's not a crime because I wasn't under oath. It wasn't perjury. And it was what I was being paid to do.... Was I lying? Yes....
> *Stahl*: (*Voiceover*) Crawford says the tobacco lobbyists, often lawyers from the top firms, call themselves "the black hats." So you took on a black hat. Why did you...
> *Crawford*: Money. Big money.... Unfortunately, the other groups are not in a position to pay the big bucks, which is necessary to hire the best people.
> ...We used to bring a scientist out of the woodwork and have this particular lab do this, and we'd have a poll pulled by some cockamamy pollster saying this, that or the other.
> *Stahl*: You're walking around with a study, and you're thinking to yourself. This study's totally bull....
> *Crawford*: Oh, sure. Just to show them that the jury's still out, that you shouldn't take away anybody's civil rights until you're absolutely sure what you're doing. How can you be absolutely sure when this—this X-Y-Z laboratory, world-famous laboratory—why... is it world famous? Because I said it is, and nobody's checked....
> *Stahl*: You know, you are describing the most coldhearted, cynical, destructive set of values—I'm sorry—because these were your values.
> *Crawford*: They were.
> *Stahl*: And you're just telling it to us as if "Sure."
> *Crawford*: It's the American way. (*60 Minutes*)

Crawford's confession is paradigmatic of the tricks of the PR trade for disguising corporate special pleading, as further discussed in chapters 4 and 5 below, including "astroturf" pseudo-grassroots support groups, phony research institutes, smearing of opponents (whom he labeled "the health nazis"), and appeals to civil-libertarian freedom of choice and fairness and balance ("the jury's still out"). A good assignment for students, and challenge to conservative polemicists, would be to ask if they can document comparable examples that have been perpetrated in recent decades by liberals or leftists such as scholars, journalists, labor unions, public employees, or civil rights and citizen advocacy organizations like ACORN—at Crawford's level of power, greed, cold-blooded deceit, and propagation of socially pernicious policies. Far from being an isolated case of the "few rotten apples in every barrel," Crawford's confession is a perfect emblem of the conservative special-interest propaganda that is indeed so ubiquitous as to be "the American way." Unless they repent like Crawford or get caught in illegal acts like Jack Abramoff and his congressional accomplices, such PR agents and lobbyists are regarded as upstanding citizens, the envy of legions seeking to emulate them, with college major programs devoted to their training. Again to avoid overgeneralization and stereotyping here, many PR agents, lobbyists, and the businesses they represent scrupulously provide useful social services, but there are far more than a few rotten apples, many of whom never repent or get caught. Conservative theorists tend to avoid the issue of what restraints in the free market, without government legislation and regulation, can prevent the possibility of corporate power corrupting the entire polity.

The Politics of No Politics

The conservative status quo in the United States is not only perpetuated through deliberate social control, propaganda, polemics, and semantic agenda-setting but through what might be termed the politics of no politics: the fragmentation of knowledge and communication, the absence of any presentation of political events or opinions within a common understanding of ideologies, the reduction of political issues to the level of personal experience, and the distractions of entertainment and sports, consumerism, and sheer busyness. The fragmentation of mass consciousness inhibits any kind of extensive, coherent understanding of politics or effective oppositional organization—thus reinforcing the conservative status quo by default, or through what Richard Ohmann once termed "the politics of inadvertence" ("MLA"). However, the conservatism of no politics is rarely acknowledged as a factor in mainstream discussions of liberal versus conservative bias, which themselves exemplify the restriction of public consciousness to the superficial and the immediate.

"I'm just not interested in politics," is the mantra of citizens and students alike whose cultural conditioning has engendered purely personal consciousness, inoculated against awareness of the inevitable impingement of the political on the personal, the fact that politics is interested in *them*. Thus, teachers face a constant struggle against students' inability or unwillingness to see beyond their personal experience on broad political issues. "My family never owned slaves, and *I'm* not prejudiced against black people. The ones I know seem very hostile. Why don't they just get over it?" "Anyone in America can get out of poverty if they work hard enough. My parents...." Virtually every student attests indignantly to have witnessed lazy poor people, welfare swindlers, street criminals, drunks and drug addicts; few have ever met a billionaire or a lobbyist like Victor Crawford, been in a corporate or investment bank headquarters, where far greater moral turpitude and swindles, at far greater expense to taxpayers, take place outside the range of public view and indignation. These students have simply not developed their cognitive scope beyond personal experience to study the distant realities of corporate power or crime and a chain of causation by which those realities might harm them more than the misdeeds of poor people. Some of my students have even said that voting and knowledge about government are only within the specialized area of political science majors. At least at public universities like Cal Poly or Tennessee, teachers who blandly evade uncomfortable political subjects tend to be more popular with students than those who confront them, so all the social pressures work toward the politics of no politics.

The conservative critique of media and education ignores the fact that, regardless of how liberal, or even radical, the message of a particular media production, publication, or teacher might be, its point will be lost if audience members and students lack the understanding of differing political ideologies that will allow them to interpret it within some coherent universe of discourse. A good case can be made that the very lack of clearly defined political controversy in the United States is a preferable alternative to countries that suffer from constant, often violent political conflict. However, at least until the recent resurgence of American right-wing militancy, in the decades after World War II we were at the opposite pole, where any distinguishable ideology was excluded from public discourse because of the attempt by both political parties to appeal to 51 percent of voters rather than to a specific constituency (in contrast to the multiparty systems and coalition governments in most other democracies), and because of the nonideological, "neutral" stance of most American mass media and education. Daniel Bell's proclaimed "end of ideology" in the fifties degenerated into nationwide ignorance of ideologies. Politicians, the media, and educators alike stampeded toward the fanatic middle of the road, where "moderate" is a euphemism for evasion of ideological consistency and where "balance" consists of a mishmash of liberal and conservative messages on diverse issues, with no value judgments or clear-cut exposition of underlying philosophical differences. As is the case with many social policies, while this politically amorphous atmosphere may not be calculatedly engineered by corporate or political powers, its inadvertent conservative results by default of articulated opposition coincide comfortably with their hegemonial interests, so that taking steps to change it is not likely to be high on their agenda.

The major challenge to this ideological mishmash in the past two decades has come from the right, with the rise of talk radio, Fox News, conservative Christian activism, and the takeover of the Republican Party by its right wing. Conservatives justify their partisan media by claiming that they simply provide a counterbalance to the alleged left bias in the Mainstream Media (commonly referred to as the MSM). However, in addition to conservative exaggeration about the extent of leftism in the MSM, as discussed above, this is a false equation because none of those media and few of their reporters or commentators expressly identity themselves as liberal (let alone leftist, socialist, or radical!); nor do they frame their news reports and commentary within a cogent ideological perspective—as their conservative counterparts do. I think it is a positive development that overtly partisan media have emerged on the right, focusing public attention on the underlying ideological divides between right and left; however, there is no mass-circulated, nationally accessible equivalent in television, radio, or print of Pacifica Radio or left-liberal-to-socialist journals of opinion like the *Nation, Dissent, American Prospect,* the *Progressive, In These Times, Mother Jones, Z Magazine,* or *Extra!* It *was* encouraging that MSNBC moved in the 2010s toward being a progressive counterpart to Fox. Its Sunday morning programs hosted by Chris Hayes and Melissa Harris-Perry came close to becoming a *Nation* of the air, and Hayes openly identified himself as a social democrat. Moreover, its panelists included scholars and intellectual journalists (mostly liberal, but in civil dialogue with conservative counterparts) discussing issues in relatively extensive length and ideological depth, despite demeaning disruptions by commercials. The most literate channel on TV, C-SPAN [Cable-Satellite Public Affairs Network] (financed by guilt-money from the commercial telecasters) also covered full conferences of both liberals and conservatives, though only rarely extended debates between them with clarification of their underlying ideologies.

Busyness as Usual

Perhaps the most important but least discussed way in which the conservative status quo is perpetuated is through habit, routine, and busyness. In the classic opening sequence of Charlie Chaplin's *Modern Times*, the little fellow is working on an assembly line, turning nuts with a monkey wrench in each hand at a frantic pace. His foreman starts haranguing him to speedup even more, and Charlie stops in exasperation to protest; but as soon as he stops, the assembly line moves ahead, the foreman orders him to catch up, and he has to leap ahead on the line and redouble his pace just to get back to his original position. Here is the emblem for the daily lives of virtually all of us except those wealthy enough to hire others to do their busy work for them—which may be the strongest of all the forms of power that wealth can buy. Concerning the conservative effects of busyness, no one in our time has improved on Thoreau's attack on the rise of nineteenth-century industrial capitalism in "Life Without Principle": "I think that there is nothing, not even crime, more opposed to poetry, to philosophy, ay, to life itself, than this incessant business" (*Walden and other Writings* 712).

The rush to get through the day's business keeps people too busy to have the energy to think about changing the system that is keeping them so busy; they are apt to shut out leftist alternatives because they create cognitive dissonance and a threat to the comforts of routine. We are all kept on the assembly line by the need to get ahead or, like Charlie, just to keep from falling behind. Students must scramble desperately to get the grade and then the degree, in order to get the job and then the promotion. The work-world is much the same whether one goes into business or the professions, the private or the public sector. Few of the debates I have heard about liberal versus conservative forces in American society talk adequately about the subservience of workers, and of students as workers-to-be, to those with the ultimate conservative prerogative—the power to hire and fire.

Whether you are going for CEO, managing editor, or higher political office, for chief surgeon or the law partnership, for tenure or a department chair, you face the same pressures to conform to the will of those above you on the ladder. Conservatives spread alarm that sixties radicals who have graduated into positions of power in academia or media are institutionalizing revolution there, but this scenario naively disregards the tendency for those who may remain leftists in theory to be co-opted into intrinsically conservative power relations and hierarchies in their institutional domain. Some of the worst academic snobs and most bureaucratic administrators I know claim to be Marxists. There the overriding imperatives are to adhere to professional rituals (e.g., administrative number-crunching, social networking, publish-or-perish, the pecking order of prestigious universities and publishers), to avoid any controversy that might rock the boat of busyness-as-usual, and to get rid any "troublemaker," political or otherwise, who might provoke the ire of those above oneself in the hierarchy. (In a footnote to chapter 6, I argue, against Allan Bloom's claim that liberal university administrators and faculty caved in to student protestors in the sixties, that they more often caved in to pressure from conservative government officials and/or to local pressures to maintain bureaucratic business as usual.)

Conservatism by Default in Education

In a multitude of ways, American education both reflects and reproduces the foregoing traits of American culture that are conservative by default. Everyone knows—though few of the hand-wringing reports on the sad state of liberal education in America acknowledge it—that the real purpose of high school and college education is to prepare the majority of students to get jobs in business and the professions, so that in most schools other than the elite prep schools and liberal arts colleges, general education and critical thinking are considered boring nuisances. The majority of university faculties outside the humanities and perhaps the social sciences, as well as most administrators and trustees, are more or less overtly in the service of big business, the political establishment, or the military, in both preprofessional training of students and in research or consulting activities. Left teachers constantly fight a losing battle against students' knowledge that they are eventually going to have to cater their political attitudes to the conservative views of businesses, professions, or government agencies in order to get and keep a job. So no amount of leftist faculty bias is apt to make a dent in a curriculum geared to uncritical service to business as usual, any more than the reputed leftists in media are apt to make a dent in a system geared toward distraction and commodity consumption.

Our schools also reflect and reproduce the politics of ideological amorphousness. At every level of education, we find the same de-emphasis of politics and absence of systematic exposure to a full spectrum of ideologies. The exposition of clear-cut ideological viewpoints gets further blurred by the convention that teachers and textbooks are expected to be blandly neutral. (As I remember my days at Roosevelt Junior High in Des Moines, though, the coaches who taught social science weren't at all inhibited from voicing their right-wing biases; around 1950, one terrorized us with grim assurances that we would be in a nuclear war with Russia within five years.) Comprehensive political understanding is still further impeded by a departmentalized curriculum of unrelated courses each jammed into a few hours a week for one semester or quarter, and each in turn broken up into discontinuous units corresponding to television's blips of information. Students and teachers alike are caught on Chaplin's assembly line, too hurried and overworked ever to gain an overview of issues that goes beyond today's exam or exercise.

How does my field, English, fit into the depoliticized, ideologically amorphous context of American society and education? In composition courses, the convention in recent decades has been to cater to students' individual, multicultural interests in assignments and to offer an eclectic menu of subject matter for writing drawn from massive textbook anthologies trying to provide something for everyone, with no cognitive coherence, no basis for recursive or cumulative learning, for developing an extended line of thought or argument. Survey courses in literature are similarly, typically structured in the standard discontinuous units of study, using textbook anthologies that reproduce fragmented, serial consciousness—in a random sequence of authors and themes with little ideological coherence. Most literature courses are organized as chronological surveys of periods and movements, as groupings of readings by genre, or as applications of diverse critical approaches. Many English majors, grad students, and professors deliberately or unconsciously turn toward literature precisely as a refuge from politics, and they often join forces with the conservatives in resenting attempts to politicize literary studies. Undergraduates taking lit courses as electives commonly bring to them the attitude of the tired worker just looking for escapism; they might not have ever heard of the New Criticism, but they are amazingly adept New Critics in their aestheticist antipathy to any literature with a political message, as they grumble, "This course should be in political science, not English."

Conservative culture warriors depict straw man leftist professors and critics who heavy-handedly reduce literary works to their political content. However, if it is an injustice to authors to focus only on the political aspects of their works, it is no less an injustice to ignore those aspects of countless writers and critics who have combined political subjects with aesthetic quality. Good politics does not necessarily produce good literature or literary criticism, but neither does it preclude them, and even this distinction does not justify the extent to which American literature, criticism, and literary education have excluded politics since World War II. Before New Left–influenced textbooks like the *Heath Anthology of American Literature*, few literature or composition anthologies included as part of their critical apparatus an overview of how authors differ in their political viewpoints. In anthologies like *The Norton Anthology of American Literature*, the selections for every period until the twentieth century included a large component of essayistic prose—letters, speeches, sermons, histories, memoirs, and so on—many of them foundational political statements, such as John Winthrop's "A Model of Christian Charity," William Bradford's "History of Plymouth Plantation," "The Declaration of Independence," the Jefferson-Adams and John Adams-Abigail Adams letters, "The Autobiography of Benjamin Franklin," "The American Scholar," "The Gettysburg Address," "Civil Disobedience," *Walden*, and Frederick Douglass's autobiography. But from the twentieth-century or modernist period to the present, the genres of fiction, poetry, and drama largely preempted nonfictional prose, especially of a political nature. The isolation of literary study from the social sciences or history has, of course, also been influenced by the inexorable drive in the academic world toward specialized scholarship, publish-or-perish, and rigid departmental lines—all in turn reflecting the development of late-capitalist division of labor, as Ohmann definitively argued in *English in America*.

The postwar hegemony of New Critical aesthetics and, more recently, poststructuralist theories of the death of the author, have obscured the simple truth that much literature—some enduring, some not—has always been engendered out of the obligations writers feel to bear witness to, celebrate or protest, the political issues of their time. The title of historian Tony Judt's 2010 book reaffirming the contemporary relevance of socialism, *Ill Fares the Land*, was an allusion to Oliver Goldsmith's 1770 poem, "The Deserted Village":

> Ill fares the land, to hastening ills a prey
> Where wealth accumulates, and men decay.

Apolitical aesthetics have likewise muted concern about the exclusion of creative writers and literary intellectuals from American political life and, conversely, their indifference to it as a literary subject—a topic I will return to in chapter 3.

Re-Politicizing Pedagogies

Various recent progressive educators have devised models of teaching aimed at counteracting all of these atomizing aspects of courses in English literature or composition and other disciplines. Gerald Graff, author of *Beyond the Culture Wars: How Teaching the Conflicts Can Revitalize American Education* and *Clueless in Academe*, criticizes the "ping-pong" effect in college education, whereby students are bounced back and forth between professors in different courses with conflicting ideological views on political or aesthetic issues, without those views ever being brought together in coherent dialogue. Graff advocates bringing those teachers, courses, and differing views together so that the conflicts among them present a dynamic means for students to learn how to understand and judge opposing views.

Other theorists and teachers to the left of Graff have developed alternatives to conventional teaching through varieties of Marxism such as Frankfurt School or Althusserian ideological critique (these include Henry Giroux and Susan Searls Giroux, Stanley Aronowitz, and James Berlin) and Paulo Freire's "critical pedagogy" (Ira Shor, Donaldo Macedo, Jane Tomkins, bell hooks, John Paul Tassoni and William Thelin, and *Radical Teacher*). Freireans, who also include a feminist, "women's ways of knowing," contingent, argue that even the teaching of left political views is likely to be cancelled out if the social relations of the classroom itself—with the teacher in an authoritarian role and students set against each other in competition for grades and financial aid—reproduce the alienation and patriarchal hierarchies of power within the larger society. So they seek to engender empowerment through centering the classroom itself on student concerns, collaboration, dialogue, and initiative in determining course content. Although I have a great deal of sympathy for this school and admiration for the positive results it can produce (ironically, most often in the hands of highly charismatic teachers such as those above), I have elsewhere expressed misgivings about its susceptibility to being co-opted toward conservative business as usual, especially through the "empowerment" of aggressively conservative students who seek to dominate classmates and teachers alike, while resisting exposure to course content that challenges their possible prejudices. (See *The Retreat*.)

Still another recent variant on Freire emphasizes student engagement in community service or social activism, sometimes extending to school-community collaborations in social-justice projects, as surveyed in collections edited by Seth Kahn and JongHwa Lee and by John Ackerman and David Coogan. While I am again sympathetic to this movement, it has in some applications been harshly criticized by conservatives for doctrinaire advocacy by teachers, and these criticisms need to be considered carefully, against the defense that such advocacy only counterbalances the far more prevalent forms of advocacy in American education for conservative business as usual.

My own approach combines Frankfurt critical theory with Graff's model for teaching it in dialectical contrast to conservative ideology. A series of my own works, beginning with "Teaching the Political Conflicts," has applied Graff's approach toward structuring courses into a cogent effort to counteract all of the atomizing, depoliticizing, and polarized aspects of American culture and education surveyed here. That effort includes the meta-polemical rhetorical schemas in my introductory chapter, as well as the pedagogical model suggested in chapters 8 and 9 for teaching the conflicts between the political right and left on economic issues, using the concrete example of a sequence of course units studying their opposing views on the escalating cost of college education.

2

Restricted-Code Conservatism

The average American is just like the child in the family....We sophisticates can listen to a speech for a half-hour, but after ten minutes, the average man wants a beer.
President Richard Nixon (quoted in Safire 314, 649)

When you speak, do not forget that a sound bite is all you have. Whatever you have to say, make sure to say it loud and clear. Keep it simple and keep it short—a slogan is always better. Repeat it often. Put it on television. Radio is good, but with few exceptions, only television reaches a public that is electorally significant. In politics, television is reality....With these audiences, you will never have time for real arguments or proper analyses. Images—symbols and sound bites—will always prevail. Therefore, it is absolutely essential to focus your message and repeat it over and over again.
David Horowitz, advice to Republican politicians, in *The Art of Political War* 15

Knowledge-Based Education—We oppose the teaching of Higher Order Thinking Skills (HOTS), values clarification, critical thinking skills and similar programs that are simply a relabeling of Outcome-Based Education (OBE) (or mastery learning) which focus on behavior modification and have the purpose of challenging the student's fixed beliefs and undermining parental authority.
2012 Republican Party of Texas Platform

My aim in this chapter is to justify a leftist viewpoint in teaching, within the particular disciplinary, or interdisciplinary, framework of the teaching of critical thinking, supplemented by a body of scholarship going back to the 1950s in the fields of social and developmental psychology, sociolinguistics, and political socialization—all pointing to a conclusion correlating lower stages of critical thinking or cognitive development with what I will call restricted-code conservatism. I reiterate that I contrast this notion to elaborated-code versions of conservatism that are on the same cognitive level with elaborated-code liberalism.

The obvious question of whether there is such a thing as restricted-code liberalism or leftism will be addressed throughout this section, but to start with continuation of the discussion of semantic agenda-setting in chapter 1, consider pertinent dictionary definitions, such as those in *Random House Webster's Collegiate Dictionary*:

> **Liberal.** Favorable to progress or reform, as in political or religious affairs.... Free from prejudice or bigotry; tolerant. Free of or not bound by traditional or conventional ideas, values, etc.; open-minded.
>
> **Conservative.** Disposed to preserve existing conditions, institutions, etc., or to restore traditional ones, and to limit change. Cautiously moderate.

Such dictionary definitions are ambiguous in failing to make point-by-point contrasts for each sense. Are all conservatives by definition closed-minded and prejudiced? Are all liberals opposed to cautious moderation? It's complicated, but I will hazard a way around these ambiguities by suggesting that, *in just one of the many senses of these terms*, liberalism can be defined as open-minded, tolerant, and so on, and conservatism as closed-minded, prejudiced, and bound by traditional or conventional ideas—what I will call restricted-code conservatism. In this sense, if self-proclaimed liberals betray these liberal traits, as they often do, they are simply not acting like liberals are supposed to.

Scholarship in critical thinking has delineated skills of analysis and synthesis that distinguish advanced levels of reading, writing, and reasoning (sometimes termed "higher order reasoning").[1] These include the abilities to reason back and forth between the past, present, and future, cause and effect, the concrete and the abstract, the personal and the impersonal, the local and the global, the literal and the figurative, the explicit and the implicit ("reading between the lines"), the actual and the hypothetical, or between what presently exists and conceivable alternatives. Also, the abilities to retain and apply material previously studied and to sustain an extended line of argument in reading, writing, and speaking, incorporating recursive and cumulative thinking (the abilities to refer back to previously covered material and to build on that material in developing stages in an argument). Still further skills involve understanding complexity and multiple levels of meaning or points of view (within personal, historical, and political contexts), and to recognize irony, paradox, and ambiguity in disparities between what is said and meant, between appearance and reality (especially between what people say and what they do), and between intentions and results—traits of the rational skepticism intrinsic to Enlightenment liberalism.

Some scholars make a further distinction, between critical-thinking *skills*, related formally or informally to traditional logic, and *dispositions* that foster or impede critical thinking within the broader context of psychological, cultural, social, and political influences. Dispositions that foster critical thinking include the development of open-mindedness, autonomous thought, and reciprocity (Jean Piaget's term for ability to empathize with other individuals, social groups, nationalities, ideologies, etc.). Dispositions that act as impediments to critical thinking include defense mechanisms (such as absolutism or primary certitude, denial, and projection), authoritarianism, culturally conditioned assumptions, egocentrism and ethnocentrism, rationalization, compartmentalization, stereotyping, and prejudice.

A related context for approaching the liberal-conservative cognitive binary is the British sociologist Basil Bernstein's terms *restricted code* (RT for short) and *elaborated code* (EC), derived from his empirical studies in language, class socialization, and workplace roles in postwar England. I have presented a fuller account of Bernstein's ideas in *The Retreat from Political Literacy in Rhetcomp*, but in brief, EC can be considered synonymous with the critical-thinking skills surveyed above, or as a shorthand, commonsense designation of the cognitive and linguistic development from childhood to adulthood, mediated both by formal education and literacy and by a widening circle of acquaintances, experience, travel, and sources of information. Likewise, RC can also be used to describe the adult consciousness of masses of people throughout most of history who have lived their entire lives in the same small geographical area, tribe, or family, whose work lives were endless drudgery, who could not read and thus, before the age of mass communication, had little knowledge of the world beyond their immediate experience, and were fixed in cognitive stages termed by psychologists sociocentric or ethnocentric. Neither children nor illiterate adults have factual knowledge of history to compare and contrast with the present, or a firm sense of sequence of events and cause and effect between the past and present (beyond oral accounts, which as Walter J. Ong and other historians of literacy have noted, may be richly extensive, but restricted mainly to chronological narration and formulaic ideas). So breadth of experience and acquisition of literacy are preconditions for both EC liberalism and conservatism. Perhaps most importantly, RC thinking tends strongly toward authoritarianism and conformity. It emphasizes "positional [i.e., role-bound, externally imposed] rather than personalized [internal] forms of social control" (Bernstein 143). "An educationally induced change of code from a restricted code...to an elaborated code...involves a shift in organizing concepts from authority/piety towards one of [autonomous] identity" (165).

Such traits of restricted-code conservatism can be identified most obviously with tribal, rural, or small-town communities, although Bernstein also discerned them in the present-day English industrial working class (much to his regret as a socialist). In modern society, the ultimate manifestation of RC thinking has been in followers of fascism on the right and communism on the left, the latter as classically dramatized by Orwell in *1984* and *Animal Farm*. (Once again, communist conformity on the left is a betrayal of the principles of liberal-left mental autonomy and questioning of any authority or social status quo, while fascism is equally a betrayal of conservatism in its elaborated-code senses like "cautious moderation.")

In the American context, I suggest that adults fixed in early stages of cognitive development are most susceptible to conservative appeals to uncritical support of authority, one's own country, race, ethnic group, class, party, and socioeconomic system (free enterprise, with low taxes and little regulation); orthodox religion, traditional family and gender roles, "the right to life," and the right to bear individual arms (as distinguished from "a well-regulated militia"); support for domestic law and order and getting tough on criminals (especially in capital punishment); xenophobia toward foreign nations, races, religions, and immigrants; eagerness to go to war and exact retribution against atrocities by the enemy Other—communists in past decades, currently Muslims and terrorists; and distrust of science and higher education. At this level, conservative attitudes toward government authority tend to be compartmentalized: reflexive support when one's own party is in office but fear and loathing when the other party is; likewise with attitudes toward the authority of conservative versus liberal teachers or scholars. (In principle, liberal teachers should welcome questioning of their authority by both conservative and liberal students, since skepticism toward authority is intrinsic to liberal thought.) Restricted-code conservatism appeals to what appear to be intuitive, immediate truths are manifestly easier to sell than the comparatively complex, counterintuitive arguments against the death penalty and for internationalism, pacifism, racial and gender equity, abortion, gun control, environmentalism, multiculturalism, sympathy for immigrants, and government restraints (including regulation and progressive taxation) on the excesses of free enterprise. (Among several recent scholarly and journalistic studies providing empirical support for these patterns, see Drew Westin, *The Political Brain*; Chris Mooney, *The Republican Brain*; Gordon Hodson and Michael Bussari, "Bright Minds and Dark Attitudes"; and George Monbiot, "The Right's Stupidity Spreads.")

Here are some examples of restricted-code conservatism based on things my students have said or written in argumentative writing courses. (Again, I contrast these with those students who have reached a stage of elaborated-code conservatism, and can make cogent arguments for conservative positions.) When asked for their source of information on the issues under study, the most frequent response is "my father," and they are apt to respond with bewilderment to any suggestion that they might engage in scholarly research about them, which has not been within their vocationally oriented conception of college study. (I suggest that some students' perceptions of teachers forcing liberal views on them might be based on incomprehension of those teachers' insistence that personal opinions be subjected to academic study of differing viewpoints and supported by evidence.) Many such students leap on every occasion to the defense of corporate executives and Republican government officials, in the manner of one who wrote about a presidential cabinet member under fire for corruption, "I don't know why people have been so hard on Secretary X. After all, he only wants what is best for the American people. That's why he was elected."

In my anonymous polls of students correlating their stated political position with their knowledge of current events and sources of information, conservative students on the whole have showed a lower knowledge level and range of news sources. Fox News is their most frequent source; almost none read the *New York Times* or any national newspaper beyond *USA Today*. More liberal students listed both Fox and the *Times* or *Washington Post*. On current events, conservatives' views have generally matched those that David Mindich reported in *Tuning Out: Why Americans Under Forty Don't Follow the News*, citing a recent poll indicating that "75 percent of young people trusted that the U.S. military would do 'the right thing,' up from around 20 percent in 1975" (4). And their views matched those that Mindich reports from a poll late in 2003 showing that over half of Americans believed that most or some of the 9/11 hijackers were Iraqi, that Saddam Hussein was behind the 9/11 attacks, and that weapons of mass destruction were found in Iraq after the invasion—beliefs that Fox News viewers were most likely to hold (105).

Many such students believe that flat tax rates seem like the most fair, because everyone pays at the same rate. It takes an extensive exposition to explain the principles of progressive taxation and to summarize the arguments that the wealthy benefit most from any flat tax rate below the top progressive rates, and that lowering taxes by the same rate in all brackets leaves far more in after-tax income, in real dollar amounts rather than percentage points, for higher incomes, far more in disposable income and surplus funds that can be reinvested, all widening the income and net worth gap. (These arguments are incorporated in a broader outline of conservative vs. liberal/left lines, for use in class study, in chapter 8.)

Conservative students at state colleges generally favor cutting taxes, but many also complain about constant tuition increases and cuts in financial aid. Few appear to have ever made an effort to trace the chain of causes and effects in a line of argument that attributes increased tuition to college budget cuts, thence to government budget cuts (nationally, statewide, and locally), thence to federal and local tax cuts. The lack here is in the critical-thinking ability to sustain an extended line of reasoning, to connect the dots. Similarly, when we have discussed the recent diversion of scholarship funds from need-based criteria to merit-based ones, favoring children from families who could afford better college preparation, I have been surprised to hear many students defending this shift, and it usually turns out their explanation is that they have been the beneficiaries. Again, it takes extensive de-centering effort to convince them that policies that benefit them personally do not necessarily benefit society at large, and that these particular policies may be contributing to an increasing level of income inequality detrimental to democracy. Once students have risen to this level of de-centering, class study can then advance to the higher level of debates on these issues between scholars and journalists on the left and right. This sequence is an instance of learning to expand critical thinking from the egocentric to the impersonal or reciprocal level.

When class discussion turns directly to income inequality, many conservatives likewise revert to rote formulas along the lines of, "Rich people work hard and deserve to keep every penny they earn." Or, "My parents worked their way out of poverty, so anyone can." Because their thinking is formulaic, fixed, and ahistorical, unaccustomed to relating the present to the past and future—"present-oriented," in Bernstein's accounts of restricted codes and Oscar

Lewis's of the culture of poverty—they are impervious to all data that indicate extreme recent changes in historical levels of inequality and that project an exponentially increasing gap as a likely future consequence. On an issue like climate change, conservative students tend to be predisposed to denials of its reality because evidence of it may not be immediately visible or tangible to them, and because they are too present-oriented to take seriously projections of its future consequences or the possible necessity of changes in immediately profitable corporate practices to avert those consequences.

Yet again, in all the debated issues here and many more, a conservative position can be supported on an informed, reasoned level, but my teaching experience indicates that arguments on that level are little more comprehensible to restricted-code conservatives than are liberal or left ones at the higher level. When I have directed conservative students or noncollege-educated conservative adults I know to the *Wall Street Journal* or *Weekly Standard*, a common response is that they are too hard to read.

In spite of my repeated acknowledgment of and respect for conservative students who show elaborated-code thinking, I predict that the conservative script in response to what I say here will be, "Lazere is just another example of arrogant academic leftists who think conservative students are idiots." To begin with, I would never characterize any student of mine as an idiot. All I say is that most conservative students in my courses have shown a more limited level and range of reading and experience than liberal ones, and that more of them are parochially ingenuous and authoritarian in their political views. I have kept a file of student writings over the years confirming this claim, which I will share with any reader who asks for it. Moreover, I assert that no one is qualified to make this kind of judgment on my or anyone else's teaching experience without firsthand knowledge of it, and that critics should refrain from making such judgments about students unless they themselves know experientially what they are talking about, from decades teaching the kind of students I have in the kind of schools I have.

Conservative polemicists will also in rebuttal posit cases where mass liberal opinions are uninformed or shortsighted. They might argue that liberals supporting deficit-spending-funded government entitlements are unable or unwilling to comprehend the long-term consequences of increasing government debt. Possibly so in theory, but scare tactics about government extravagance driving us over the brink of financial ruin certainly have wider gut appeal in America than defenses of government spending and higher taxes to support it. Nor is there by any means a consensus among policy analysts that deficit spending is in fact a clear and present danger, or that the major fault for current deficits lies with liberal constituencies and policies rather than conservative ones like unfunded wars or irresponsible financial institutions, which conservative polemicists rarely mention in their anti-deficit, antitax arguments. Or conservatives might respond to my positing liberal skepticism toward authority as a trait of higher cognitive development by arguing that such skepticism might sometimes indicate knee-jerk, childish insubordination or unwillingness by adults to accept the necessity of authority. This too is possible in theory, but it would need to be verified on a case-by-case basis. I also acknowledge widespread instances of ingenuous, "bleeding heart" liberalism or leftism, but suggest that they at least represent one developmental stage beyond that of conservatives whose reasoning is restricted to what directly benefits themselves and their sociocentric circles or to xenophobia. I can only speak from my own experiences of growing up in Middle America and teaching for four decades at Middle American colleges, where restricted-code conservatism is by far most prevalent. Granted, I would not vouch a priori for the level of rationality and economic knowledge in everyone who took part in the Occupy Wall Street demonstrations, or for followers of shrill media liberals like Bill Maher, Keith Olbermann, and Chris Matthews.

RED-STATE RESTRICTED CODES

In another arena of restricted-code conservatism, the most conservative states in America, especially in the South, generally have the lowest taxes, spend the least on education, and have the lowest levels of both individual and institutional educational achievement, while a plutocratic elite (Democratic before the sixties, now mostly Republican) controls the status quo. Tennesseans have long refused to implement a state income tax, even as K-12 and higher education funding has been decimated, especially since 2008. These states also have the highest rates of crime and population in prison, other than urban inner cities. Contrary to Republican polemicists' at-a-distance sentimentalizing of their base as the Andy-Griffith-like "real America," solidly Republican East Tennessee is an urban and rural area with tragically extensive poverty among whites and blacks alike, low wages, and inadequate schooling. Knoxville news reports consist largely of a daily parade of murders, armed robberies, shootouts with police, theft and drug rings, rapes, child abuse, meth labs, corrupt politicians, judges, police, and entrepreneurs. (Of course, media sensationalism gives a distortedly negative image of a region that I have generally found quite civil and increasingly cosmopolitan, largely through the relatively liberal influence of the faculties at the University of Tennessee and Oak Ridge Nuclear Laboratory; thus suburban Oak Ridge has one of the highest ranked public school systems in the state.[2]) I have relatives and acquaintances in rural, virtually all-white areas of Tennessee, Missouri, and Iowa who have clung to their lower-middle-class conservatism even as their sources of livelihood have disappeared in recent decades and they have sunk into poverty and sickness, without health insurance; they continue to rail against welfare, unemployment insurance, and "Obamacare" as they blame themselves for their failures and idolize distant billionaires and multinational corporations as "job creators."

Circumstances like these throughout the South, compounded by the legacy of slavery and segregation, have long bred a high incidence of the right-wing pathologies of white supremacists, militias, and neo-Nazis. Last year I heard a caller from Georgia get through C-SPAN's screening and, after reciting the most bizarre right-wing claims about President Obama, conclude, "Obama is a nigger piece of shit." In 2008, a US Army veteran burst into the Knoxville Unitarian Universalist Church firing a shotgun, killing two people and wounding seven others. According to a police affidavit, "Adkisson stated that he had targeted the church because of its liberal teachings and his belief that all liberals should be killed because they were ruining the country, and that he felt that the Democrats had tied his country's hands in the war on terror and they had ruined every institution in America with the aid of major media outlets. Adkisson made statements that because he could not get to the leaders of the liberal movement that he would then target those that had voted them into office." He further testified that his wish list of targets included those in conservative commentator Bernard Goldberg's book *One Hundred People Who Are Screwing Up America*. Among Adkisson's other grievances were that he couldn't find a job and that his government food stamps had been cut. (Source, *Wikipedia*.)

In October 2011, the *Knoxville News Sentinel* reported the arrest of a Georgia militia member and white supremacist who drove to Madisonville, Tennessee, carrying a handgun and an AK-47 rifle with the avowed intent of taking over the town in protest of the earlier arrest of a fellow "birther" after their group tried to force a grand jury there to indict President Obama for treason. They had attempted to make "citizen's arrests" of the grand jury and local officials for refusing to indict the president.

The following letter appeared in the *News Sentinel* on 22 Oct. 2011:

> Just after the 10th anniversary of the 9/11 attack, I can hardly believe the left-stream media has not made the comparison to al-Qaida and the Occupy Wall Street radicals.
>
> Both groups have attacked our major financial district. Both groups hate the Jews, with Occupy Wall Street protesters carrying blatantly anti-Semitic signs.
>
> Envy and jealousy is a major motivator for both groups. Al-Qaida attacked our nation's capital, and the Occupy Wall Street thugs are planning to do the same.
>
> Why hasn't the media been warning about this obvious parallel? Unless, of course, they agree with the radical agenda of both of these terrorist groups.
>
> Al-Qaida wanted to destroy our democratic form of government and our capitalist way of life. Isn't this exactly the same thing that the Occupy Wall Street gang wants, since they openly advocate violent revolution? Yes, it is, and they should be treated the same way—put on terror lists and sent to Guantanamo.
>
> Bottom line is, there is no difference between the goals of the radical Islamic terrorists and the Marxist commie terrorists marching on Wall Street. In fact, supporters like Michael Moore and Roseanne Barr have even called for beheading.
>
> Where is homeland security when we need them?

The *News Sentinel* regularly prints letters by conservatives that are only slightly less factually challenged. Some letters there from liberals are poorly reasoned and hotheaded, but not at this level of derangement.

My aim in all this is not the facile one of cherry-picking a few extreme examples with which to smear conservatism in general. I am not implying that these fringe cases are typical of most current American conservatives, and conservative readers can probably dig up an equal sampling of irrationality on the American left. Still, my own experience from living the past decade in East Tennessee, and from previous stretches in "red-state" America, indicates that conservative politicians, media, and intellectuals try to minimize or deny altogether the persistent extent of right-wing pathology in "the real America," which eclipses any counterpart on the American left since the long-forgotten days of Stalinists, Lee Harvey Oswald, the Black Panthers, the Symbionese Liberation Army, and the Weathermen. We all tend to project from our own limited locales; liberals or leftists like me living and teaching in conservative areas are probably inclined to overestimate the strength and extremism of the right elsewhere, while conservatives in liberal areas do the opposite.

My longtime acquaintance David Horowitz has lived his whole life in the radical chic enclaves of New York (where he went to Columbia), Berkeley (where he was a grad student in English, and where I met him), San Francisco, and Los Angeles, where until recently his home office was on Wilshire Boulevard near UCLA; it is now in upscale suburban Sherman Oaks. Thus he understandably exaggerates the dominance of the left nationally and romanticizes provincial conservatism on the basis of his Potemkin-Village lecture visits to college towns under the auspices of conservative student organizations and foundations. When I described my experiences with conservative students while teaching at Cal Poly and University of Tennessee to Horowitz in an email, he tipped his hand in replying, "So you've taught in some conservative backwater schools in the South [San Luis Obispo?]. Who cares and what has this got to do-except as a marginal anomaly—with the state of higher education in America?" (email 17 Jan. 2006). Horowitz and other conservative polemicists would never use this language in their public pronouncements, which extol "the heartland," "the real America," and conservative colleges in contrast to liberal elite universities that are themselves alleged to be the "marginal anomaly," out of touch with the vast majority of Americans and college students, in those "backwaters," with their more sensible beliefs. Heads I win, tails you lose.

Whenever leftists like me make arguments like these, conservative polemicists' boilerplate response is to accuse *us* of contempt for the masses (though, like Horowitz, they will on occasion let slip their own contempt for the "backwaters"), rather than blaming the upper-class conservatives who posture as champions of the common people while insulting their intelligence and dragging mass discourse down to the level of Rupert Murdoch's tabloid and TV empire. Conservative media executives and politicians claim they are just "giving the people what they want." So does the drug pusher peddling *his* narcotics. I ask conservative intellectuals: Shouldn't you hold corporate executives to any standards of ethics or literacy in their practices other than maximizing profits, politicians to no standards other than winning elections? The older conservative notion of a patrician class exercising a sense of social responsibility seems to have been jettisoned in the wake of global corporate hegemony and take-no-prisoners Republican politics, with few expressions of protest by conservative intellectuals. (Laudable exceptions here included David Frum, Sam Tanenhaus, Ross Douthat, Andrew Sullivan, and Bruce Bartlett.) By the 2010s, the Republican candidates for president and other high offices were competing in disparagement of the value of higher education and dismissal of science, epitomized by Herman Cain after repeatedly being caught in ignorance of major world affairs: "Who knows every detail of every country or every situation on the planet? Nobody! We've got plenty of experts. We need a leader, not a reader" (Saulny).

Another instance of the conservative elite manipulating the mass base is the neoconservative followers of Leo Strauss who embrace his notion of "the noble lie," by which the ruling intelligentsia manipulate, for the people's own good, simplistic mass beliefs in religion, patriotism, and conventional morality, without practicing those beliefs themselves. Irving Kristol was on record avowing this kind of manipulation in support of wars and of Reaganomics, which he did not really believe in but which worked to elect Republicans (see Kristol, "American Conservatism").

Do those at the higher cognitive levels of liberalism similarly exploit those at the lower ones? Undoubtedly in communist countries, and sometimes American "limousine liberals" also do so, though the political and financial rewards tend to be lower and turned toward conservative ends; if presidents like Clinton and Obama sold out their liberal constituencies, it was to corporate powers, not to labor unions, the poor, pacifists, or environmentalists. There is a significant asymmetry here. The fact that those like Clinton and Obama build their public image and get elected by appealing to liberal and left constituencies indicates that the American populace is farther to the left than is generally acknowledged, but that Democratic politicians pose as liberals only to gain office and impose many aspects of a conservative agenda, such as crony capitalism and war-making, where they are pressured to show themselves more Republican than the Republicans.

TELEVISION'S RESTRICTED-CODE CONSERVATISM

[It is] "inconceivable that we should allow so great a possibility for service to be drowned in advertising chatter." If a presidential message ever became "the meat in a sandwich of two patent medicine advertisements," it would destroy broadcasting.

Republican Secretary of Commerce Herbert Hoover, in 1922, opposing the introduction of commercially-sponsored radio. (quoted in Barnouw 15)

It is manifest that the individual cognitive traits of restricted codes diagnosed by Bernstein correspond to those transmitted and engendered by commercial television, and it is equally manifest that these traits form a major impediment to education for critical thinking. When Howard Jarvis, sponsor of Proposition 13, the momentous 1978 tax-cutting ballot initiative in California, was asked why he spent all his advertising money on TV and radio rather than newspapers, he replied, "People who decide elections today don't read" (quoted in *Los Angeles Times*, Feb. 10, 1980, Pt. 2, p. 1). The professional consultants who developed the rapid-fire, "action news" format for local newscasts justified it by claiming, "People who watch television the most are unread, untraveled, and unable to concentrate on single subjects for more than a minute at a time" (quoted in *San Francisco Examiner*, 16 Mar. 1975, 14).

It would verge on conspiracy theory to attribute every restricted-code trait of TV to political machination by conservative forces, rather than to the quest to maximize corporate profits. Analyzing this quest ultimately leads to basic questioning of the conservative imperatives of a capitalist economy, but that is a later point for argument. More immediately, what are the indirect political *consequences* of TV's restricted codes? This question has been addressed by a long line of scholars and cultural critics, going back to at least the 1950s, who have seen conservative implications in commercial TV's sound-bite oversimplification, stereotypes and slogans, atomized thought, consumerist mentality, distraction, and confusion of the significant and trivial, the long-term and the ephemeral. (I surveyed these themes in a section of readings and works cited, titled "Media, Literacy, and Political Socialization" in *American Media and Mass Culture*.)

No one has summed it up better than Aldous Huxley in *Brave New World Revisited*: "A society, most of whose members spend a great part of their time, not on the spot, not here and now and in the calculable future, but somewhere else, in the irrelevant other worlds of sport and soap opera, of mythology and metaphysical fantasy, will find it hard to resist the encroachments of those who would manipulate and control it" (267–68). Like the Frankfurt School, Huxley stressed the points of similarity between the use of propaganda and social control in totalitarian dictatorships and modern capitalist democracies, where there may be a generic "Dr. Jekyl" devoted to democratically elevating public intelligence, but also "Mr. Hyde," a motivational-research analyst seeking only "to find out the best way to take advantage of [people's] ignorance and to exploit their irrationality for the pecuniary benefit of his employer" (278). "His employer" is the media corporations or the political parties that "merchandize their candidates and issues by the same methods that business had developed to sell goods.... Candidates need, in addition to rich voices and good diction, to be able to look 'sincerely' at the TV camera" (285).

Similar lines of analysis have been pursued by more recent critics like Robert Putnam in *Bowling Alone: The Collapse and Revival of American Community*, Jeffrey Scheuer in *The Sound-Bite Society: How Television Helps the Right and Hurts the Left*, and Todd Gitlin in *Media Unlimited: How the Torrent of Images and Sounds Overwhelms Our Lives*. Gitlin sums up this line as follows:

> As Jeffrey Scheuer has powerfully argued, American broadcasting is systematically biased because it gains our attention by virtue of being kinetic, episodic, personalized, and conflictual, because it systematically breaks large subjects into small chunks. Automatically, then, it leads to simplification. Since conservatives tend to be more Machiavellian than liberals, and more zealous about their politics, conservatives play better on the air, and so, for commercial reasons, television and talk-radio will be disproportionately right wing. (164–65)

I would only qualify Gitlin's account by noting again that Orwell's *1984* and *Animal Farm* depict a conceivable left-wing version of all these traits, largely realized in communist countries. It would be a far stretch, though, to claim to find such traits dominating the present-day American left, notwithstanding a disturbing movement in that direction by MSNBC's liberal screamers like Chris Matthews and Al Sharpton or Bill Maher on HBO. After all, the most common rap against Democratic leaders is that they are overly cerebral wusses, like Al Gore failing to contest the 2000 election result, John Kerry not fighting back against his Swift Boat attackers, and Barack Obama naively expecting cooperation from Congressional Republicans.

Gitlin continues:

> If the media flow is central to our civilization, where is democracy? The answer is: largely reduced to a sideshow. This is partly because of the media's political skew toward the hypervaluation of private

life and the devaluation of public life.... But skew, much castigated by critics, is the least of media's political impacts. The bigger story is demobilization. The ceaseless quest for disposable feeling and pleasure hollows out public life altogether. If most people find processed images and sounds more diverting, more absorbing, than civic life and self-government, what becomes of the everyday life of parties, interest groups, and movements, the debates, demands, and alliances that make democracy happen? (165)

Gitlin cites Putnam's conclusion that "among all the factors that might predict civic disengagement, 'dependence on television for entertainment' was 'the single most consistent predictor.' The additional hour a day Americans on average spent in front of the TV in 1995 as compared to 1965 might account, by itself, for 'perhaps one-quarter of the drop in civic engagement'" (Gitlin 166). Several studies in empirical research correlating TV-viewing with political views have concluded that the more commercial TV people watch, the more traits of restricted-code conservatism they tend to show (see Gerbner et al.). At least two academic studies have indicated that heavy viewers of Fox News are more misinformed about political issues than consumers of other news media (Kull et al.; Cassino).

Gitlin next adds:

> Moreover, if Putnam is right, it would follow not only that television weakens civil society, but also that national politics will tilt to the conservative side. Governing interests thrive when there is no popular mobilization to contest with. Those who wish to conserve their economic power have less need to mobilize voters. On the other hand, those who want to shift the balance of power toward the left—the poor, minorities, and labor—need to stir up action. This media saturation certainly retards. (166)

Conservatives will counter by arguing that it is the poor (represented by lobbies like ACORN), minorities, labor, liberals in media and education, and other left constituencies—backed by George Soros—who hold the balance of power, so that it is populist conservatives like the Tea Party who are compelled to stir up action against the status quo, with the selfless support of backers like the Koch Brothers who view conservatives as underdogs fighting the entrenched power of the left. Here again, these opposing views need to be adjudicated through impartial weighing of evidence in their support. Still, it is hard to imagine a substantial conservative rebuttal to the argument that, whatever accommodations to liberal interests those owners and advertisers might make, their bottom line is the bottom line, the maximizing of profits that keep the wheels of capitalism turning, and that this necessitates appeal to the lowest common denominator.

Where are the trends in commercial television and other media in recent decades leading?[3] Incessant speedup in manufacturing, communication, and politics has led to ever more shoddy and wasteful commodities, news reporting, and government policies. The Internet has admirably expanded the range of information and viewpoints beyond any other medium, but it too has become captive to speedup, as daily newspapers are pressured into hourly updates and as weekly journals (even the *Chronicle of Higher Education*) have become dailies, with serious slippage of editorial vetting. Talk radio, cable news channels, the explosion of information in the blogosphere, have exponentially compounded the tendencies to propagate information with little or no fact-checking, to fixate on the trivial and ephemeral in a constant present tense in which no one cares about historical continuity or correcting past errors. Sponsors of dishonest political ads calculate that by the time fact-checkers research their claims, the corrections are relegated to the back pages; nor is there any legal means for preventing false claims in these ads, other than suing for slander.

Probably the most corroding cognitive influence since the 1980s has been the arrival of cable news and sports networks pouring out information 24/7, mainly driven by the insatiable corporate quest for multiplying markets and advertising profits. Corporate control over the Federal Communication Commission has led to loosening of restrictions on advertising time on TV, including restoration of hard liquor ads, in which hip yuppies are shown endlessly, riotously partying. (Why doesn't this debasing image of American youth provoke the ire of neoconservatives like Norman Podhoretz and Irving Kristol who denounce liberal moral rot and decadence?) Robert McChesney's *The Problem of the Media* documents this expansion of advertising:

> Until 1982, commercial TV broadcasters operated under a non-binding self-regulatory standard of no more than 9.5 minutes per hour of advertising during prime time and children's programming.... By 2002, advertising accounted for between 14 and 17 minutes per hour of prime-time programming.... The amount of time devoted to advertising on television during prime time grew by more than 20 percent between 1991 and 2002. (145–46)

My main argument here is not that viewers are hypnotized into buying particular advertised products. Advertisers themselves admit that the success of any given technique or campaign is unpredictable—although there is substantial evidence that constant repetition of particular commercials does influence buyers subliminally, even if they say they are annoyed by it. Many analysts on both the right and left point to instances of audience resistance, mediation, and reappropriation in response to mass media in general and advertising in particular. That line of argument, however, seems to me irrelevant to the *intention* of media owners and advertisers, which is ever-increasingly, as Herbert Marcuse put it definitively, "the systematic moronization of children and adults alike by publicity and propaganda" ("Repressive Tolerance" 83).

The increase in advertising time leads to more commercial breaks and longer strings of commercials in each break. As advertising time increases, content time decreases and is broken up into ever-shorter sound-and-vision bites. The same commercials are repeated incessantly, every few minutes. To provide additional filler between commercials, the same video news clips are also repeated over and over, in the same broadcast segment, day after day. In "Propaganda Under a Dictatorship," Huxley compared the "arts of selling" to Hitler's formula: "Only constant repetition will finally succeed in imprinting an idea upon the memory of a crowd" (274). CNN and other cable news networks now make a game out of a round of pundits compressing their take on current events into 30 seconds or less. Cable news and talk programs include teaser previews of stories to be covered right after the next commercial break, only to be followed by repetition of the same teaser and another round of commercials.

As noted earlier, constantly expanding election campaigns profit TV and other media that hype up audience numbers and consequent advertising revenue from the extended news coverage and political advertising. The longer campaigns and increased number of debates could facilitate more intelligent debate formats, with in-depth discussions, substantive rebuttals and counter-rebuttals, and voices from parties other than Democrats and Republicans, but to this date, the result has just been more extended, mind-numbing repetition of the same sound-bite slogans, scripts, talking points, and frenetic background music played over news reports, further compounding cognitive overload.

Sports channels now also broadcast 24/7, not only ESPN but those for MLB, NFL, NBA, and PGA, even through their off-seasons!

Every sport and game from little league baseball to skateboarding provides further filler between commercials. In live coverage, telecasts now switch from one game to another every few minutes in the middle of play or show several games at once on a split screen, again with an overlay of hyperactive music. During every pitch in televised baseball games, ads are projected onto the fence behind the batter. Gratuitous time-outs are now called in televised sports to allow for more commercials. Profitable expansion of leagues and seasons, leading to overlap of baseball, football, and basketball telecasts, has created further cognitive overload for fans. Fans in previously unserved areas justifiably welcome having a local big-league team, but did the national TV audience actively "want" all this expansion, or have they passively taken what the TV producers and advertisers have given them in the quest for hyped-up profits? It seems hopelessly crankish to raise the question of what it says about Americans' atrophied sense of community and country that televised sports is our strongest common bond. How different might things be if anywhere near the amount of time and emotional investment that mass media and millions of Americans—men at least—devote to spectator sports, was devoted to becoming informed about political and economic issues at the local, national, and international levels?

The definitive prophecy of the attitude of modern corporate executives and producers of mass culture toward their workers and consumers of their products was voiced by Dostoyevsky's Grand Inquisitor: "We shall show them that they are weak, that they are only pitiable children, but that childlike happiness is the sweetest of all.... Yes, we will set them to work, but in their leisure hours we shall make their lives like a child's game, with children's song and innocent dance" (*Brothers 307*). The immediate context of Dostoevsky's fable of the Grand Inquisitor was more religious than social, its target the corrupted Christianity of the medieval Catholic Church, but the fable tied in thematically with Dostoyesky's fundamentalist-Christian rejection of modern mass society, in which he identified the secular equivalents of the Church's reign variously (perhaps confusedly) as democratic, socialistic, and materialistic: "Interpreting freedom as the multiplication and rapid satisfaction of desires, men distort their own nature... They live only for mutual envy, for luxury and ostentation" (376).

In our time, Dostoyevsky's image of social infantalization has become a keynote for dissenters from the rule of corporate grand inquisitors, such as Mario Savio speaking in the Berkeley Free Speech Movement in 1974: "America is becoming evermore the Utopia of standardized, sterilized contentment. The 'futures' and 'careers' for which American students now prepare are for the most part intellectual and moral wastelands. This chrome-plated consumers' paradise would have us grow up to become well behaved children." ("An End to History," quoted in Cohen 332).

An additional, more literal dimension of contemporary infantilization originated with the discovery by Madison Avenue in the 1950s of a highly lucrative "youth market." That discovery has been increasingly exploited through marketing to children and adolescents to pressure their parents for buy things for them, through lowering the taste level of media productions, and through reducing the age of those who appear in mass media to match this target demographic. So we have witnessed the steady lowering of the age of TV journalists and anchors, characters in film and TV dramas and the actors who portray them, and pop musicians—say, from Benny Goodman and Frank Sinatra to younger-and-younger teen favorites like Justin Bieber, who became famous at 14.[4]

In conclusion, I beseech my conservative intellectual peers: Where is your voice decrying all of these trends in corporate television and consumer society in general, the ultimate in what neoconservaiaves attribute to the moral rot and decadence in *liberal* culture? It will not do to revert to threadbare scripts extolling the free market and the sovereign consumer, with claims that no one is forced to watch TV, and so on, and so on. Those scripts evade several issues. Children get addicted to TV and its consumerist worldview before they reach the age of rational choice, and the pressures against parents preventing their children from heavy viewing are overwhelming, especially for poorer parents without the time or cultural resources to give their children alternatives. Does commercial TV, the most pervasive modern medium of information, foster a free market for interests other than the corporations that own and advertise on it? Does it provide a market for debate of public issues, or even a sales medium, at the level of a literate, discerning audience, or does it aim solely at the level of those who are "unread, untraveled, and unable to concentrate on single subjects for more than a minute at a time"? What ever happened to Thomas Jefferson's ideal of an educational system and national culture that would "[raise] the mass of people to the high ground of moral respectability necessary to their own safety, and to orderly government" (*Writings* 1308)? How can multimillionaire producers of this degradation of audiences claim that they are just giving people what they want, and should they be held to no ethical responsibility? Conservative media critics like Michael

Medved, Bernard Goldberg, Ann Coulter, and David Horowitz cherry-pick instances of overt liberal bias out of the whole flood of TV's output, while evading all of these more pervasive and invasive conservative influences. They, along with conservative educators like the National Association of Scholars and American Council of Trustees and Alumni, generally refuse to consider that public education might have a responsibility to provide an explicit corrective to all the cognitive damage inflicted by commercial TV and other media. It is easier just to reduce any such effort by teachers to imposition of leftist political correctness. So I hereby invite conservative polemicists to engage in extended dialogue on these issues.

3

SOCIALISM AS A COGNITIVE ALTERNATIVE

I reiterate that to the extent all the forces I have discussed here bolstering the capitalist status quo in America involve issues of cognition, conceptualization, and semantics, they become legitimate and necessary subjects of study in liberal education—as do socialist alternatives. In this post–Cold War, postmodern, neoliberal age, one is subject to ridicule, even in some sectors of the left, for insisting on any remnant of value not only in democratic socialism but even in social democracy.[1] Aside from Senator Bernie Sanders and the late, lamented Paul Wellstone, the lone avowed socialists in the Senate, it is taboo for any prominent American politician, journalist, or media pundit to say anything in favor of social democracy. Only in America can conservatives smear both Democratic liberals and social democrats through guilt by association with communists—an infantile equation in the eyes of Europeans who have witnessed over a century of often-bloody conflict between socialists and communists. And only in America is the whole, wide range of Marxist scholars of economics, history, social science, literature, or cultural studies tarred with guilt by association with communist dictatorships. Thus there is little challenge in mainstream politics or media to outlandish claims like that of Michael Boskin, former chair of President H. W. Bush's Council of Economic Advisors, that "the Western Europeans have seen their standard of living decline by 30% in a little more than a generation because of their high taxes" (quoted in Jonah Goldberg, 2007). Such claims lead many of my students who have never traveled abroad to picture Western European countries as police states like *1984*, with storm troopers on every corner and everyone living in shanties. So the main issue here is not the debatable efficacy of social democracy, but conservatives' monolithic propaganda campaign against it and their ludicrous exaggeration of the power and extremism of "the left" in the United States, which obstruct any evenhanded evaluation of the relative merits of America's political economy versus social-democratic ones.

Among the few recent prominent defenders of social democracy was the dean of American sociologists, Nathan Glazer, one of the mentors of neoconservatism along with Irving Kristol, but never bound to its orthodoxies as Kristol was. In 2005 Glazer wrote in a retrospective on the journal the *Public Interest* (edited by him and Kristol) in its final issue, "I flip through past issues of the *Public Interest* and am happy to see a few articles in defense of the more developed welfare states of Europe, which to my mind have created a better society than we have in the United States" ("Neoconservative" 12). Likewise, historian Tony Judt's last book, *Ill Fares the Land* (2010), was an eloquent defense of what remains viable in social democracy, with substantial evidence refuting the conservative case against it, along with a similar analysis to mine of the constrictions in our cognitive universe and public discourse that disable us (Europeans as well as Americans) from imagining any way out of the current order, no matter how far it deteriorates.

> The materialistic and selfish quality of contemporary life is not inherent in the human condition. Much of what appears "natural" today dates from the 1980s: the obsession with wealth creation, the cult of privatization and the private sector, the growing disparities of rich and poor....We cannot go on living like this. The little crash of 2008 was a reminder that unregulated capitalism is its own worst enemy....And yet we seem unable to conceive of alternatives. This too is something new. (2)

The recent debt and currency crisis in Greece, Italy, and the rest of Europe has provided the latest opportunity for conservatives to crow about the death of socialism, as they also do every time a European socialist party temporarily loses control of government. In rebuttal, I will pursue two lines of argument: first, it is extremely difficult to distinguish what antisocialist arguments may be valid and what ones stem from the perpetual campaign by capitalist propagandists to discredit any and every argument in favor of socialism; and second, even if socialism were at least for the present and immediate future discredited as an attainable economic model, it would retain its value as a cognitive and critical perspective outside the mainstream of American ideology.[2]

I make no claim to being an authority on global economics, but as a rhetorician; I see a systematic bias in mainstream American politicians' and journalists' accounts of the recent European crisis. (This is another instance where the left-of-liberal media like *The Nation*, *Dissent*, and Pacifica Radio provide a needed alternative.) European countries are in truth a mixture, under democratic government, of capitalist and socialist economies, or more precisely are capitalist economies maintaining great wealth in individuals and corporations, with some quasi-socialist curbs. In conservative propaganda, however, everything positive in those societies in comparison to America has long been suppressed, while everything negative has been attributed to "the nanny state." "Blame Socialism First" is the all-purpose mantra. Thus in American media and politics, responses to the recent European crisis downplayed the coincidence between that crisis and the Wall Street meltdown in 2008, with its repercussions on now-global financial markets and policies. Such responses further downplayed the extent to which England and other European countries have succumbed in recent decades to Reaganite-Thatcherite policies of austerity and privatization rolling back the welfare state, without considering the possibility that those policies themselves may have contributed to their economic crises.

In Europe multinational corporations have gained increasing control over governments, epitomized by recent revelations of the infiltration by Rupert Murdoch's enterprises of both the Conservative and Labor parties in England. The most shocking aspect of Stieg Larsson's best-selling "Millenium" trilogy of novels was not the lurid sexual violence but the depictions of capitalistic corruption and neo-fascist politics in "socialist" Sweden. Further pressures on those countries have come from the globalization of labor and from immigration as a source of cheap labor from the postcolonial world, the former Soviet bloc, and Muslim countries, on a scale surpassing that which prompts fury here in conservatives. In sum, if the survival of European social democracy is in jeopardy, shouldn't the possibility be considered that the primary cause has not been its socialistic elements but its capitalistic ones and the impossibility of avoiding worldwide economic disruptions? The fact is that some of the more socialized European countries like Germany, Norway, and Finland have best survived the international crisis.

In Europe, and even more in America, political policies in response to the recession following 2008 have increasingly followed the lead of free market conservatives rather than of social democrats, as in the Democratic cave-in to the agenda set by Republicans of panic over governmental debt, to which the proposed solution was still-further tax cuts and ever more austere cuts in government agencies and "entitlements." The subsequent failure of the economy to improve has not led to consideration of a reversal of direction but to still greater doses of the same medicine. (Within a rhetorical framework, the situation can be examined through a standard topic in causal analysis: Has a policy been unsuccessful because it has been pushed too far or not far enough?) The next predictable conservative campaigns include delaying retirement age, privatization of Social Security, Medicare, K-12, and college education, accompanied by dismantling of government agencies (the US Postal Service appears doomed) and of public employment and its employee unions, with Governor Scott Walker in Wisconsin leading the way and, at this writing in 2013, having triumphantly survived a recall election through outspending the opposition 7–1, thanks to the Koch Brothers and other conservative donors. Is there any foreseeable reversal of these trends, and if not, where will they lead?

Within a historical perspective on the period since World War II, compare the United States to European democracies that have had large socialist or labor parties and presses and far more unionized labor. After François Mitterand's election in 1981, one-third of the members of the French National Assembly were teachers, who continue to exert much more power in European parties than in the Democratic Party, in comparison, say, to corporate lobbies. Neither that conservative bogey, the "all-powerful teachers' unions" nor any other unions usually have any prominent members in the legislative, executive, or judicial branches of American federal and local government. European social democracy also includes (or did until recently) state ownership of some major industries like utilities and transportation; sharply progressive taxes; national health insurance; free education in the best secondary, undergraduate, and graduate schools; government family subsidies for home purchases; childrearing and daycare; five-week vacations for all workers; a workweek as short as 35 hours; early retirement; and far more extensive public broadcasting than in America. These features have not to this date been rolled back very much even after recent economic crises or temporary control of government by conservative parties pursuing Reaganomic and Thatcherite policies; the dominant conservative parties there are still to the left of the Democratic Party. In 2012, a French politician was quoted by Steven Erlanger in the *New York Times* affirming that the vast majority of Europeans believe in the welfare state: "The British Tories can't touch the National Health Service without being beheaded."

The financial crises following 2008 prompted a revival of European left parties along with mass protest against austerity measures, on a scale unimaginable in America, at least before the Occupy Wall Street movement. When the French Socialist Party (SP) regained power in 2012 for the first time since 1988, the op-ed by Erlanger, *Times* Paris bureau chief, asked, "What's a Socialist?" This was indeed an enigma in an era when *l'embourgeoisement* of the SP had become personified by the abominable, satyric plutocrat Dominique Strauss-Kahn. Even so, Erlanger reported, the French state represented 56.6 percent of gross domestic product, and President François Hollande proposed "hiring 60,000 more teachers over five years, raising the minimum wage (the highest in the European Union) and creating a state bank for innovation."

What Socialist Media?

As I argued in chapter 1, even if conservatives were correct in every instance they cite of liberal biases in American politics, media, and education, pointing to any number of random instances of liberal bias does not necessarily lead to the conclusion that any of these fields, or American society on the whole, are dominated by leftist ideology—especially socialist ideology. The sum total in recent years of all the liberally oriented American films, television newscasts and dramas, or print media dealing explicitly with political issues is offset by the fact that such expressions still form a minute percentage of the total media output; the dominant climate of self-absorption, apolitical distraction, and promotion of commodity consumption dissipates any political message, whether of the left or right. A 2009 study by James Curran and other prominent media scholars in the *European Journal of Communication*, comparing commercial media systems in countries like the United States with public service models in other countries concluded, "Public service television devotes more attention to public affairs and international news, and fosters greater knowledge in these areas, than the market model. Public service television also gives greater prominence to news, encourages higher levels of news consumption and contributes to a smaller within-nation knowledge gap between the advantaged and disadvantaged" (Curran, "Media System").

The success of Michael Moore's *Capitalism: A Love Story* and other documentaries, or of MSNBC's recent movement toward being a TV version of the *Nation*, provides evidence that leftist views can occasionally attain corporate funding, a mass audience, and profitability; but such successes would need to be multiplied thousands of times over really to sink into public consciousness. Only if and when business as usual ever breaks down, say, under an economic or environmental catastrophe, might the necessity of considering alternatives become viscerally evident. (Other, unpredictable points of rupture or Emperor's New Clothes moments are also possible, like the recent Occupy Wall Street movement, which touched a popular nerve on economic issues that had been marginalized in the mainstream public agenda, and the long-running cover-up of child abuse by a football coach at Penn State University, which sparked a long-suppressed questioning of the business-as-usual corruption of higher education by commercialized intercollegiate sports.)

Consider the proportionate power of the American left and right this way. Imagine a national democratic socialist party with equal resources to Democrats and Republicans. Imagine that in broadcast media and public broadcasting, newspapers and news magazines, and their Internet versions, corporate ownership and management was equaled by that of socialists, labor unions, environmentalists, feminists, pacifists, militant minority groups, advocates for the poor and consumers, liberal arts faculties, and K-12 teachers. (For just one point of contrast, France has long had two nationwide socialist daily newspapers, now online—the Communist Party's *L'Humanité* and the independent *Libération*, which originated as a voice of the protest movements of 1968.) Further imagine that every commercial advertisement in all the media—including the maddening daily flood of junk mail, telemarketing, and spam—was matched or refuted by one from these groups. "Hello, this is Rachel calling from the International Socialist Organization." (Not that I really wish for any increase in this surfeit.) Imagine that among all the magazines in supermarket checkout lines and in waiting rooms that are saturation-bombs for apolitical distraction, celebrity worship, and commodity consumption—aimed at a subadolescent literacy level—at least a few spoke for leftist interests. (My late auto mechanic in Knoxville, bless his heart, was an old lefty whose waiting room featured the *Nation*.) If such prospects strike you as facetious, isn't that the ultimate proof of how far American public discourse is skewed toward conservative business as usual, and of how overblown most allegations of left-wing bias are?

The most feasible democratic alternative in the United States to the present media monopolies, a system of broadcast and print communications providing a forum for a full range of ideological positions, is effectively precluded by lack of capital or political support for a true public broadcasting system. The virtual monopoly of corporate-owned media creates a vicious circle wherein lack of a profitable or politically sizeable constituency for left media precludes their funding—and the lack of left media precludes the growth of that constituency. Who could object, simply on the grounds of a free market of ideas, to the premise that capitalist ownership of virtually all our major sources of public information might not be in the best interests of a free society, and that a broader range of expression would result from the creation of some mass media with a socialist viewpoint, or at least from some prime airtime and print space being made available to that viewpoint? Every conceivable niche market—hobbies, beauty advice, shopping, single sports—down to skate-boarding and poker—has a 24/7 national TV channel, so why not the Socialist Channel or at least the Labor Channel? Yet even in the absence of such media, a 2009 Rasmussen survey found that only 52 percent of respondents saw capitalism in a favorable light—the lowest level since World War II—while 29 percent looked favorably on a socialist alternative (Montopoli). And a Gallup Poll in 2010 found that 36 percent of Americans and 53 percent of Democrats have a favorable image of socialism (Newport). So why should there not be something close to this proportion of representation in American politics, media, and education? In its absence, I maintain that college liberal arts courses are justified in providing *some* semblance of that representation.

In conservative polemicists' claims of leftist bias in the media, exhibits A and B are the *New York Times* and public broadcasting. However, they are demonstrably to the right of the *Nation* and other left journals of opinion, Pacifica Radio, or websites like Commondreams.org—except in the eyes of those conservatives who have so little sense of discrimination that they can see no difference among media that are to their own left but that fiercely disagree with one another from different positions on a center-to-left spectrum. The *Times* and NPR-PBS are the prime targets for claims of conservative bias in the mainstream media by left media critics like FAIR and Media Matters. (FAIR and MM provide useful classroom sources as a counterpoint to all the claims of liberal/left bias in the *Times*, NPR-PBS, and others, by conservative critics like Bernard Goldberg and Brent Bozell's Media Research Center). The *Times* editors periodically avow that their viewpoint simply accords with that of the urban, professional profile of its target audience. (Conservatives are all for media giving the people what they want—except when the people in question happen to be liberals.) Even so, the liberalism of *Times* writers like Frank Rich, Paul Krugman, Bob Herbert, Charles Blow, Gale Collins, Joe Nocera, and David Cay Johnston (who actually describes himself as a libertarian conservative) is somewhat offset by one or more regular conservative columnists (currently David Brooks and Ross Douthat), editors like Charles McGrath and Sam Tanenhaus, and reporters like Richard Bernstein and Judith Miller (a conduit for Bush administration disinformation in pushing for the Iraq War, who left the *Times* for the Heritage Foundation). The liberal elements are also dissipated by their juxtaposition with corporate-friendly business reporting and huge feature sections on upscale style, larded with ads for Gucci handbags, Tiffany jewelry, and multimillion-dollar houses (likewise for the editorially liberal *New Yorker*).

As for public broadcasting, in an historical survey in *The Death and Life of American Journalism*, Robert McChesney and John Nichols note that European countries were able to establish well-funded public systems early in the twentieth century before commercial broadcasters gained power, and that systems like the BBC have steadfastly maintained ideological independence from both government and business. Here, however, the first movement for public broadcasting in 1934 was squelched by corporate media. When PBS and NPR were finally established in the sixties, a supporting Carnegie Commission report envisioned them as "producing cutting-edge political and creative programming that commercial broadcasters found unprofitable and serving poor and marginalized audiences of little interest to advertisers" (193–94). Ever since then, however, PBS and NPR have been underfunded and steadily depoliticized—(think Lawrence Welk, "Antiques Roadshow," old British sitcoms, Suze Orman ("The Courage to be Rich"), Yonni, rock concerts and reviews, "Car Talk," "The Elegant Table". Underfunding by government has forced PBS and NPR to pitch programming to an affluent audience that attracts corporate foundation funding and contributes to interminable pledge drives. In recent decades, several PBS public affairs programs have been produced by conservative think tanks—indeed "Think Tank" was hosted by Ben Wattenburg at the American Enterprise Institute. Corporate "underwriting" has also oozed into PBS's programming, as in the PR pitches for Chevron Oil and Archer-Daniels-Midland beginning each "News Hour" and featuring inane musical jingles, unctuous narrators, and plain-folks testimonies to multinational corporations' deep concern for small business, environmental protection, and most recently education (as promoted of course by corporate programs), repeated insultingly every day, year after year—"OK, listen," the earnest, average teenage girl implores the camera on behalf of Chevron.

The range of political opinion on PBS is epitomized by the ubiquitous moderate conservative David Brooks and the soporific Democratic centrism of Mark Shields, Jim Lehrer, and Jon Meacham, the *Newsweek* editor who replaced "Bill Moyers' Journal" when the feisty progressive Moyers (temporarily) retired. Despite Moyers, "Frontline," "Independent Lens," some other liberal documentaries and arts programming, the overall political identity of PBS and NPR is just amorphous. It is one more index of how far the American media spectrum is skewed to the right that conservatives constantly try to eliminate government support for them because of their alleged leftist bias. Conservatives anomalously appeal to fear of socialistic government control over public broadcasting in America, while it is conservative administrations that have acted most unscrupulously to control—or kill—it, as in the episode of the Republican chair of the Corporation for Public Broadcasting, Kenneth Tomlinson, who pressured PBS to cancel Moyers' program. It seems as though conservatives designate as "leftist bias" the airing of *any* liberal opinion in media like the *Times* and PBS that are at heart, that is, in their corporate management, bastions of capitalism and American nationalism.

Cognitive Deprivation

As chapter 1 suggested, the "business as usual" of capitalism and nationalism is immediate and familiar, while socialist alternatives are hypothetical, distant, and alien. The ideology of capitalism and nationalism is propagated less through theoretical discourse than through constant, saturating repetition of its everyday manifestations. Socialism entails a completely different system of thought that takes more time to explain than is available in any area of American public discourse except for advanced scholarship and intellectual journalism. (A major anomaly of cultural politics in contemporary America is that access to socialist thought has largely become restricted to intellectuals, especially academic ones, whose own class position in many cases is ultimately inimical to socialism.)

Suppose then, if only hypothetically, that democratic socialism (not its totalitarian perversions in communist countries) did in fact present some preferable alternatives to capitalism in America. In the present ideological climate, the vast majority of the public would never even have access to knowledge of those alternatives. People suffering from immediate, intense oppression—the situation of the proletariat in Marx's scenario for socialist revolution or Third World colonies after World War II, of American blacks who waged the civil rights movement and feminists who fought for women's rights—need little abstract information or theoretical sophistication to be persuaded that change is in their interests. In present-day America, however, the grosser forms of injustice have been greatly reduced, and the majority of the population has been socialized into a mood of at least passive assent. Even as they have lost ground economically over the past three decades and become increasingly disgruntled, most have little understanding of the dynamics of the global and domestic forces squeezing them, including the exploitation of Third World (and now Chinese) labor and resources on which the West's relative affluence depends. In order for people to perceive and effectively oppose such realities, they need not only to have access to a diversity of information sources, many of which are in print and written at an advanced level of literacy, but to have the analytic reasoning capacities to evaluate distant events and abstract data. The information and explanations necessary for analysis simply aren't widely accessible. Having lived most of my life in various Middle-American communities, I can testify that the Chamber of Commerce view of reality, in which what's good for business is good for America and the world, is the only one most people in such communities are ever exposed to from cradle to grave.

In another historical perspective, a cover story in the *Time* magazine issue of April 24, 1989, was titled "Living: How America Has Run Out of Time.". It noted, "In 1967 testimony before a Senate subcommittee indicated that by 1985 people could be working just 22 hours a week or 27 weeks a year or could retire at 38. That would leave only the great challenge of finding a way to enjoy all that leisure" (Gibbs 59). Those predictions of vastly increased leisure time even led Milton Friedman and President Nixon, as well as neoconservative senator Daniel Patrick Moyniham, to propose paying people not to work, through a negative income tax or guaranteed minimum income.

However, *Time* lamented, after the economic reversals of the seventies and eighties, "The amount of leisure time enjoyed by the average American has shrunk 37% since 1973. Over the same period, the average workweek, including commuting, has jumped from under 41 hours to nearly 47 hours. In some professions, predictably law, finance and medicine, the demands often stretch to 80-plus hours a week" (Gibbs 58). Typical of the failure of mass media to place concrete events in an ideological context, *Time* simply treated these economic developments as if they were acts of God, without analyzing what political policies may have produced them or who benefits from them, for example, globalization, the downscaling of wages by American corporations, and the growing gap between the rich and everyone else, accelerated by Reaganomic policies. The same mystifications have marked mainstream accounts of subsequent decline among most Americans.

Analyzing the even worse acceleration of the trends noted by *Time* in the subsequent two decades, Susan Searls Giroux presented a more precise causal analysis in a 2005 article in *Journal of Advanced Composition*:

> In addition to a massive tax restructuring that has starved social programs for the benefit of the very rich, we've also seen the stagnation of wages for working people.... The pay gap between top executives and production workers grew from 42:1 in 1980 to a staggering 419–1 in 1998 (excluding the value of stock options), according to *Business Week*'s "Forty-ninth Annual Executive Pay Survey." The same report notes that "Had the typical worker's pay risen in tandem with executive pay, the average production worker would now earn $110,000 a year and the minimum wage would be $22.08" instead of the current wage of $5.15. And how does this wage figure in terms of yearly salary? A 40-hour week at $5.15 per hour "nets a pre-tax annual income of $10,3000, or about $6,355 below the official 1998 poverty line for a family of four." In contrast to these poverty wages, "the average large company chief executive was paid $10.6 million, a 36 percent jump over 1997." (970–71)

Giroux went on to examine the impact of these trends on individuals: "Citing Bureau of Labor Statistics, [Jeff] Gates reports that 'the typical American now works 350 hours more per year than a typical European—almost nine full weeks.'... 'They have less parental leave, less affordable day care, and the least number of paid holidays and vacations of all industrialized nations.'" (971)

Giroux concluded with a poignant account of the cognitive consequences on citizens and, tacitly, on college students, which brings her article within the scope of humanistic studies including composition (hence its publication in *JAC*):

> Citizenship requires time for the task of locating and researching various positions on key policy debates (a task even more complicated

given the paucity of alternative views in the dominant media sources), for reading and critiquing, sorting out ideological claims buried in "the facts," and weighing alternative positions in terms of the human costs and social costs as opposed to simply financial costs. Without that time, Paul Street concludes, "brain-weary worker-citizens tend to become over-reliant on the often bad, generally biased, and heavily filtered information manufactured by those whose salaried task is to shape mass opinion in the interests of those who pay their salaries." The upshot is apparent public approval for policies that mitigate against the interests of ordinary people.... It is a function of deprivation, of being deprived of the information one needs to make informed decisions on matters of grave social concern, of being deprived of time to think through the choices and consequences of public policy decisions,... and deprived of any sense of security to foster anything other than the frightened reactions of the besieged. (972–73)

Neither Democratic nor Republican leaders have been able to implement effective policies for dealing with the widening wealth gap or the return of high unemployment and poverty rates in the recent decades, and these trends might be irreversibly structured into the long-term declining economic picture for all but the wealthy. I have heard no prominent Democrat invoking those rosy forecasts from the sixties about ever-increasing leisure time, in order to revive those earlier proposals by conservative economists for a guaranteed minimum income even without work, or to float the idea of creating more employment through *earlier* retirement, not later, and cutting the workweek and year, with more vacation time, without cutting wages. If socialist concepts like these were to disappear from consciousness, and if the present American and global economic system were to collapse or lead to environmental catastrophe—which are less outlandish prospects than they would have appeared before 2008—society might be at a loss in envisioning possible ways to start over.

Isn't there something to be said, then, for at least preserving in the human imagination the socialist ideals of an economic common community, guaranteed employment and living wage, reduction of required work time, democracy in governance of work and of employers' economic and political activities—and an ultimate end to the long-established bonds between work and basic subsistence, with the corollary power of employer over worker? And mightn't college liberal arts teachers perhaps be indulged in this role, like the monks who preserved the manuscripts of classical humanists through the Middle Ages?

Socialism and the Privatizing of Politics in American Culture

In chapter 1, I discussed the reduction of social issues to personal experience in postwar American politics, mass media, education, and literature and the corollary exclusion of political dimensions of such issues—a fortiori the exclusion of socialist perspectives. Barbara Kingsolver is currently one of the most committed, astute American political novelists and essayists. Her 2009 novel *The Lacuna* is an account of the intersections of art and politics in Mexico in the 1930s, focused on Leon Trotsky's fatal sojourn with Frida Kahlo and Diego Rivera. According to an interview about it with Cynthia Crossen in the *Wall Street Journal*, she started working on it in February 2002, "when a 'long-term ache' to write about the estrangement of art and politics in the U.S. was fired up by the events that followed 9/11." Kingsover says, "For the past 20 years, I have often found myself on the defensive when people ask if it's appropriate to write novels about power imbalances related to gender or ethnicity. I've wondered why art and politics seem to have an uneasy relationship in the U.S., while they travel hand in hand in most of the world. People elsewhere look to art and literature for commentary on the social and political aspects of the culture.... I had a hunch it was related to historical events... the McCarthy era and that period of ferocious political censorship of art. Art and politics were forced apart at that time, and we've never gotten over it." (Crossen, "Kahlo.")

Thus as previously noted, in undergraduate literary survey courses after World War II, the strong tendency of literary anthology editors was to steer clear of political writings. In American surveys, Jack London is typically represented by "The Law of Life" or "To Build a Fire"—rarely by any of his socialist works. Charlotte Perkins Gilman has likewise been represented by "The Yellow Wallpaper" rather than by *Herland* or her socialist works. "The Yellow Wallpaper" is also typical of the preference of anthology editors for stories dealing with mental illness and suicide as reflections of purely personal, psychological conflicts divorced from any political context. The political writings of Thoreau, Emerson, Melville, Whitman, Twain, Howells, and Wharton have similarly been downplayed (see chapter 10). Likewise in mass entertainment media. Here is a description in a cable TV guide of a film version of *The Mysterious Stranger*, Twain's savage existentialist fable that attacks, among other political targets, racial bigotry and religious hypocrisy in justification of imperialism and war, written out of Twain's anger over the Spanish-American War: "In a film adaptation of Mark Twain's delightful fantasy, a printer's naive apprentice from Missouri daydreams himself into a medieval European castle and meets a magical youth called 44, who displays fascinating powers"—fascinating powers in the original version like, in emulation of both God and warring nations, wiping out whole populations of miniature humans like swatting flies, with the offhand explanation, "It is no matter; we can make plenty more." (*Great Short Works* 289). (Twain's suppressed political writings were detailed in Philip S. Foner's case for Twain as a staunch socialist in *Mark Twain Social Critic*, published in 1958 by the Communist Party's International Publishers in New York—an audacious enterprise in that beleaguered time.)

When I teach works like Rebecca Harding Davis's *Life in the Iron Mills*, Gilman's *Herland*, Upton Sinclair's *The Jungle*, Simone de Beauvoir's *The Mandarins*, Isabel Allende's *The House of the Spirits*, Doris Lessing's and Nadine Gordimer's African fiction, or even Orwell's *1984* and Huxley's *Brave New World* and *Brave New World Revisited*, I have found it necessary to preface them with lengthy handouts and lectures glossing the historical background and basic vocabulary these books presuppose in readers—for example, the spoils system, monopoly and trusts, populism, progressivism, colonialism, socialism, plutocracy, and labor versus capital. Even with such explanations, the completely predictable response of most students is to respond only to the personal conflicts while skimming or blanking out the political content. Students and teachers often skip the long "Goldstein's book" section in *1984*, but I consider it the heart of the book, a profound commentary on the course of twentieth-century history and social psychology, in regard to capitalism and socialism, authoritarianism, war, colonialism, poverty, mass society, and literacy. I would hope that conservative culture warriors like the National Association of Scholars and William J. Bennett whom I discuss in later chapters will concur with me, in their calls for more study of history in K-12 and college education, on the need for emphasizing *these* aspects of history.

These diminutions of politics in American culture have long been analyzed by Marxist-influenced critics. I recently rediscovered the posthumous 1962 collection of Robert Warshow's essays titled *The Immediate Experience*. Warshow was one of the most brilliant critics associated with the "New York Intellectuals," and particularly *Commentary*, until his untimely death in 1955. Immersed by family upbringing in the culture wars on the left between communists and democratic socialists, Stalinists and Trotskyists, he was most adamant in his essays in debunking the fraudulence in popular cultural works of the thirties and forties that parroted the Communist Party's vulgar Marxism and Popular Front propaganda; these essays made him a mentor for later neoconservative polemicists. His anti-Stalinist essays, however, are counterbalanced by ones like an exemplary Marxist analysis of conservative mystification of socioeconomic issues in the Academy-Award-winning 1946 film *The Best Years of Our Lives*, along with many other products of mass culture.

> The falsehood has many aspects, but its chief and most general aspect is a denial of the reality of politics, if politics means the existence of real incompatibilities of interest and real *social* problems not susceptible of individual solutions.... Every problem [is presented] as a problem of personal morality.... A conscious effort is made to show that class differences do not matter.... The problem of the monopoly of capital is reduced to a question of the morals of banks; if bankers are good men, then they will grant small loans (not large loans, apparently) to deserving veterans (those who are willing to work hard) without demanding collateral.... The small loan is apparently conceived to be some kind of solution to the economic difficulties of capitalism—cf. *It's a Wonderful Life*. (Warshow, 128–29)

Warshow, writing just before the cultural Cold War set in, was examining the deeply rooted, privatizing tendency in American culture, which Toqueville noted in *Democracy in America*. This tendency was to take a new turn in literature and criticism during the Cold War with a retreat from the kind of holistic social critique associated with Marxism, which Warshow was practicing—now unjustly considered discredited by its Stalinist vulgarizations and displaced throughout the culture by fixation on problems of personal morality and psychology.

By the sixties, however, New Left critics revived Warshow's theme with an assault against the Cold War "culture of narcissism," in the book title of historian Christopher Lasch, one of the leading critics of the time. Another of his definitive titles, "The Cultural Cold War," subtitled "A Short History of the Congress for Cultural Freedom" was a chapter in his 1968 book *The Agony of the American Left*. Lasch wavered between a Frankfurt School-ish perspective on capitalist society and conservative nostalgia for precapitalist communitarianism. Louis Kampf expressed a more directly Marxist view than Lasch's in "The Scandal of Literary Scholarship" (1968): "A totally self-centered individualism is not necessarily a sign of heroism or nobility; it may, in fact, serve as a mask for the competitive depredations of capitalism. The narcissistic obsession of modern literature for the self, the critical cant concerning the tragic isolation of the individual—these are notions which tie our hands and keep us from the communion necessary for meaningful action" (56–57). (See the related sections in my *American Media* titled "Capitalism and American Mythology" and "Moments of Historical Consciousness.")

In a brilliant *Film Quarterly* article in 1975, reminiscent of Warshow, Peter Biskind analyzed Elia Kazan's *On the Waterfront* (1954) as a thinly coded justification of Kazan's cooperation with the House Un-American Activities Committee and a portrayal of crypto-communist union corruption, depicted in isolation from the larger political economy from which such corruption arises. Biskind concluded: "Kazan twists and turns to avoid confronting the implications of American power and power in America.... Power struggles in the public sphere are displaced into moral struggles in the private sphere" (Lazere, *American Media* 196). (Biskind would later go the way of all flesh in becoming a celebrity journalist, writing best-sellers like a tell-all biography of Warren Beatty—which did at least thoughtfully explore the anomalies of Beatty's limousine liberalism.)

New Left critics also identified the pattern in Cold War culture of an animus toward not only socialist governments but also liberal ones. Thus they analyzed films glorifying the solitary hero who bypasses inept government authority by dispensing vigilante justice, à la *High Noon* or Clint Eastwood's *Dirty Harry* and spaghetti-western movies, or those, from *The Blackboard Jungle* in 1955 to *Dangerous Minds* in 1995, about the charismatic individual teacher (usually white) inspiring inner-city minority students, against the odds of poverty and bureaucratic administration—thus evading the root causes of poverty and discriminatory funding in poor versus rich school districts. More recent variations on the vigilante hero theme identified by Marxist critics include films like the Batman and Iron Man series, in which billionaires alone are able to stand up to villainous criminals or terrorists who have overpowered police and government, through their plutocratic power in the private sector. (For similar recent Marxist studies of film, TV drama, comics, pop music, and other popular culture, see Jameson [*Signatures*], Aronowitz and Giroux; Willis; Grossberg; Ehrenreich; Dorfman; and Dorfman and Mattelart.)

Unfortunately, even the invigorating attention in cultural studies to the politics of gender and racial issues in recent decades has been moving toward displacement into the private sphere in its tendencies toward unlimited pluralism or exclusively individual identity and concepts of empowerment, as Walter Benn Michaels argues in *The Trouble with Diversity*. I have been struck by the fact that my students, who are mostly middle-class whites and not feminists, tend to respond more positively to literature about the personal tribulations of women and minorities than to those that deal with broader political themes (and, as noted above, they invariably focus on the personal rather than the political dimensions of works that contain both). I suspect this response goes beyond purely aesthetic judgments and reflects the traits of American individualistic socialization, restricting consciousness to personal experience and psychology to the exclusion of the political context in which the personal is formed. These student responses are pertinent to debates among cultural leftists over whether issues of race, gender, or class should take precedence, or, more broadly, whether questions of race and gender can or should be addressed independently of (or in opposition to) a Marxist or other "master discourse" placing race and gender issues in a larger socioeconomic context. Arguments about whether patriarchy and racism have preceded or superseded capitalism and socialism historically are important, to be sure, but they sometimes obscure the essential relationship of racial or gender issues to political economy in contemporary society.

It is noteworthy here that feminism, multiculturalism, and gay rights have been more readily assimilated into mainstream culture and education than have class and labor issues or socialist voices—largely because the former causes can be absorbed without addressing the latter ones, as can be seen in the increased presence of upscale minorities, "liberated women," and gays perpetuating the corporate status quo in journalism and entertainment. A *New York Times Magazine* full-page color ad (9 May 2010) depicted in their upscale Connecticut kitchen "Paris-born designer Robert Couturier and his partner Jeffrey Morgan," who "live elegantly among centuries of antique treasures. Brand new among them is the six-burner, 48-inch gas range and double oven in their new GE Monogram kitchen." It is not so easy to imagine Madison Avenue co-opting poor people, labor unions, or socialists.

In 1990, historian Elizabeth Fox-Genovese (then a Marxist, though tending toward neoconservatism) said about revision of the academic canon toward identity politics:

> The new literary studies in race and gender have focused on recovering personal experience rather than a systematic view of the central

dynamics of American society and culture. The haste to dismiss Marxism thus merges with a general disinclination to engage general theories of social and cultural relations and leaves many of the new studies hostage to the models that they are attacking. ("American Culture" 22–23)

Elsewhere Fox-Genovese wrote:

> At some point the attack on the received canon shifted ground.
>
> Increasingly, the attack has been waged in the name of the individual's right to education as a personal history, a parochial culture, and a private epistemology. The worst of it is that the "radical" critics of the purportedly irrelevant canon have sacrificed the ideal of collective identity that constituted its most laudable feature. To settle for education as personal autobiography or identity is tacitly to accept the worst forms of political domination. ("The Claims" 133)

"The ideal of collective identity" here seems related to "the central dynamics of American society and culture," not to the simplistic celebrations of national chauvinism advocated by Republican propagandists like William J. Bennett and Lynne Cheney. One can say by the same token that to settle for political democracy defined as everyone's freedom to affirm personal autobiography or identity, at the expense of critical education and communication media for comprehensive critique of capitalism and conceiving possible socialist alternatives, is also tacitly to accept the worst forms of political domination.

Part II

Countering the Conservative Counter-Establishment

4

THE CONSERVATIVE ATTACK MACHINE: "ADMIT NOTHING, DENY EVERYTHING, LAUNCH COUNTERATTACK"

> The difference between the well-thought-out, unending and no-holds-barred hostility of the left and the acquiescent, friendship-seeking nature of many of my Republican colleagues never ceases to amaze me.
>
> Newt Gingrich, quoted in Ferguson, "What Does Newt Know?" 21

> According to Horowitz, conservatives often fail to understand that there is a political war at all, or disapprove of the fact that there may be one. The conservative paradigm is based on individualism, compromise, and partial solutions, and regards politics as a management issue, an effort to impose limits on what government may do. This puts conservatives at a disadvantage in political combat with the left, whose paradigm of oppression inspires missionary zeal and is perfectly suited to aggressive tactics and no-holds-barred combat.
>
> Jamie Glazov, introduction to David Horowitz's *Left Illusions* xxxii

> In fields ranging from education to art to law, the attack on truth has been accompanied by an assault on standards. The connection is seldom made clear. Indeed, one of the characteristics of postmodern thought is that it is usually asserted rather than argued, reasoned argument having been rejected as one of the tools of the white male elite.... So much that follows from denying the idea of truth is deeply unsettling. We have to worry not only about whether our educational and cultural institutions will pass along an accurate and balanced history to our children, but also about whether they will communicate to them the importance of reason, of trying to overcome bias, of using evidence to arrive at conclusions.
>
> Lynne Cheney, *Telling the Truth* 18–20

The conservative assault on academic political correctness must be viewed in the context of a continuous series of political and cultural offensives, engineered by the Republican Party and its allies since the 1970s. The Republican strategy of attack and polarization has persisted up to the present, indeed reaching new levels of shrillness since the elections of 2010, as in recent assaults against public employees and their unions, including in education, as well as against government agencies in general, targeted for demolition in the ginned-up panic over deficits and debt ceilings, all in the wake of the recession triggered by the Wall Street crash of 2008. Among the strategies of this offensive has been to scapegoat alleged misdeeds on the academic and cultural left as a distraction from far more pernicious activities on the right and to distort the proportions between the two. The mainstream media, with their present tense fixation, have been remiss in not considering these recent Republican campaigns as reiterations of an historical pattern, so this should be another responsibility of scholars and teachers. The next four chapters develop my earlier references to the deliberate mimicry by conservatives of every line of argument and piece of evidence supporting the left, toward the ultimate aim of obfuscating any possibility of the truth being ascertained, through what I term "right-wing deconstruction." Again, I argue that the pervasiveness and unscrupulousness of this apparatus far exceeds any counterparts on the American liberal or far left, despite the constant attempt by conservatives to claim analogies or equivalencies between the two.

Above all, my entire survey of conservative misdeeds here exposes the hypocrisy of all those American conservatives who claim to champion traditional religious or ethical morality and intellectual probity against the "rot and decadence that was no longer the consequence of liberalism but was the actual agenda of contemporary liberalism" (Irving Kristol, *Neoconservatism* 487) and "the attack on truth" through "name-calling and invective" (Lynne Cheney, *Telling the Truth: Why*) on the left, but who fail to see the beam in their own eye. Hypocrisy is by no means lacking in Democrats, liberals, and leftists, but it is especially glaring in a party that since President Nixon's time has incessantly proclaimed itself the upholder of moral standards and religious faith against their corruption by the left, as epitomized by Vice President Spiro Agnew denouncing liberals in 1972 as "the elite...the raised eyebrow cynics, the pampered egotists who sneer at honesty, thrift, hard work, prudence, common decency, and self-denial"—precisely at the time the crimes of Watergate and

Nixon's gangster-like conversations with his aides in the Whitehouse tapes were unfolding, and shortly before Agnew's own resignation under corruption and tax evasion charges (quoted in Nobile 5). As Montaigne said, "Between us, these are things that I have always seen to be in remarkable agreement: super-celestial thoughts and subterranean conduct" (601). The mainstream media have also for the most part been acquiescent in being stenographers to Republicans' claims of higher morality without holding them accountable on this hypocrisy.

These four chapters do not deal directly with teaching about these issues, which *is* the subject of chapters 8 and 9. However, I tacitly put forth these arguments as subject matter for general education courses and frame them within rhetorical topics like establishment of accurate proportions and identification of logical fallacies such as false analogies and equivalences, double standards, selective vision, and not practicing what one preaches.

In refutation of the constant claims by conservative polemicists that their "team" is only fighting back against the stronger and more unscrupulous agencies of the Democrats and leftists, I argue throughout these four chapters that, although the Democratic Party, liberals, and leftists (especially in education and media) undeniably have their realms of power and their faults, they simply do not possess anywhere near the scale of the coordinated infrastructure or the capacity to launch political and cultural offensives that the Republicans have built, which have become associated with terms like "staying on message," "scripts," and "talking points." Individual Democratic politicians like the Clintons and Obama have built their own efficient machines, but they are mostly ad hoc, not continuous for different candidates over the years like the Republicans'. Certainly there are liberal and left echo chambers, with similar conformity, clichés, and unverified citations of allies as putative documentation—I do this at times myself in this book—but they are far less organized. (Democrats come across ineptly when they try to emulate Republicans in repeating a script rather than directly answering a question.) Indeed, after lamenting for years about their failure to build a competing infrastructure, Democrats finally launched the Center for American Progress and persuaded George Soros to fund some kindred liberal projects, such as MoveOn.org—since which time, of course, conservatives have jumbled the causal and temporal sequence to claim that their projects are just an attempt to "balance" these. During the debate in 2010 over President Obama's health care reform bill, on C-SPAN I watched Mitch McConnell on the Senate floor reading nearly word for word the talking points distributed by the Republican National Committee on its website, with invocations of catchphrases coined by Republican semanticist-in-chief Frank Luntz like "death panels," "government takeover," and "deprival of individual choice," which were similarly echoed through the conservative media. (On Luntz's role, see http://www.huffingtonpost.com/2010/02/01/frank-luntz-pens-memo-to_n_444332.html.) Whenever Democrats try to raise income taxes on multimillionaires back to their levels before 1980 or even 2000, the conservative echo chamber's script is "class warfare" and "punishing job creators." I have found no such counterpart for "scripts" on the website of the Democratic National Committee or the White House during these debates, nor have I on other such occasions. (In *Don't Think of an Elephant* and *Thinking Points*, George Lakoff has proposed such scripts, based on economic truths, but his proposals have not been widely adopted by the Democratic Party.)

In another recent product of the conservative echo chamber, after the British Petroleum spill in the Gulf of Mexico in May 2010, FAIR quoted from an array of influential conservative commentators who in the preceding months had declared as in a chorus, suggesting a script provided by the oil industry, that drilling technology was now so advanced as to make the danger of offshore spills obsolete. ("E-mail Alert, Drilling Disasters Can't Happen Here," 25 May 2010.) Stephen F. Hayward's cover story in the 26 Apr. 2010 *Weekly Standard*, "Fill 'er Up," had proclaimed:

> The two main reasons oil and other fossil fuels became environmentally incorrect in the 1970s—air pollution and risk of oil spills—are largely obsolete. Improvements in drilling technology have greatly reduced the risk of the kind of offshore spill that occurred off Santa Barbara in 1969. There hasn't been a major drilling related spill since then, though shipping oil by tanker continues to be risky, as the Exxon Valdez taught us. To fear oil spills from offshore rigs today is analogous to fearing air travel now because of prop plane crashes. (24)

Hayward's article was widely praised and linked to in conservative websites—until it was followed within days by the BP spill. The article identified Hayward as the F. K. Weyerhauser Fellow at the American Enterprise Institute (which also posted his article), and he was the producer of a documentary film refuting Al Gore's *An Inconvenient Truth*. Although Hayward subsequently expressed some embarrassment about being compared to those who proclaimed that the Titanic was unsinkable ("How to Think"), none of the others, to my knowledge, later acknowledged what they had said before, which went down the memory hole as they shifted to new lines of argument rationalizing offshore drilling.

The primary origin of the conservative offensive has long been identified as "Confidential Memorandum: Attack on American Free Enterprise System," published in 1971 in the US Chamber of Commerce's *Washington Report*, written by Lewis F. Powell, a corporate lawyer and former president of the American Bar Association, whom President Nixon would appoint to the Supreme Court the next year; Nixon had started to implement similar plans to counter-attack those on his "enemies list" during the run-up to Watergate. Powell argued that the American system of free enterprise was under attack by four institutions that shaped American public opinion: the academy, the media, the political establishment, and the courts. Business needed to "stop suffering in impotent silence, and launch a counter-attack" harnessing its "wisdom, ingenuity, and resources" against "those who would destroy it." Powell proposed that heavily subsidized "scholars, writers, and thinkers," speaking for "the movement," would press for "balance" and "equal time" to penetrate the media, thereby shaping news coverage, reframing issues, influencing the view of political elites, and changing mass public opinion (Powell, "Confidential Memorandum"). Basically, conservative corporations set out to recruit the best minds money could buy. This judgment might be unfair to those conservative intellectuals, especially older ones, motivated to accept this patronage out of conviction rather than reward, but that has always seemed to me to put them in an equivocal situation in relation to the many others, especially younger ones (including several of students of mine) who have been attracted to conservative activism as a lucrative career path.

The key institutions in this counterattack would become foundations and research institutes like the Scaife, Heritage, and Bradley Foundations, American Enterprise Institute, Manhattan Institute, Cato Institute, and the Hoover Institution; the John M. Olin Foundation was equally influential until its charter ended in 2005. (For further sources on these institutions, see Lazere, "*Partisan*," "Patriotism," "Neoconservatism.") In recent years, similar cultural fronts sponsored by Charles and David Koch have become prominent players, as will be seen in chapter 5. Eric Alterman's *What Liberal Media* contains several chapters with detailed documentation of their operations. Among the highlights:

William Baroody, the former president of the American Enterprise Institute, explained:

> "I make no bones about marketing...We hire ghost writers for scholars to produce op-ed articles that are sent to the one hundred and one cooperating newspapers—three pieces every two weeks."...Burton Pines, a Heritage vice president, has added, "We're not here to be some kind of Ph.D. committee giving equal time. Our role is to provide conservative public-policymakers with arguments to bolster our side."...Heritage provides lawmakers and talk-show guests with colored index cards stating conservative positions in pithy phrases on every imaginable issue. According to Heritage's "vice president for information marketing," these cards have been "wildly successful" with Republicans in Congress for media appearances. (Alterman 82–83)

"Ghost writers for scholars!" "We're not here to be...giving equal time!" Thus does the conservative counter-establishment uphold standards of intellectual integrity and impartiality against their alleged abuse by liberal and left academics and media. Again, although some reputable scholars have worked with these think tanks, I have never understood why they do, in light of how tainted association with them is because of such crass avowals. Conversely, how many liberal or left academics, especially in the humanities—the main target of conservative attacks—hire ghost writers, are paid to make partisan arguments by an employer, or have this kind of access to newspapers, radio, and TV?

One succinct firsthand testimony appeared in *Up from Conservatism*, by Michael Lind, a disillusioned protégé of Irving Kristol and William F. Buckley, who asserted: "American conservatism, then, is a countercommunism that replicates, down to rather precise details of organization and theory, the communism that it opposes" (94). And, "The network orchestrated by the foundations resembled an old-fashioned political patronage machine, or perhaps one of the party writers' or scholars' guilds in communist countries. The purpose of intellectuals was to write essays and op-eds attacking liberals and supporting official Republican party positions....Once the party line had been adopted, any conservative scholar who questioned the new dogma in print would find himself the victim of a whisper campaign about his 'liberalism'" (85–86).[1] David Brock's confessions about his apostasy from the conservative counter-establishment in *Blinded by the Right* confirmed Lind's account. As a former, self-described, journalistic "right-wing hit man" (164), Brock provides further personal testimony for the case against what he calls the big lie machine operated by the right wing of the Republican Party and its multimillionaire backers like Richard Mellon Scaife, the late William Simon, Reverend Sun Myung Moon, the Coors family, Rupert Murdoch, and the Koch brothers. These "Leninists of the right" (48), as Brock calls them, exercise control "far more rigidly doctrinaire than the PC crowd that had so offended me [as an undergraduate] in Berkeley" (22), over a large network of think tanks, political operatives, lobbies, jurists, newspapers, magazines, book publishers, talk radio hosts, and TV pundits. Brock admits that he and other conservative journalists did the bidding of Republican leaders in cover-ups of right-wing atrocities in Chile and Central America, of the Iran-Contra scandal, and of Clarence Thomas' guilt in Anita Hill's charges against him, a cover-up accompanied by character assassination of Hill and her defenders. He was one of many journalists who enriched themselves with the millions that Richard Mellon Scaife poured into a crusade to bring down President Clinton from the day he was elected. (Many conservatives who now dismiss Brock as a congenital liar eagerly embraced his lies when he was on their side. And while *Blinded* has been challenged on a few specifics, to date his larger case about the Republican apparatus has gone unrefuted.)

Brock reveals the prescribed rhetorical tactics he was coached in, beginning with the postures of sneering derision and apoplectic indignation. Other standard devices: Always stay on the attack, never admit fault or concede any points to the opposition. Make sensationalistic charges (even without adequate evidence) to credulous mass media through publicity agents. Hyperbolically stereotype and demonize opponents, while sentimentalizing your own side and whitewashing its sins. Disguise partisan polemics behind professions of objectivity and evenhandedness (see chapter 5 for more on Brock).

"Attack, Attack, Attack—Never Defend"

The ethical and rhetorical standards of Republican Party leadership famously plummeted under President Nixon with his "dirty tricks team," which morphed into "the plumbers unit" responsible for the Watergate burglary. Other phrases originating with the Nixon administration were "wedge issues," "the Southern strategy" (Republican exploitation of the backlash by white Dixiecrats against the civil rights movement), and "positive polarization," Attorney General John Mitchell's phrase for the strategy of provoking anti–Vietnam War demonstrators into violence and antipatriotic rhetoric—forming a deadly codependence with some of the protesters' own belief in polarization to prime the pump of revolutionary change. The quintessential expression for subsequent Republican rhetoric was voiced by Nixon dirty-trickster Roger Stone: "Politics is not about uniting people. It's about dividing people.... Attack, attack, attack—never defend." And "Admit nothing, deny everything, launch counterattack" (quoted in Toobin). This credo has been espoused, explicitly or tacitly, by a continuous series of Republican strategists including Lee Atwater (who wrote a deathbed recantation of his dirty tricks, such as the infamous Willy Horton ad), Roger Ailes (who went on to be the director of Fox News), Newt Gingrich, Jack Abramoff, Ralph Reed, Tom DeLay, David Brock, Frank Luntz, David Horowitz, and Karl Rove. (Their cohorts in mass media include Rush Limbaugh, Ann Coulter, Bill O'Reilly, Glenn Beck, and Fox News, the very models of an "acquiescent, friendship-seeking nature.")

Conservative polemicists have long accumulated evidence claiming to show that academic leftists are cynical moral relativists and deniers of objective truth toward deceptive ends and winning through intimidation, an accusation repeated by countless conservative books and research reports that appear credible to the general public, though close scrutiny reveals that it is often *they* who resort to deceit in accusing leftists of doing so. For example, in her 1995 book *Telling the Truth*, Lynne Cheney alleged that leftists, deconstructionists, social constructionists, and postmodernists believe "truth was not merely irrelevant, it no longer existed," therefore, "might makes right... and so intimidation was a perfectly natural way to try to gain assent" (16). But she failed to cite any specific texts that make precisely such a claim, especially advocating intimidation (she distorted several in the effort, as I showed in "Ground Rules"), and I have never seen one in any reputable scholarly or journalistic publication. In fact, the left authors to whom conservatives attribute this belief are often attributing it to the *right*, not claiming it as their own.

An ironic echo of Cheney's passage came to light in Ron Suskind's widely cited 2004 article about George W. Bush's administration in the *New York Times Magazine*, "Faith, Certainty, and the Presidency of George W. Bush," quoting from an interview with an anonymous White House aide, generally assumed to be Carl Rove (though, to be sure, the quotation does not seem to have been acknowledged or verified):

> The aide said that guys like me were "in what we call the reality-based community," which he defined as people who "believe that solutions emerge from your judicious study of discernible reality." I nodded and murmured something about enlightenment principles and empiricism. He cut me off. "That's not the way the world really works anymore," he continued. "We're an empire now, and when we act, we create our own reality. And while you're studying that reality—judiciously, as you will—we'll act again, creating other new realities, which you can study too, and that's how things will sort out. We're history's actors...and you, all of you, will be left to just study what we do."

Here was the epitome of right-wing deconstruction. No comment was forthcoming from the then–Second Lady.

The website for a PBS "Frontline" report on Gingrich reproduced the text of a talk he gave to College Republicans (CR) in 1978, including:

> The great strength of the Democratic party in my lifetime has been that it has always produced young, nasty people who had no respect for their elders.... And I think that one of the great problems we have in the Republican Party is that we don't encourage you to be nasty. We encourage you to be neat, obedient, and loyal and faithful and all those Boy Scout words, which would be great around the camp fire, but are lousy in politics. ("The Long March")

In 1984 *Mother Jones* reported on a speech that Gingrich gave to Republican activists:

> "The number one fact about the news media," he told them, "is they love fights." For months, he explained, he had been giving "organized, systematic, researched, one-hour lectures. Did CBS rush in and ask if they could tape one of my one-hour lectures? No. But the minute Tip O'Neill attacked me, he and I got 90 seconds at the close of all three network news shows. You have to give them confrontations. When you give them confrontations, you get attention; when you get attention, you can educate." (Osborne)

A cover letter for the GOPAC training tapes sponsored by Gingrich explained, "As the tapes have been used in training sessions across the country and mailed to candidates, we have heard a plaintive plea: 'I wish I could speak like Newt.' That takes years of practice.

But we believe that you could have a significant impact on your campaign and the way you communicate if we help a little. That is why we have created this list of words and phrases." The list provided boilerplate demonizing words for Republicans to use on every occasion: "Apply these [words] to the opponent: destructive...sick...pathetic...unionized bureaucracy...traitors...hypocrisy...radical...permissive attitudes...corrupt...selfish...criminal rights" ("Language: A Key Mechanism").

Terry Dolan (the closeted homosexual who was a leader of the homophobic, religious-right Council for National Policy and the National Conservative Political Action Committee before dying of AIDS), was quoted on the CNP Web site avowing that the secret of conservative fund-raising is to "make them angry and stir up hostilities. We are trying to be divisive. The shriller you are, the easier it is to raise funds" (http:www.seekgod.ca/cnp.d.htm). (Conservative mimics like Rush Limbaugh are of course quick to attribute these motives exclusively to liberal nonprofit fund-raisers, where they possibly may also be found on occasion, but as far as I know, conservatives have failed to produce smoking-gun evidence like this against liberals.)

Horowitz noted in *The Art of Political War*, "Aggression is advantageous because politics is a war of position, which is defined by images that stick. By striking first, you can define the issues as well as your adversary. Defining the opposition is the decisive move in all political war. Other things being equal, whoever is on the defensive generally loses.... In attacking your opponent, take care to do it effectively. 'Going negative' increases the risk of being defined as an enemy" (12). Horowitz again claims to reconcile this kind of advice to conservatives with his contradictory statements like the one in the epigraph above by saying it is liberal Democrats who practice such aggressive tactics, so conservatives are forced to go against their better nature in responding in kind. But this claim is based mainly on his own interpretation of liberal behavior, not on direct quotations confirming devious motives on the left, and his blindness to all the evidence of initiatives of aggression on the right that I partially catalogue here discredits on the face of it his claim to intellectual or ethical evenhandedness. Even if Horowitz and other conservatives had adequate evidence that Democrats and leftists are the ones who initiate unscrupulousness, for them to rationalize that they are forced to fight fire with fire is to succumb to the fallacies of tu quoque, two wrongs make a right, an eye for an eye, and ultimately Orwellian doublethink: "To use logic against logic, to repudiate morality while laying claim to it, to believe that democracy was impossible and that the Party was the guardian of democracy" (Orwell *1984*, 25).

JACK ABRAMOFF: "OUR IDEA OF A SUCCESSFUL DAY WAS TO OBLITERATE OUR OPPONENTS"

Jack Abramoff's 2011 memoir, *Capitol Punishment*, can be read as the ultimate playbook for the Republican attack mode, as well as a refresher course on the extremist sources of recent conservative attacks on the academic and political left, going back to the 1970s. It is fascinating to compare Abramoff's ostensibly confessional but self-excusing, expurgated accounts of key episodes with more critical ones like Nina Easton's in *Gang of Five* (2000) and Thomas Frank's in *The Wrecking Crew* (2008), and this would make a good assignment for classes in which to apply my Semantic Calculator for Bias in Rhetoric.[2] Abramoff boastfully recounts his rise to influence in the Republican Party by means of winning through intimidation, deception, and sabotaging opponents. This began with his election in the late seventies as president of the College Republicans at Brandeis, then the Massachusetts and national organizations, when he already formed part of a triumvirate with Grover Norquist and Ralph Reed, who both took equal pride in unscrupulous methods. Abramoff says about the College Republicans, "To us, politics was war without the benefit of armed forces. 'Kill or be killed' became an unspoken mantra, contrary to all I believed and was raised to believe [as an orthodox Jew]" (30). Easton's *Gang of Five*, a well-researched and evenhanded account of conservatives' own views, studied five leaders of the national conservative movement who rose to prominence in the 1980s, including Reed and Norquist, in their collaborations with Abramoff (who in 2000 was not yet widely known to the public; this part of his history was downplayed by the media covering his spectacular fall from power as a lobbyist in 2004). Easton quotes a 1983 interview with Abramoff published by the CR National Committee: "It is not our job to seek peaceful co-existence with the Left. Our job is to remove them from power permanently.... This means removing Leftists from positions of power and influence in every area of student life" (Easton 143). A typical CR campus campaign was against Naderite Public Interest Research Groups (PIRGs), which CR described as "tyrannical," "radical," "a major threat to democracy on American campuses." Easton describes CR members putting up a military-style map with pins locating the PIRG chapters they intended to "take out" (151). (Their immediate cause was the requirement on some campuses that a portion of student fees be allocated to PIRG, a policy that CR caused to be annulled.)

Describing Reed's bizarrely grandiose "take no prisoners approach," even toward a rival candidate in Abramoff's 1980 campaign for president of the national CR, Abramoff quotes Reed, "I want to be invisible. I do guerilla warfare. I paint my face and travel at night. You don't know it's over until you're in a body bag" (30). According to Easton, Reed required CR recruits to memorize George C. Scott's bloodthirsty lines in *Patton*, substituting "Democrats" for "Nazis": "The Democrats are the enemy. Wade into them! Spill *their* blood! Shoot *them* in the belly!" (Easton 143). With all of their Rambo-esque posturing, few of these militant post-draft-era patriots ever volunteered for military service, nor did many of their "war wimp" elders in the Vietnam war or their neoconservative successors in Iraq and Afghanistan.

Abramoff's College Republicans early mastered the art of red-baiting, lumping together communists with anticommunistic, democratic socialists (like the Independent Socialists that I belonged to at Berkeley), and even with liberal Democrats. In 1982, Abramoff repeated the canards about a "cadre of 12,000 Marxist professors" and "their beloved Soviet Union" (*Review of the NEWS*, 8 Sept. 1982), with no documentation or distinction among the diverse definitions of "Marxist." CR recycled the claim by an allied right-wing South African student organization that the liberal American campus movement for divestment from South Africa was a "very effective KGB disinformation campaign" (Easton 169). College Republicans' favored reading included the 1980 novel *The Spike*, by Robert Moss and Arnaud de Borchgrave, which depicted the liberal media, the campus protest movement, and a Washington think tank obviously based on the Institute for Policy Studies as KGB fronts (the name of the think tank in the book had to be changed when IPS threatened to sue).

While expressing no regrets in his book about the behavior of the College Republicans, Abramoff does acknowledge that the College Democrat organizations he opposed were under-organized and underfunded compared to the Republicans, that they were pushovers in aggressive debate, and that the debate settings were rigged to favor the Republicans. He also confirms that he, Norquist, Reed, and later Karl Rove, were budding financial entrepreneurs who turned the College Republicans into a profitable business, following the widespread pattern that Tom Frank traces of conservative zealotry combining with self-enrichment, domestically and internationally.

All this once more gives the lie to the Republican tactic of pretending that Democrats and liberals are the powerful, ruthless, wealthy ones against the penniless and pitiful but gallant forces of conservatism. Abramoff makes the interesting claim that "the domination of the College Republicans in the early 1980s inadvertently spawned the unfortunate creed of political correctness, which has since ruled academia" (31). His causation is dubious (conservatives are more apt to attribute PC to the ascension of sixties radical students into faculty and administrative positions), but this is one of the rare instances when a conservative views a leftist movement as reaction against a conservative one rather than vice versa.

The unabated rancor against the intellectual left that runs throughout Abramoff's book is another instance of conservatives' distorted sense of the proportionate power and ethics of the left and right in America. Here is a man who was already connected by birth to corridors of national power through his father, a Beverly Hills international big-business executive, and who still boasts about having become the highest-paid lobbyist in Washington. He was a regular guest at the White House under presidents Reagan and George W. Bush. He represented some of the world's wealthiest, most powerful interests—including Microsoft (his first lobbying position was with the Seattle law firm headed by Preston Gates, Bill's father), the apartheid government of South Africa, former Philippine First Lady Imelda Marcos, the government of the Mariana Islands (allied with the proprietors of garment sweatshops and an infamous prostitution industry there), post–Soviet Russian top officials and billionaire entrepreneurs, and finally several billion-dollar chains of Indian gambling casinos, which he was convicted of swindling. His lobbying for and investments in these and other gambling enterprises earned him the nickname Casino Jack.[3] Yet, after having attained all this power and wealth, Abramoff seethes with resentment, not only against academic and intellectual leftists, but even against liberals in government and business who, like Preston Gates and Microsoft executives, were partial to Democrats and, worse yet, gave "wine and brie" cocktail parties (twice mentioned)—as though wealthy Republicans, including those Abramoff entertained on the cuff every day at his own upscale Washington restaurant, touch nothing but Budweiser and Velveeta!

The behavior of Abramoff, Norquist, and Reed as College Republicans carried over into their later careers. Abramoff boasts that his Washington lobbying firm included "some of the roughest, toughest street-smart killers who ever walked the halls of well-heeled law firms" (93). "Our idea of a successful day was to obliterate our opponents" (152). And about his lobbying partner and eventual coconspirator in fraud, a former aide to Congressman Tom DeLay, "Mike Scanlon knew how to bury the hatchet—in his opponent's head" (153–54). Norquist, the influential head of Americans for Tax Reform, was famously quoted in a *National Journal* interview in 2003 saying, "Our goal is to inflict pain. It is not good enough to win; it has to be a painful and devastating defeat. We're sending a message here. It is like when the king would take his opponent's head and spike it on a pole for everyone to see" (Maggs, "Grover at the Gate"). In a 1999 article in *American Spectator*, and several related pieces on the ATR website, Norquist outlined in detail a program "to crush the structures of the left" ("Winner Takes All" 67).

By his own account, Abramson's lobbying enterprises were directly tied to the upper circles of the Republican Party, frequently including a policy through which Republican Congressional or executive-branch officials' favoritism toward his corporate and foreign-government clients was granted through extortion for large campaign contributions and exclusive employment of Republican lobbyists by the clients. Abramoff describes "enjoying the awkward meeting" between Congressman Tom ("The Hammer") DeLay and "quivering executives" of Microsoft whom DeLay threatened with unfavorable legislation unless they shifted their contributions from Democrats to Republicans, a meeting that resulted in a $100,000 contribution to the Republican Congressional Committee (65). (A few pages earlier, Abramoff has said about his close friend DeLay, "What struck me about Tom was how sincerely religious he was" [59].) This variety of extortion was part of a carrot-and-stick combination, whose incentive side consisted of dangling lucrative lobbying job offers in front of government officials and their staff after they left office, again a common practice by Democratic as well as Republican lobbyists. These policies reached their pinnacle after the Republicans gained control of Congress in 1994, in their K Street Project, led by DeLay, Gingrich, Abramoff, and Norquist. Then-junior partners included Senator Rick Santorum and Congressman John Boehner, who in the 2010s (like Gingrich and DeLay in the nineties) would become distinguished for their representation of the Republicans as the defender of Christian piety, family values, and other culture-war distractions from their own complicity with the kind of financial corruption that eventually brought Gingrich and DeLay down. Abramoff says Democrats also indulged in these practices, but again admits they were far outdone by Republicans.

Norquist's account of the K Street Project similarly claimed that its model was the practices of Democrats in the 1970s and 1980s; however, in Norquist's characteristic manner, his mode of "catching up" extended to display-the-opponent's-head-on-a-spike excesses. (On the K Street Project, see Frank, *Wrecking* 186–93). Aside from the debatable relative proportion of culpability between the two parties, the long-running complicity of both with lobbying corruption, primarily corporate (along with the failure of the corporate media to foreground it) was prime evidence of the need for the presence in American politics of forces outside the two-party monopoly, such as higher education and noncorporate media.

Abramoff's descriptions of his lobbying strategies read like a manual for sophistic calculations in making the weaker argument appear the stronger one, rationalizing the motives of even his seemingly most unsavory clients by claiming they were acting in the interest of the public and free enterprise, just defending themselves against communism, excessive government power or regulation, and greedy labor unions. An exemplary case is his account of lobbying in the 1990s on behalf of the government and corporations (virtually indistinguishable) of the Commonwealth of the Northern Mariana Islands (CNMI), an America protectorate east of the Philippines, whose capital is Saipan. In this locus classicus of globalization, lauded by DeLay as "a perfect petri dish of capitalism" (Frank, *Wrecking Crew* 210), the ruling elite made billions in the two previous decades because they were exempt from mainland laws on minimum wage, unions (banned), immigration, tariffs, and occupational safety and health regulations, which enabled them to exploit garment workers imported from the Philippines and China in the worst sweatshop conditions, with an infamous sex slavery trade on the side, while their products were sold as American brand names with "Made in USA" labels. According to a 2006 article in *Ms.* by Rebecca Clarren, Abramoff received nearly $11 million in fees between 1995 and 2004 to lobby against Democratic efforts in Congress, supported by mainland and Hawaiian unions, to bring the Marianas into compliance with mainland laws; only after Abramoff's disgrace in 2004 did reform legislation start slowly to progress, although Clarren indicates that not much had changed by 2006. In a classic case of conservatives mimicking the ethos of the left, one of Abramoff's strategies was to defend the islands' local governmental and corporate oligarchy as "an indigenous people" whose critics were racist and colonialist oppressors—a mind-boggling two-step around the fact that most of the workers were imported to drive down local wages. A representative of the Saipan Chamber of Commerce flown in to testify in Congress quoted Martin Luther King against stripping a native people's "pride, dignity, and respect" (Frank, *Wrecking* 233). (Abramoff would later resort to a similar strategy in attacking as racist, against Indians, the *Washington Post*'s initial revelations of his shady operations lobbying for tribal casinos, although the subsequent exposure of his private emails revealed him referring to these clients whom he swindled out of millions as "monkeys" and "morons.")

Abramoff also arranged multiple junkets, paid for by the Marianas government, for dozens of members of Congress, led by DeLay, to fly halfway around the world for Potemkin Village tours to witness how responsible the factory owners were, in spite of harassment by "meter-maid-like citation writers from the Occupational Safety and Health Administration" (73). But, "Of course these trips were not all hard work. The Marianas are exotic and beautiful, not to mention equipped with golf, the favorite pastime of Congressmen and lobbyists alike.... Consider, if you're trying to influence someone from the Congress, why meet them in their stuffy, overcrowded office... when you could meet at a pastoral, posh country club where the only interruptions are from a waiter offering you Courvoisier and a fine cigar, or a caddy offering you a five-iron?" (78). But no wine or brie. Or prostitutes. Around the same time, a Saipan politician writing in a newspaper owned by the manufacturers blamed liberal attempts to raise the minimum wage or restrict immigration on greedy union leaders, whose imposed dues on workers would swell the riches of "bigwigs in the States who drive around in limousines and smoke big cigars" (Frank, *Wrecking* 224).

A recent report by Bill Moyers and Michael Wincroft dug up another juicy bit of Marianas history, concerning Ralph Reed, who by the nineties had brought his lobbying prowess and tactics with him to an executive position in the Christian Coalition. Abramoff hired Reed's political direct mail company to conduct a phony grass roots campaign urging Alabama Christians to write their local congressman to oppose the reforms. Reed didn't tell those Christians he was being paid to help keep running sweatshops that exploited women. Instead, he told them the reforms were a trick orchestrated by the left and organized labor. Limits on Chinese workers would keep them from being "exposed to the teachings of Jesus Christ." His company explained it was just trying to encourage "grass roots citizens to promote the propagation of the Gospel" and that many of the workers were "converted to the Christian faith and return to China with Bibles in hand" ("Ralph Reed in the Marianas Trenches").

In another cosmeticized section of his book, about Africa in the 1980s, Abramoff says nothing about his leading role in the International Freedom Foundation, a lobby initiated in 1986 and secretly financed by right-wing military factions in South Africa, whose activities included depicting Nelson Mandela and the African National Congress as Moscow-sponsored terrorists. Abramoff does proudly describe organizing a 1985 conference of Third World anticommunist "freedom fighters" (Abramoff's epithet, picked up by President Reagan) in Angola, hosted by Jonas Savimbi, leader of the rebel movement UNITA against the Soviet and Cuban-backed government there, but he again fails to mention the facilitation of the conference by the South African apartheid government, with which Savimbi was allied. (Norquist, one of the organizers, ghostwrote articles from there under Savimbi's byline for Heritage Foundation and the *Wall Street Journal*, predictably praising free markets and low taxes.) Nor does Abramoff discuss the more extreme right-wing elements represented. Easton sums up the dark side of these "so-called 'freedom fighters': the roots of Nicaragua's contra leaders in the repressive Somoza regime; the El Salvadoran government's tolerance of well-documented terror and assassinations of labor and human rights leaders by right-wing security forces; the documented slaughter of civilians by Mozambique's Renamo forces [another of Norquist's favorite clients]; the persistent rumors of murders ordered up by the leader of Angola's UNITA" (154). Although Easton's book was published the year before 9/11, she might also have mentioned, as Frank does in *Wrecking Crew*, these conservatives' passion for the resistance to Soviet rule in Afghanistan, which included the incipient Taliban and Al-Qaeda, with figures like Gulbadin Hakmatyar, head of a group praised by *Freedom Fighter* magazine in 1986 for its "strongly Islamic orientation." Frank notes that Hakmatyar in 2008 was "currently a terrorist ringleader sought by the U.S. Army" (64).

From today's comfortably post–Cold War perspective, there appears to have been a tragicomic symmetry from the sixties through the eighties between the ingenuous romanticizing of Third World revolutionary leaders by many (not all) American leftists and that of counterrevolutionary leaders by conservatives like those in Abramoff's circle, accompanied by Manichean demonizing of domestic opponents on both sides. Many of those leaders on opposing sides, both communists and anticommunists, turned out to be butchers and plunderers. (Others, like Nelson Mandela, didn't.) Still, there were some differences. American Third World–liberation promoters like Tom Hayden, Jane Fonda, the Black Panthers, and fans of Fidel

Castro and Che Guevara were never endorsed by Democratic leaders, while Abramoff and his allies, foreign and domestic, were embraced (often literally) and financed by Republican administrations, though they did antagonize some more moderate Republicans. Abramoff's idol Oliver North was elevated into a hero by many conservatives and media for his crimes on behalf of the Nicaraguan Contras, although it has been suppressed from conservative memory that he illegally sold arms to Iran a few years after that country's Islamic rulers had taken Americans hostage in Teheran, and that they at the moment happened to be the enemies of our then-ally Saddam Hussein in Iraq. (Maybe conservatives would claim North was just wisely though prematurely anti-Saddam, though all of this got hopelessly muddled by the time George W. Bush lumped Iran and Iraq together as part of an "axis of evil" with far-distant North Korea.) Finally, American leftists have generally been more willing to express regret for their romanticizing of Third World revolutionaries than have Abramoff and his friends, who voice no regrets for their onetime championing of South African apartheid, Savimbi, the Contras, Renamo in Mozambique, or the El Salvadoran right, with its death squads directed by the psychopathic Roberto D'Aubuisson.

In Abramoff's account of his downfall, in *Capitol Punishment*, he is all whining self-pity against both his resentful political rivals and "the liberal media," who conspired to bring him down for practices that he says were no different than those practiced by virtually everyone in Washington. Even now, he insists that the root cause of corruption in Washington is the inordinate growth of government, without ever considering the possible opposite historical causation, that the inordinate growth of corporations and their lobbies were what corrupted government. He pretty much whitewashes the lurid history of corporate crime and ineptitude over the time-span of his book.

The Psychology of Self-Contradiction and Projection

The lurches from bellicose bullying to religious piety and hypersensitive self-pity in Abramoff and many of the other conservatives I discuss here, reflecting a Manichean worldview that rationalizes whatever one's own side does in the cause of fighting "evil-doers," bring to mind a comment by John Dean, of Watergate fame, in his 2006 book *Conservatives without Conscience*, which astutely applies psychological studies of the domineering, authoritarian personality to precisely this variety of Republican—Nixon, Abramoff, Gingrich, DeLay, and Karl Rove are among his central targets. About them, Dean says, "Not surprisingly, the very conservatives who love to hurl invective against the ranks of their enemies prove to have the thinnest of skins when the same is done to them" (26). This observation has certainly been confirmed in my personal contacts with antagonistic conservative polemicists, who tend to seethe with righteous indignation about the slightest questioning of their arguments.

Another psychological explanation for their authoritarian selective vision lies in the notion of projection, especially in relation to paranoid tendencies. This explanation is confirmed in Brock's *Blinded By The Right*, when he admits that he and his fellow conservative ideologues assumed that liberal political and journalistic circles were just as tightly organized and unscrupulous, so that conservatives told themselves they were just fighting fire with fire. But he eventually realized that "I unconsciously projected onto the liberals what I knew and saw and learned of the right wing's operations" (114). About Republican control of media conservatives, he acknowledged in an earlier *Esquire* article, "There is no 'liberal movement' to which these journalists are attached and by which they can be blackballed in the sense that there is a self-identified, hardwired 'conservative movement' that can function as a kind of neo-Stalinist thought police" ("Confessions" 107).

I see this projection as the key to the whole line of conservative polemicists that I have been discussing, when they are not just hypocritically dissembling. Their demonizing image of the left—perhaps a justifiable one in the era of Stalinism, but long outdated—seems to derive less from empirical reality than from projections of their own skewed mentality and that of right-wing organizations. Thus their lack of perspective constantly leads them into strategic and rhetorical overkill against the left, in the manner of Gingrich, Abramoff, and Norquist. They may believe that they are only fighting fire with fire, but the result is usually that their firepower ends up far exceeding that of their opponents. "Overkill" and lopsided "kill ratios" (between enemy deaths and our own) were literally the American military strategy in the Vietnam War, and some progressive historians of the Cold War suggest that it also characterized American military and rhetorical policy against the Soviet Union, in exaggerating Soviet strengths and aggression so as to justify constantly escalating expense on American defense that would swamp the other side. Some neoconservatives like Midge Decter, in *The*

Old Wife's Tale, have confirmed after the fact that the latter was the secret goal all along, and it succeeded

Of course, the perception of bias always lies to some extent in the eye of the beholder, and conservatives rush to claim equivalent abuses on the left to match all those I have cited on the right. So a defense of the Koch brothers in a cover story by Matthew Continetti in the *Weekly Standard* in 2011—the cover drawing depicted the brothers about to be burned at the stake—claimed the Kochs are "the latest victims of the left's lean, mean cyber-vilification machine" and "the buzz saw of the contemporary left." "The left-wing counter-counter-establishment was a juggernaut investing vast energy in destroying the reputations of its favorite targets: Sarah Palin, Michele Bachmann, Rush Limbaugh." (Continetti is the author of *The Persecution of Sarah Palin.*) And, in the obligatory Orwell allusion, the Kochs were "objects of the progressives' latest two-minutes hate." This is just boilerplate mimicry, however, and although Continetti's article contained more substantive points, which I explore in chapter 5, he made no effort to weigh liberal vilification of the Kochs against conservative vilification of George Soros, or against the whole history of the conservative attack machine I have traced here. Indeed, the most conclusive evidence of bad faith in conservatives is their suppression of this entire 40-year history of misbehavior on the American right, in order to magnify the sins of Democrats, liberals, and the academic and journalistic left out of any relative proportion. As I said at the outset, I have no stake in whitewashing the left, but I assert that its sins can only be judged accurately in proportion to a full accounting of those on the right, and such an accounting should be incorporated into our courses in argumentative rhetoric, combined with the best conservative rebuttals we and our students can find.

5

RIGHT-WING DECONSTRUCTION: MIMICRY AND FALSE EQUIVALENCIES

My introductory chapter raised the topic of conservatives devising a mirror, or mimicry, effect in the recent American culture wars, with the example of David Horowitz writing, "I encourage [fellow Republicans] to use the language that the left has deployed so effectively on behalf of its agendas...." And I invoked Jonathan Swift's dilemma that "everything spiritual and valuable has a gross, revolting parody, which looks exactly like it." Lewis Powell's conception in 1971 of a conservative counter-establishment had a precursor two decades earlier when American cold warriors like ex-Marxists James Burnham and Irving Kristol (who, not coincidentally, became a key figure in forming the new Republican apparatus) formulated a strategy for neutralizing the elaborate Soviet propaganda apparatus in international politics and culture by devising counterpropaganda efforts like the Congress for Cultural Freedom, with the result that, as Michael Lind put it, "American conservatism, then, is a countercommunism that replicates, down to rather precise details of organization and theory, the communism that it opposes." (Also see Saunders, *The Cultural Cold War.*) And even this aspect of the Cold War was anticipated by Orwell in both *1984* and *Animal Farm*, with their grim vision, based on the Communist and Fascist revolutions and on World War II, of rival governing elites on the right and left emulating each other to the point where, as with humans and pigs, "already it was impossible to say which was which" (*Animal Farm* 128.) Thus Orwell's concept of doublethink embodies the psychology of needing to deny the similarity in one's own side's behavior to the other side's by convincing compatriots, and oneself, that their own side is different and superior: "To believe that democracy is impossible and that the Party was the guardian of democracy" (*1984*, 25); or, as in *Animal Farm*, "Four legs good, two legs bad" (40).

One of the most elaborate forms of conservative mimicry has been to emulate the protocols of academic and intellectual discourse in order to launder right-wing propaganda. In *Blinded*, David Brock mocks the pseudo-academic trappings of think tanks he worked for like the Heritage Foundation, where "though I had no advanced degrees, I assumed the grandiose title of John M. Olin Fellow in Congressional Studies" (79). *Blinded* also gave a fascinating account of how his *The Real Anita Hill* in 1993 (which he later confessed was a fraud) was edited at the Free Press, a highbrow press that largely became a neoconservative organ in the eighties under editors Erwin Glickes and Adam Bellow, both of whom claimed to have rebelled against New York liberal-intellectual backgrounds. (However, Bellow's father, Saul, had evolved from Trotskyist to neoconservative and prompted his friend Allan Bloom, with whom Adam studied at Chicago, to write *The Closing of the American Mind*, with support from Irving Kristol and the Olin Foundation.)

> Even more than Erwin, Adam had an instinctive knack for how to cover a conservative argument with a patina to make it more appealing to the liberal eye.... The key to success, as Adam explained it to me, as if he had a secret formula, was to "capture" the center with rhetorical sleight of hand, just as a right-wing pol might lure swing voters. Persuading the liberal or moderate reader that a conservative book's point of view was "reasonable" would give it a crack at a favorable review in the *New York Times* and elsewhere.... The climb up the best-seller lists would be aided by having an author with the talent for presenting extreme views in a "reasonable" fashion on the book promotion tour, as D'Souza did. [Free Press had published Dinesh D'Souza's *Illiberal Education*.]...
>
> Before my book tour in the spring of 1993, I practiced my shtick with a media trainer hired for me by Erwin. Because the liberal media was out to discredit conservatives, Erwin coached me, the price of media credibility, of being taken seriously as a journalist, was to call black "white," to deny that I had a political agenda. (*Blinded* 116)

Adam Bellow, incidentally, has recently discarded the patina of "reasonability" and centrism in editing an expressly conservative series called Broadside Books, with titles like *Revolt! How to Defeat Obama and Repeal His Socialist Programs—a Patriot's Guide*.

My own long-running efforts to call out conservative culture-war mimicry have drawn heavily from the books of Thomas Frank, going back to *One Market under God: Extreme Capitalism, Market Populism, and the End of Economic Democracy*, which have brilliantly delineated the ways American conservatives have stood on its head the left's traditional claim to working-class populism and opposition to elites. In Frank's more recent *Pity the Billionaire*, a definitive, hair-raising chapter titled "Mimesis" suggests that conservatives have emulated the children's taunt, "I'm rubber, you're glue; what you throw bounces off me and sticks to you." Frank focuses on the rise of the Tea Party, partially guided by FreedomWorks, headed by Richard Armey, formerly a powerful Republican senator, later a high-paid lobbyist for an international corporate and foreign-government law firm, allied with Abramoff in lobbying for Mariana Islands sweatshops. Citing Armey's book *Give Us Liberty: A Tea Party Manifesto* (coauthored with Matt Kibbe) and other footnoted Tea Party sources, Frank says about FreedomWorks:

> There is reportedly a deliberate effort to look and sound like a left-wing organization. The idea, according to Armey, was "not just to learn from their opponents on the left but to beat them at their own game." The outfit's leaders write that after the Tea Party conquers the GOP and Congress, it "will take America back from The Man," explaining helpfully to readers that this is "the term the New Left used to refer to the political establishment." [More precisely, it was the term "blacks" had long applied to the white power structure, so the implication is that blacks now rule whites.] Activists that the group trains are asked to learn the leadership secrets of the Communist Party and to read a book by the famous neighborhood organizer Saul Alinsky. (117)

Leftists will be surprised to learn that Alinksy was "famous." Maybe we should take heart from the right's fixation on obscure figures like Alinsky, Francis Fox Piven, Van Jones, ACORN, and other advocates for poor people's movements. This fixation might indicate that left movements have been more successful than their supporters think, although it might instead simply indicate a classic demagogic invention of scapegoats. Note, however, the semantic inversion here of the meaning of "community organizing." In 2011, Matthew Continetti wrote a long defense of Charles and David Koch in the *Weekly Standard*, which described the Koch organization that in 2004 split into Americans for Prosperity and FreedomWorks:[1]

> In 1984 [!] Charles and David established Citizens for a Sound Economy.... CSE was an exercise in community organizing. It rallied grassroots voters in support of reduced spending and lower taxes. "What we needed was a sales force that participated in political campaigns or town hall meetings, in rallies, to communicate to the public

at large much of the information that these [conservative] think tanks were creating," David said. "Almost like a door-to-door sales force that some of the cosmetics organizations have." CSE was an innovation in interest group politics, marrying business practice and libertarian ideology: Mary Kay meets von Mises.

In other words, CSE was an innovator in Astroturf, and the meaning of community organizing was twisted from organizing within communities into organizing from outside by sales forces from corporate-funded think tanks: Mary Kay *replaces* Saul Alinsky. The most prominent accomplishment of these campaigns to date has been the apparent role of these sales forces in Tea Party "campaigns or town hall meetings, in rallies," to oppose President Obama's health care reform bill and to win elections in 2010. Continetti says, "David Koch chairs the AFP [Americans for Prosperity] foundation. 'I see AFP as having a huge number of boots on the ground,' David said. Its ranks have swollen to upward of 1.6 million people." However, Jane Mayer's article on the Kochs in *The New Yorker* says about Tim Phillips, (director of AFP): "Last year, Phillips told the *Financial Times* that Americans for Prosperity had only eight thousand registered members" ("Covert" 53).

FALSE ANALOGIES AND EQUIVALENCIES

These mirror effects characterize several other fronts in the conservative counter-establishment's attack campaigns, in the form of arguments by analogy, which claim two situations are similar, or by equivalency, which claim they are exactly the same. These fronts include analogies between (a) the political attitudes of college teachers and students or journalists versus those of the public at large, with the implied assumption that the two should have the same proportion of conservatives versus liberals; (b) liberal/left scholars and their professional associations versus conservative counterparts financed by corporate foundations; and (c) liberal versus conservative foundations and think tanks, and wealthy backers of liberal versus conservative causes, the most prominent recent cases being George Soros and the Koch brothers. Consider the general lines of argument conservatives make on each of these fronts:

> *Academics and journalists are overwhelmingly liberals and Democrats, in comparison to the American public at large. This is a bad thing, and the proportions should be more similar.*

This line of argument commits the *ad populum* fallacy. Thus Larry Mumper, the Republican introducing David Horowitz's "Academic Bill of Rights" in the Ohio legislature, asked in an interview with the *Columbus Dispatch*, "Why should we, as fairly moderate to conservative legislators, continue to support universities that turn out students who rail against the very policies that their parents voted us in for?" (DeForest.) The implication is that professors and their students should tailor their political views to follow the latest public opinion polls or election results. Likewise for liberal or leftist journalists whose judgments run contrary to majority conservative opinion.

Politicians like Mumper, along with many media pundits and members of the public who revile professors, appear to have little more familiarity with the nature of humanistic scholarship than they do with that of brain surgery—though they would not presume to tell brain surgeons how they should operate, even in a tax-supported hospital. Scholars are at the disadvantage that they sometimes address public issues on which everyone does and should have an opinion. There is a difference, however, between just any such opinions and those derived from standards of professional accreditation (upwards of ten years graduate study for a PhD and seven more for tenure), systematic scholarship, and academic discourse. That discourse is based on the principles of reasoned argument, rules of evidence and research procedures, wide reading and experience, and historical perspective on current events, and open-minded pursuit of complex, often-unpopular truths. (For a fuller, excellent discussion of the differences between popular and academic discourse, see "From Ideology to Inquiry," by Anne Colby and Thomas Ehrlich). This also means that academic discourse should stand independent from government or corporate pressure and public opinion, in a similar manner to the ideal of a free, independent press. To put it more bluntly, by the very nature of their professions, academics and intellectual, independent journalists are supposed to be better informed on the issues they address than is the populace at large. That is why taxpayers should be willing to support the autonomy of the academy as well as independent journalism, within reasonable limits, whether or not it agrees with their personal views. This is not to exempt academics or intellectual journalists from bias, error, or debate on any given issue, or to downplay the extent of such bias, but it is to exempt them from wholesale attack campaigns by individuals or groups who would demand equal time for uneducated versus educated opinions. Incidentally, when it has served their rhetorical advantage, conservative intellectuals like Leo Strauss, Allan

Bloom, and Peter Shaw have made similar arguments for protecting the autonomy of the liberal arts as a Socratic gadfly to the body politic (see Lazere, "Political").

I know I am on thin ice making this argument as a leftist, since it runs contrary to traditional left populism and skepticism toward elites, the professional-guild mentality, and authorities in general as conservative by definition. It also runs contrary to the self-styled progressivism of postmodern/poststructuralist pluralists who would level all hierarchical concepts, a position I do not consider progressive at all; see my *Retreat* and Marlia Banning's "When Poststructural Theory and Contemporary Politics Collide," which similarly argues that the skeptical epistemology prevalent in recent academic theory has ingenuously provided a paradigm for what I have described as right-wing deconstruction. My position is a reaction against the conservative mimicry that has sought to reverse the binary of left-wing populism versus right-wing elitism, through selectively stigmatizing the intellectual elite but not the economic one. So current right-wing populism champions lower over higher levels of education and knowledge—with college dropouts like Rush Limbaugh and Glenn Beck accorded authority as historians, political theorists, and theologians for their error-laden, bigoted rants, which have made them multimillionaires. (I surveyed some of Limbaugh's howlers in "Is Rush Limbaugh a Racist?") Right-wing populism, most recently in the Tea Party, has further been both encouraged and exploited by figures who themselves belong to the corporate elite, like Herman Cain ("We need a leader, not a reader"), Newt Gingrich (whose consulting firm was paid $1.6 million from Freddie Mac in the 2000s), Rupert Murdoch, Dick Armey, and the Koch brothers. The very defense of higher knowledge obliges us to defend intellectual elitism, which in present-day society is at least meritocratic, responsible for reasoned defense of one's judgments, and inclined to sympathize out of a sense of justice with the left-populist constituencies of low-income workers, minorities, immigrants, and women's rights.

> Conservative foundations and think tanks simply serve to counterbalance more highly funded interests on the left, such as liberal foundations, professional organizations like the American Association of University Professors and the Modern Language Association, and the totality of university faculties. Likewise for overtly conservative media, which simply counterbalance the liberal media.

These are false analogies on the following points:

1. As surveyed in chapter 4, the conservative media, foundations, and think tanks established since the 1970s were designed to be,

in effect, public relations agencies or lobbies for the Republican Party (with the fig leaf of a few conservative Democrats) and the politico-economic interests of their corporate sponsors, many of whose executives have also been visibly partisan, influential figures in that party, such as Rupert Murdoch, Richard Mellon Scaife (Scaife Foundations), the Coors family (Heritage Foundation), William Simon (Olin Foundation), William Baroody (American Enterprise Institute), and the Koch brothers (Cato Institute and multiple foundations). They typically exert top-down control, in the manner of the Heritage executive stating baldly, "We're not here to be some kind of Ph.D. committee giving equal time. Our role is to provide conservative public-policymakers with arguments to bolster our side." Jane Mayer's profile of the Koch brothers in the *New Yorker* quotes Koch biographer Brian Doherty: "David Koch has asserted that the family exerts tight ideological control. 'If we're going to give a lot of money, we'll make darn sure they spend it in a way that goes along with our intent.... And if they make a wrong turn and start doing things we don't agree with, we withdraw funding'" ("Covert" 59). (So much for libertarian fostering of freedom of speech!) The same cannot be said for more liberally inclined foundations like Ford, Rockefeller, Carnegie, MacArthur, in relation either to corporate sponsors or the Democratic Party. These foundations and their executives are independent of their parent corporations, and although they spend more money, much of it is spent on projects that are not political or partisan (Ford at one time funded Irving Kristol). (The unique case of George Soros's Open Society Foundation is discussed below.) They generally do not select projects and grantees to promote their executives' own ideological or financial self-interest, but more often respond to applicants' initiatives, in the manner of academic grants, although there are exceptions that conservatives are quick to jump on, as with some ideologically driven social-justice activism programs—but not even these serve the self-interest of the executives or parent corporations. The very fact that these foundations fund projects that are often antithetical to their patrons' class interests is evidence that their motives are philanthropic, not propagandistic; they fund precisely the kind of projects least likely to attract corporate sponsorship. Leftist journalistic media are in a similar situation. As Victor Navasky, who has been editor and publisher of *The Nation*, recounts in *A Matter of Opinion*, such journals throughout their history have delighted in opposing the class interests of their corporate-wealthy financiers, who for the most part have had enough noblesse oblige to

give them free rein—in contrast to the top-down control exercised by Republican-allied media moguls like Rupert Murdoch (preeminently in *Fox News*) and Sun Myung Moon (*Washington Times*).
2. Academic professional associations democratically represent their membership, and are primarily funded by dues. Their officials are not appointed by, and are not accountable to, any higher power or special interest other than the majority rule of their members. Thus, whatever political biases they may have are those of their own constituencies, not of executives, sponsors, or party organizations. Likewise, faculty employees and administrators at the level of dean and department chair are generally appointed through election by peers, not nonacademic administrators, patrons, or parties. Whatever political biases university faculty members in the humanities and social sciences may have, individually and collectively, are in general the consequence of their years of independent study, not influenced by outside sponsorship or affiliation with party apparatuses. (Faculty conflicts of interest are far more common in the more conservative fields like natural science, technology, and economics, which are rife with corporate influence.) No one ghost writes their lectures for them; the top ranks of research professors are provided research assistants whose work all too often has been appropriated without credit, but the ideological bent is that of the professor, not some agency. None that I have ever known has press agents like those provided for "fellows" at conservative think tanks or a "media trainer" like Brock did as a conservative. (However, I have noticed an uptick in slickness of TV performance as the lefty journalists and academics of *The Nation* and *Mother Jones* have become regulars on MSNBC and Current TV—most recently Michael Eric Dyson, sociology professor at Georgetown and scholar of black culture, has guest-hosted Ed Schultz's nightly commentary program on MSNBC.) Most academics vote Democratic, but, with rare exceptions—President Obama himself, or Robert Reich and John Podesta in Clinton's administration, come to mind—faculty liberals, and especially radicals, in recent decades have not had the kind of top-level roles in the Democratic Party or presidential administrations, or had the high public profiles, that Republicans with academic backgrounds have, like Newt Gingrich, William J. Bennett, Lynne Cheney, Irving and William Kristol (Irving was a professor at NYU and William has a Harvard PhD), Dick Armey, Phil Gramm, and Chester Finn—all also beneficiaries of the conservative foundations. Cass Sunstein, a University of Chicago law professor, worked

as administrator of the White House Office of Information and Regulatory Affairs in the Obama administration but kept a low public profile, as did several other advisors who were academic scientists, economists, and political scientists, including Samantha Power, who was a foreign policy advisor to President Obama and was married to Sunstein. Of course, Glenn Beck inflated Sunstein into "the regulatory czar" and "the most dangerous man in America." (Leibovich 54). (In the Republican, Luntzian lexicon, only Democratic officials are "czars.") According to Media Matters, "Beck claimed Sunstein's office at OIRA was 'a new role' and compared it to the 'Reichstag.' On May 17 Beck said, 'He holds the office—the White House office of information. Jawohl. Is that a new role, do we know?' Beck continued, 'The office of information—that doesn't sound too Reichstag, here, does it?' In fact, OIRA was formed in 1980 under the Paperwork Reduction Act of 1980. According to Beck, though, 'If the financial reform bill passes Congress, it will put 60 percent of the economy under 'government control,' and that as a result Sunstein 'will control your every move'" (Allison). . In fact, the most prominent academic Democrats have tended to be free market economists like Lawrence Summers, Ben Bernanke, and Austan Goolsbee, while Republicans in Congress have, infamously, shot down left-liberal academic nominees for executive branch positions like Elizabeth Warren and Van Jones under Obama, Lani Guinier under Clinton. It is a breathtaking bit of sleight of hand that so many conservative intellectuals' high-minded protests against liberal politicizing of higher education, journalism, and government appointments have come from individuals and organizations with direct ties to the top ranks of the Republican Party.

3. Conservative invective against the disproportion of Democrats to Republicans in liberal arts faculties is reductive on several other levels, in addition to the compensatory function against "business as usual" and restricted-code conservatism that I have defended in part I. Can many liberal arts professors reasonably be expected to identify personally with a party that is not only increasingly anti-intellectual and antiscientific but that is committed to defunding public education at all levels and turning it into a source for corporate profit? This is no more reasonable than it would be to expect there to be more socialists in the top ranks of the military or corporations. (Professors should, however, allow a fair hearing in their courses and scholarship for reasoned conservative arguments on controversial issues.) Another line of argument here is supported

by Matthew S. Woessner, a conservative professor of political science at Pennsylvania State University in Harrisburg, author of "Rethinking the Plight of Conservatives in Higher Education," in the AAUP journal *Academe*. Woessner and his wife, April Kelly-Woessner, have been conducting empirical research on the issues involved in conservative allegations about liberal faculty bias, and he admits that their findings largely fail to support those allegations. Among their general conclusions, "Like the vast majority of Republicans in our study, I've never been the victim of mistreatment as a result of my political views" (26). Concerning the ideological gap in doctoral programs:

> Whereas liberal and conservative students have very similar grades and nearly identical levels of satisfaction with their overall college experience, right-leaning students are far more likely to select "practical" majors that are less likely to lead to advanced degrees. Their emphasis on vocational fields such as business and criminal justice permits them to move directly into the workforce. (24)

THE KOCH-SOROS IDENTITY

All the familiar paradigms of the mirror effect between the American left and right have been on display in several recent issues in which the media have focused either on Charles and David Koch, George Soros, or analogies and equations between them. To begin with the Koch brothers, in 2011 they had a combined fortune of some $50 billion, putting them between Bill Gates and Warren Buffett at the top of the *Forbes* 400; Soros was seventh with $22 billion. *Forbes* ranks Koch Industries, mainly in oil, other energy sources, and chemicals, as the second largest private company in the country. Soros Fund Management is one of the largest and most profitable hedge funds. The Koches have been high-spending backers of conservative lobbies and Republican candidates for decades, as was their father, a John Bircher, in the fifties. (In Thomas Frank's 2004 *What's the Matter With Kansas*, their Kansas-based operations were already referred to as "The Kochtopus.") However, the brothers' libertarianism sometimes puts them at odds with the Republican establishment, as in their opposition to the Iraq War, and they kept a relatively low public profile until 2009, when their role in the Tea Party uprising, through their advocacy organization Americans for Prosperity, attracted wide attention. Herman Cain boasted about the Kochs's financial support of him in the 2012 primaries, proclaiming that he was "the black Koch brother."

As noted in my introduction, comparisons between the extent of the Koch's financial support and control of the Tea Party versus Soros's of Occupy Wall Street (OWS) have been one recent source of dispute, to which I will return. A second is the Kochs's academic philanthropy. A Koch foundation in 2011 donated $1.5 million for faculty positions in Florida State University's economics department, and in return, Koch representatives get to screen and sign off on any hires for a new program promoting "free enterprise." (Hundley, "Billionaire's Role"). The Koches had previously founded the Cato Institute in 1977 and contributed more than $30 million to George Mason University, another public university, partly to establish the nonprofit Mercatus Center, which bills itself as "the world's premier university source for market-oriented ideas—bridging the gap between academic ideas and real-world problems." George Mason's faculty in general has become a bastion of libertarianism, as we will see. Regarding the Koch foundations' support of research in general, a 2004 report by the liberal National Committee for Responsive Philanthropy concluded, "These foundations give money to nonprofit organizations that do research and advocacy on issues that impact the profit margin of Koch industries" (Mayer, "Covert" 50).

Increasing criticism of the Kochs in the media over the late 2000s culminated in the long article in the *New Yorker*, in August 2010, titled "Covert Operations," by Jane Mayer, persistently liberal reporter on the culture wars going back to the Clarence Thomas-Anita Hill dispute. Mayer presented several specific examples in which the Kochs sponsored tax-exempt research and policy institutes that promoted their companies' interests or their personal gain, as in tax policies and environmental regulations. Among the other charges against the Kochs that Mayer documented at length is their energy companies' long-running record of air pollution, toxic oil leaks, a fatal butane gas explosion, and carcinogen discharges; in several cases, criminal or civil charges were brought by the Justice Department and local prosecutors against their companies, including for covering up violations of regulations, and they settled with payments of multimillion-dollar fines. In another charge, a Greenpeace report identified the Koch network of foundations, think tanks, and "political front groups" as a "kingpin of climate science denial" (45–46). Mayer surveyed the Kochs' power in the Republican Party through their campaign contributions and lobbying, most prominently against President Obama and his policies on health care, taxation, financial, and environmental regulation. Much of their partisan political spending is concealed behind tax-exempt shell organizations like the Economic Education Trust, which, according to Mayer, spent millions on attack ads against Democrats in several House and Senate races (52–53), or Citizens for the Environment, which called acid rain and other environmental problems "myths," but which when investigated by the *Pittsburgh Post-Gazette*, had "no citizen membership of its own" (52). Mayer did not discuss one especially controversial branch of Koch political spending, the American Legislative Exchange Council (ALEC), which has lobbied in state legislatures for a broad agenda of conservative causes including loosening of restrictions on campaign contributions, more stringent voter ID laws, "stand your ground" gun policy, and assaults on unions and public employees—most famously that by Wisconsin governor Scott Walker, an ALEC loyalist and Koch campaign-fund beneficiary.[2]

The accumulation of critiques like Mayer's in 2010 provoked concerted rebuttals by the Kochs, partly generated by their hiring several PR agents to counterattack (see Vogel, "The Kochs Fight Back" in *Politico*). In several cases these agents and other Koch beneficiaries defending them concealed their affiliation or downplayed it until they were called on it. "Errors in Jane Mayer's New Yorker Article Attacking the Kochs," by Ilya Somin, appeared in September 2010 in *The Volokh Conspiracy*, a libertarian lawyers' blog named after Eugene Volokh, professor of law at UCLA. Somin followed much the same lines of argument as those of other critics of Mayer including Matthew Continetti, discussed below, focusing more on disagreement in interpretation of the Kochs' activities than on specific errors of fact by Mayer, of which such critics have provided few instances. Somin's article ended with a postscript:

> CONFLICT OF INTEREST WATCH: I am an adjunct scholar at the Cato Institute (an unpaid position). I have also done work for the Institute for Justice, Cato, and a couple other organizations that the Kochs donate to. Much of this work was pro bono, while in some cases I received small payments (Given the vastly greater amount of research funds available from liberal foundations, I could almost certainly have gotten as much or more from liberal funders had I been a left-wing academic). I suppose I should also mention that I have published articles in journals and spoken at conferences sponsored by organizations that got some of their funding from George Soros.

Somin linked to an earlier defense of the Kochs on Volokh Conspiracy by David Bernstein, which concluded, "Disclosure: I've received money from organizations that are or were Koch grantees, such as the

Cato Institute—though I've never taken any money directly from the Kochs—and I only wish it was the kind of money Ford Foundation or MacArthur Foundation favorites get!"

In yet another *Volokh Conspiracy* rebuttal to Mayer, Todd Zywicki acknowledged, "I'm involved in all sorts of ways with the Koch Foundation and many organizations that it supports" ("On Charles and David Koch"). While piling up examples of cases where the Kochs might have exerted self-enriching governmental or financial influence but didn't, Zywicki fails even to mention any of the numerous allegations in Mayer of cases where they *did*, or her claim that "their companies have benefitted from a hundred million dollars in government contracts since 2000" (53). He then turns around and defends the Kochs for their biographer's quotation, "If we're going to give a lot of money, we'll make darn sure they spend it in a way that goes along with our intent" on grounds that, *if they chose to*, they would be perfectly entitled to spend limitless money (especially after the Supreme Court Citizen's United decision) exerting such influence. I wonder how Zywicki and everyone else hired under such conditions in corporate-front think tanks and media feel about being under the constraint that any deviation from the boss's party line might cause them to be fired. Once again, libertarian freedom of the press would seem to be limited to those who own a press.

In one typically nasty exchange in 2011 between Democratic and Republican bloggers, Lee Fang at *Think Progress* and John Hinteraker at *Powerline*, Fang charged that in Hinteraker's repeated rebuttals to *Think Progress* in defense of the Kochs, he failed to disclose that the Kochs are clients of his law firm ("Blogger from Koch Law Firm"). Hinteraker responded that the Kochs are only one among the firm's multiple clients and that he has never personally represented them. He added, "When I have a relationship to a company or person that is relevant to the subject matter of a post, I do disclose it. Thus, I did say I had participated in one of the Koch-sponsored seminars in Aspen" ("Think Ignorance").

The most prominent rebuttal to Mayer appeared in Matthew Continetti's "The Paranoid Style in Liberal Politics: The Left's Obsession with the Koch Brothers," in the *Weekly Standard* of 4 Apr. 2011. (This title was another co-optive simulation of a liberal source, historian Richard Hofstadter's *The Paranoid Style in American Politics*, which traced this strain in American conservatism, culminating in McCarthyism.) Comparative analysis of Mayer versus Continetti would be a perfect course assignment for students to apply the heuristics in my introductory chapter, since Continetti attempts to refute Mayer point by point, and does so skillfully in general, especially as he plays up the Kochs's positive accomplishments, like their extensive cultural philanthropies (Mayer does acknowledge these, but perfunctorily) and their companies' recent environmental scrupulousness. Pending more extensive comparison, here are a few salient points.

Continetti downsizes Mayer's long list of the Kochs' criminal infractions of environmental regulations to, "Making matters worse was a series of industrial accidents and environmental violations that drew the attention of Clinton's EPA." Mayer described a 2010 Americans for Prosperity summit in Texas as "a training session for Tea Party activists," with details of projects directed by Peggy Venable, a longtime AFP staff member (46). And, "In the weeks before the first Tax Day protests, in April 2009, Americans for Prosperity hosted a Web site offering supporters 'Tea Party Talking Points'" ("Covert" 47).[3] Continetti, along with all the other critics of Mayer that I have read, ignored her evidence here as he insisted, "Neither brother has attended a Tea Party. If anything it was the Tea Partiers who used Americans for Prosperity." Like other Koch defenders, Continetti waffles between boasting about AFP's millions of "boots on the ground" in their Mary-Kay-strength sales force directed at the Tea Party constituency, and denying that their forces exert any influence on the Tea Party or have any responsibility for the more raucus displays at their events. (See "Semantic Calculator," #4. a-3 and b-3, in my introductory chapter.) Whenever I have heard rank-and-file Tea Party members interviewed, or read their websites, they have insisted that they are equally opposed to big government, to Republicans and Democrats, and to big corporations, especially as they exert "crony capitalism" through lobbying and campaign contributions. However, they seem oblivious to the corporate empires, lobbyists, political action committees, and Republican officials behind their boosters like Americans for Prosperity and FreedomWorks, and news interviewers rarely press this point.

Continetti refuted Mayer's evidences of Koch-sponsored research programs coinciding with their corporate interests, by arguing, "It was impossible for the liberal activists to acknowledge that libertarians might actually operate from conviction. Charles and David believed in low taxes, less spending, and limited regulation not because those policies helped *them* but because they helped everybody." Maybe so, but evidence for this distinction is not demonstrable, while it is demonstrable that their support of lobbies and research promoting these beliefs does immediately help their companies and contribute to the escalating increase in their share of the nation's wealth, most obviously in opposition to the kind of environmental regulatory laws that they have broken and to rescinding President Bush's tax cuts for the wealthy. Continetti adds, "'If I wanted to enhance my riches,' said David, 'why do I give away almost all my money?'" These are constant lines of argument by other Koch defenders like Zywicki, who pile up instances of their unselfish spending on both philanthropic and political causes or, in a variant, instances where, true to libertarian principles, they have *not* sought to buy government favor when they might have. But does the amount of money the Kochs (and other philanthropists, conservatives, or liberals like Soros) spend on unselfish causes (or do not spend on selfish ones) nullify the verifiable effects of the amount on selfish ones? With a current net worth of some $22 billion, Koch is a long way from having given away "almost all" of his money, in the manner of Andrew Carnegie. Besides, aren't libertarians *supposed* to believe in "the virtue of selfishness"?

In another conflicting view between Mayer and Continetti, she says:

> Koch Industries has been lobbying to prevent the EPA from classifying formaldehyde, which the company produces in great quantities, as a "known carcinogen in humans."... Major scientific studies have concluded that formaldehyde causes cancer in human beings—including one published last year by the National Cancer Institute, on whose advisory board [David] Koch sits.... David Koch did not recuse himself from the National Cancer Advisory Board [which guides NCI], or divest himself of company stock while his company was directly lobbying the government to keep formaldehyde on the market. (A board spokesperson said the issue of formaldehyde had not come up.) ("Covert" 55)

It is ambiguous here whether the board was that of NCI (National Cancer Institute) or NCAB (National Cancer Advisory Board). It would apparently be necessary to research the NCI report to see if it was published during the time Koch was on that board. Continetti says, "Particularly outrageous was Mayer's claim that David used his position on the National Cancer Advisory Board to lobby against classifying formaldehyde as a carcinogen. David was on the board for almost seven years. Not once did he hear formaldehyde discussed." Continetti not only evades the question of whether or not Koch was on the NCI board when it was studying formaldehyde but of whether Koch Industries lobbied Environmental Protection Agency (EPA) about formaldehyde. Mayer does not claim here that he lobbied

NCAB, but that it was an intrinsic conflict of interest for him to be on the board of either NCAB or NCI when he had investments in and lobbied elsewhere for a product these scientific agencies were studying.

> Does the author have anything personally to gain from the position she/he is arguing for, any conflicts of interest or other reasons for special pleading? ("Semantic Calculator for Bias in Rhetoric")

None of the vituperative conservative critics of Jane Mayer's work I have read claims that she is on the payroll of any liberal outside financial or political interest. Nor, despite the *New Yorker*'s many decades of political liberalism, have any of its various owners had a direct affiliation with the Democratic Party. Likewise for any of its editors until 1992, when Hendrik Herzberg, who was a speechwriter for President Carter, became executive editor. David Remnick, current editor in chief, wrote a sympathetic biography of Obama in 2011 but had no direct Democratic affiliations. Its current owner is billionaire S. I. Newhouse, whose Condé Nast company publishes mainly glossy magazines; he has a reputation for staying out of both politics and control over the political content of his magazines. (Direct ties of executives to the Democratic Party, beyond social ones, are also rare between the most influential "liberal media" like the *New York Times*, *Washington Post*, PBS, and NPR.)

Continetti was employed by the *Weekly Standard* (*TWS*), edited by William Kristol, a ubiquitous TV talking head for the Republican Party, former chief of staff to Vice President Dan Quayle and, simultaneously, cofounder in 1991 of The Committee to Confirm Clarence Thomas. (Continetti is Kristol's son-in-law, continuing the neoconservative tradition of nepotism, surveyed in chapter 6.) The magazine was founded by Rupert Murdoch, who was on the original board of directors of the Cato Institute and whose Fox News, *Wall Street Journal*, *New York Post*, and multiple other worldwide media have been champions of the Tea Party and other Koch political causes. (On Murdoch's and director Roger Ailes' Republican-slanted editorial control over Fox News, see Robert Greenwald's documentary *Outfoxed*.) Murdoch's power in the Republican Party was matched in counterparts in England, where the 2011 scandal over his tabloids hacking emails and phone messages and bribing police officials for inside information revealed that former Murdoch executives held high positions in both Conservative and Labor governments. (Fox News and Murdoch's print publications in the

United States were the last place to look for coverage of the scandals in England.) In 2009 Murdoch sold the magazine to Philip Anschutz, who also publishes the conservative daily *Washington Examiner* and has attended the Kochs' regular summits and fundraisers for influential conservatives.

Continetti and *TWS* opinion editor Michael Goldfarb received fellowships in 2007 and 2008 at the libertarian Phillips Foundation for young journalists, modestly funded in part by the Kochs ("Phillips Foundation"), and Goldfarb was deputy communications director for John McCain's 2008 presidential campaign. In 2010 Goldfarb left *TWS* to work for Orion Strategies, as part of the Kochs' PR counteroffensive; Orion's head, Randy Scheunemann, was McCain's foreign policy adviser and also an adviser to Sarah Palin. (Bizarrely, Orion worked for both the Kochs and George Soros—lobbying and PR do make strange political bedfellows!) Early in 2012, Continetti left *TWS* to partner with Goldfarb in starting the Center for American Freedom, a conscious simulation of the Democratic-affiliated Center for American Progress (CAP), where they started a daily online conservative journal, *Washington Free Beacon*, dedicated to refuting liberal journals and blogs like *Politico*, *Talking Points Memo*, and *Think Progress* (the latter being an outlet of CAP and widely considered a surrogate for the Obama White House). This prompted considerable buzz in the blogosphere about where the funding came from; early liberal rumors about the Kochs apparently were erroneous, and no other information has become available at this writing.

As a general rule, this kind of revolving door between media owners or journalists and party organizations, partisan foundations and think tanks, PR and lobbying agencies has been more prevalent among Republicans than Democrats, and even more prevalent than among left-of-liberal media. On the TV nets, especially MSNBC, past Democratic administration staffers and/or PR consultants like Paul Begala, James Carville, George Stephanopolis, Chris Matthews, and Lawrence O'Donnell are designated liberal talking heads. However, to the left of these designated Democrats or of the *New Yorker* and *Think Progress*, media like *The Nation, Mother Jones, IFairness and Accuracy in Reporting (FAIR)* Alternet, Common Dreams, and Truthdig are far distant from most Democratic Party leaders and more critical of them.

Concerning Continetti's article, let's try to skirt the endless back-and-forth charges, rumors, and innuendos by considering it this way. At a minimum, The *Weekly Standard* has had a history of direct and indirect ties to the Kochs. Continetti's article appeared soon after the Kochs launched a PR counteroffensive against its critics (partly conducted by former *TWS* editor Goldfarb, whom Continetti would join the next year in the Center for American Freedom), and it reflected greater access to the brothers, including interviews, than any previous major publication about them. Considering that the editors and author were well aware of all this, shouldn't they have bent over backward to acknowledge in the article more of the substantial criticisms of the Kochs and instances of vilification by Koch allies of wealthy liberals like Soros comparable to that alleged against the Kochs, so as to avoid giving it the appearance—which it undeniably has—of a PR-generated puff piece? The gist of the article is, why are liberals saying such awful things about this couple of saintly guys who only have the country's best interests at heart? Sticks and stones.... In the *New Republic* Jonathan Chait ridiculed Continetti's sympathy for the Kochs' self-pitying selective vision, which included their hurt feelings over receiving abusive emails:

> Is this clear? The Kochs and Koch-financed groups are merely a collection of largely like-minded people using research, argument, polemic and other tools to advance their political viewpoint. The liberal version of this, by contrast, is a "Death Star." Your side is composed of passionate citizens expressing their genuine concern for the country. The other side is a vilification machine. Nobody associated with the Tea Party would ever send a mean e-mail.

Returning to Soros, his defenders, like those of the Koch brothers, play up the millions he has donated to laudable nonpolitical or nonpartisan causes worldwide, a point that his critics, like those of the Kochs, generally concede. In both cases, however, this is a distraction from the more controversial areas. Soros does have Democratic Party ties comparable to those of the Kochs and other wealthy Republicans. He has contributed hundreds of millions to Democratic candidates, campaign organizations, PACS, and unions, along with advocacy groups like Common Cause, MoveOn.org, Media Matters, and the Center for American Progress, which are counterparts to Republican-aligned groups like Americans for Prosperity, FreedomWorks, and the Cato Institute. Few leftists consider Soros, in his history of financial speculation and manipulation, a poster boy for the left; nor are many happy to have to depend on wealthy people to fight their battles for them. In *American Foundations* (2002), journalist Mark Dowie reports on a meeting at Soros's Open Society Institute to resolve a disagreement about grant-making priorities, Soros is alleged to have announced, "'This is my money. We will do it my way.'" At which point a junior staff member interjected that roughly half of the money in the foundation was not his money, but the public's money, explaining, "'If you hadn't placed that money in OSI...about half of it would be in the Treasury'" (247. Dowie comments that the junior staffer did not last long in the Soros foundation's employment. Dowie does not specify what the disputed issue was, or whether Soros was motivated by profit or just vanity.

So it would a big stretch for conservatives to make a case that either Soros's political contributions or his most high-profile philanthropy advances his financial interests. Mayer made this contrast between the Kochs and Soros in her article. Continetti in rebuttal cleverly dug up Mayer's 2004 *New Yorker* article on Soros, "The Money Man," in which he admitted starting a think tank in England through which he made connections enabling him to make a big killing in the British bond market. In Mayer's account, however, the connection was not direct; a routine conference there happened to be attended by "British notables," from whom Soros got a tip while chatting about matters unrelated to the conference (6).

Beyond these few tenuous instances, much of Soros's and his grantees' writings warn against capitalists like him gaining too much wealth and power, and his organizations lobby for higher taxes on the wealthy and corporations, more financial and environmental regulation—diametrically opposite from the Koch forces. (Mayer's article on Soros began with an account of a "clandestine summit meeting" in 2004 at the Aspen Institute, also the scene of Koch summits, attended by Soros and several other Democratic billionaires, all dedicated to such liberal policies contrary to their personal interests; the meeting was stated to be "clandestine" because of the discomfort many leftists feel about being bedfellows with rich people and corporations, and because of conservatives' fondness for labeling such alliances "hypocritical." This kind of thing unfortunately fuels parallel conspiracy theories on the left and right.) Soros made this case himself in a 2011 article, "My Philanthropy," in *New York Review of Books*, where he is a regular contributor: "I do not hesitate to advocate policies that are in conflict with my business interests" (12). Soros, like everyone on opposing sides in the culture wars, evoked Orwell against his critics, especially Fox News:

> Newspeak is extremely difficult to contradict because it incorporates and thereby preempts its own contradiction, as when Fox News calls itself fair and balanced. Another trick is to accuse your opponent of the

behavior of which you are guilty, like Fox News accusing me of being the puppet master of a media empire.... Those in charge of Fox News, Rupert Murdoch and Roger Ailes, have done well in identifying me as their adversary. They have done less well in the methods they have used to attack me; their lies shall not stand, and their techniques shall not endure. (16)

A pertinent question would be whether Soros funds *New York Review*, but conservatives haven't come up with any evidence of this that I can find.

Conservative media have gone to extreme lengths to concoct devious motives for Soros's ostensibly altruistic activities, like the allegation by Glenn Beck and dozens of online sources that the projects of the Open Society Foundation to promote free markets, free elections, and human rights in the former Soviet Union and elsewhere throughout the world are intended to impose a one-world socialist (or, in some versions, fascist) dictatorship—presumably with Soros as dictator. (Mayer's article on Soros asserted that Richard Mellon Scaife has funded several media campaigns dedicated to attacking Soros, including David Horowitz's Center for Popular Culture and the magazine *Newsmax*, which has been a favorite source for Fox News, just as Scaife financed devious efforts to bring down the Clintons in the nineties—see Brock's *Blinded*—and John Kerry in 2004.)

As noted earlier, when Occupy Wall Street emerged in 2011, conservatives eagerly sought to mimic left criticism of the Kochs' role in the Tea Party by fastening on Soros as designated puppet master, most crudely in the manner of Rush Limbaugh and Bill O'Reilly: "This is a George Soros operation." For a slightly more refined version, consider "Liberal billionaire behind left-wing organizations and media celebrating anti-capitalist protests," (13 Oct. 2011), by Iris Somberg, posted by the Business and Media Institute, a branch of the Media Research Center in Washington, which is headed by L. Brent Bozell III and dedicated to "prove—through sound scientific research—that liberal bias in the media does exist and undermines traditional American values" (home page). Herman Cain was previously on the advisory board of the Business and Media Institute's advisory board, which currently includes several libertarian economists and policy analysts at Cato Institute and George Mason, including Walter Williams, John M. Olin distinguished professor of Economics at George Mason, also a board member of Americans for Prosperity and guest host for Limbaugh's radio show.

Somberg begins, "George Soros is at it again. While he may claim he's not behind the Occupy Wall Street protests,...his foundations funded groups that back the protests and steer their 'progressive' message."

Somberg once again focuses on the Tides Center and Tides Foundation, which she says have received $25,991,845 since 2000 from the Open Society Foundations—much more than Reuters acknowledged. She concedes that Adbusters, which started OWS, has received only $184,721 from Tides over a decade, but she goes on to identity other "organizations that joined the protesters" and that have received much more from Open Society or Tides. These included not only the Democratic-aligned Common Cause and MoveOn.org, but "the Independent Media Center, which received more than $70,000 from...Tides" and which funds the *Occupy Wall Street Journal*, as well as the Media Consortium (an umbrella organization for mainly nonprofit media groups like Independent Media Center and Alternet that criticize "the liberal media" and the Democratic Party from the left), which has received $425,000 from Open Society, while Alternet has received $495,000. (It would be significant if Somberg or other conservative polemicists presented some evidence of these left media groups catering their coverage to Soros's financial profits, but to this date I have seen none.)

Somberg continues, "Additional funding went to the Service Employees International Union (SEIU), Community Voices Heard, Coalition for the Homeless, Neighborhood Economic Development Advocacy, and 350.org [a liberal environmental organization headed by Bill McKibben, mainly addressing climate change]." The implied relation here between SEIU, Soros, and OWS is unclear. I emailed Somberg to ask for clarification, and received a reply from Dan Gainor at Business and Media Institute (BMI), who provided the information that the Open Society Foundations gave grants to the SEIU Education and Support Fund of $26,000 in 2006 and $75,000 in 2007. So all Somberg and Trainor seem to be saying is that Soros contributed to SEIU, and both supported OWS. Trainor included a link to a SEIU blog (5 Oct. 2011) endorsing OWS and saying the union was joining forces with its activities (without mentioning financial support).

Somberg's account still leaves several large questions dangling. How does the amount of Soros' funding of OWS and these other left causes compare to that of conservative ones, especially the Tea Party, by the Kochs, FreedomWorks, and other wealthy conservatives? How much power has OWS exercised in comparison to the

Tea Party? Does Soros or organizations he funds "steer [OWS's] progressive message," and again, what would he or they have to gain by doing so? Both Soros and OWS leaders deny any active association. Drawing the line about the extent to which either the Tea Party or OWS is a grassroots movement or has been instigated by outside interests is a complex chicken-and-egg problem that needs to be addressed through extensive empirical research—another good class assignment for students. Going back to the admission by their own leaders that Americans for Prosperity and FreedomWorks employed Mary Kay–style sales campaigns, or to Mayer's description of Americans for Prosperity offering workshops and talking points for the Tea Party, do conservatives have evidence that a similar controlling (and financing) role was played by Soros-connected or other left organizations, or were the latter only joining forces with their natural political allies in OWS?

But above all, what would Soros, whose wealth derives from market speculation, hedge fund management and stock ownership, plausibly have to benefit financially or politically from support of OWS, of labor unions, of media that are mostly nonprofit alternatives on the left to infinitely larger and wealthier corporate media (whether they lean Republican or Democratic), of anticorporate environmentalists, or of advocates for the poor and homeless? Can anyone honestly believe that Soros has selfish motives for supporting organizations to aid the poor, or that these organizations have political power comparable to big unions like SEIU, to say nothing of big businesses like the Kochs' and their lobbies like Americans for Prosperity, with its $40 million annual budget? For that matter, weigh the Independent Media Center's $70,000 from Tides or the Media Consortium's $425,000 from Open Society (Somberg does not say over how many years) and its annual budget of under $500,000, against the Media Research Center's budget in 2008 (the last year available online) of over $12 million and net assets of about $10.7 million ("MRC Annual Report 2008"), from conservative donors including Exxon-Mobil and the Scaife, Olin, Bradley, and Carthage foundations. (Source: the leftist Center for Media and Democracy: http://www.sourcewatch.org/wiki.phtml?title=Media_Research_Center#Funding.) (And what about CMD's funding? The conservative ActivistCash.com lists CMD's 2003 revenue as about $336,000 and net worth as about $156,000, mainly derived from liberal foundations including Open Society and Ford. And what about ActivistCash's funding? Are you dizzy yet?) These infinitely proliferating echo chambers on the left and right enabled by the Internet are the most compelling reason for the creation of a bipartisan Truth and Reconciliation Commission to referee the opposing claims.

The waters are further muddied here by the conflation by Somberg and other conservatives of media and organizations that support the Democratic Party (including the wealthiest unions and corporate interests comparable to those supporting the Republicans) with those that oppose the Democrats from the left or would move them much more to the left than at present. Aside from these gross exaggerations of the power of organizations that speak for the far left or for the poor and homeless (including ACORN, which was rapidly hounded to death on the basis of false accusations), conservatives' search for self-interested motives behind philanthropy on the left equal to those on the right would seem to reflect a mix of deliberate obfuscation with another psychological projection of the selfish mind-set of corporate-conservative circles (whose very gospel is Ayn Rand's *The Virtue of Selfishness*) onto supporters of left causes, who some conservatives cannot imagine acting out of a disinterested sense of social justice and fair play to support forces too weak to compete on their own against corporate wealth.

I might have been able to find instances where Soros' defenders, like the Kochs', receive money from him without disclosing it, at least without pressure. But how egregious would that be, if the beneficiaries' own enterprises do not promote Soros's financial or political interests (as the Kochs' generally do) or if they are diametrically opposed, as many are? These attempts by conservatives to make a false equation between the Kochs and Soros epitomize the overall asymmetry of forces on the American right and left that my last two chapters have traced.[4] Suppose that on one side, there are scholars, scientists, and journalists whose views derive from their professional commitment to seek the truth—whatever personal and professional biases they might have—and on the other side, there are basically corporate public relations agents employed by executives who make unabashed statements like, "We're not here to be some kind of Ph.D. committee giving equal time. Our role is to provide conservative public-policymakers with arguments to bolster our side." If something like this is true, mightn't we be suckers in a rigged game, whose riggers employ people to fabricate contradictions and imitations of every argument we make, and who resort to boilerplate smearing and ad hominem evasions to poison the well of opposing arguments—while accusing us of doing all that?

Case in point: Did I poison the well by prefacing my critique of Somberg's article from Business and Media Institute with background on its ties to the Cato Institute, George Mason libertarian economics, and the Olin and Koch foundations? As noted, Dan Gainor at BMI helpfully sent me information about the connections between Soros, SEIU, and OWS, so was providing a perfectly legitimate, valuable service. Although I was grateful to him for this information, I would also like to ask him frankly and without malicious intent, whether he is employed to pursue the truth of these contested issues impartially and evenhandedly or "to provide conservative public-policymakers with arguments to bolster [their] side" (Pines, cited in chapter 4), and whether he is subject to being fired by his employers for any departure from that role, consistent with libertarian principles? He and other conservatives will predictably respond with a tu quoque volley of alleged instances of conservatives being censored, fired, or not even hired, by liberally dominated institutions. Even if all these allegations were accurate (they are often disputable), the more important question would be: How many instances can you cite of calculated bias and blatant autocracy comparable to those I have cited by William Baroody, Burton Pines, and David Koch—"If they make a wrong turn and start doing things we don't agree with, we withdraw funding" —by liberal administrators in universities and academic departments or scholarly organizations, foundations, media, or think tanks? (The closest counterpart might be found in some labor unions and academic labor education programs, which are expressly opponents of corporate interests and their agents in partisan academic fields like business administration.) In the last analysis, this may be the best test for distinguishing valuable originals from gross parodies: Which institutions and individuals are *at least in principle* dedicated to the disinterested pursuit of knowledge and justice, and which are dedicated to the pursuit of profit and suppression of internal voices questioning that pursuit, not as exceptions to the rule but as the rule of business as usual?

6

FROM *PARTISAN REVIEW* TO *FOX NEWS*: NEOCONSERVATIVES AS DEFENDERS OF INTELLECTUAL STANDARDS

> Most neoconservatives believe that the last, best hope for humanity at this time is an intellectually and morally invigorated liberal capitalism.
> Irving Kristol, *Reflections of a Neoconservative* 77

> I would rather be ruled by the Tea Party than the Democratic Party, and I would rather have Sarah Palin sitting in the Oval Office than Barack Obama.
> Norman Podhoretz, *Wall Street Journal*, 2010

This chapter will explore the relations, direct and indirect, between the movement of intellectual neoconservatism since the late 1960s and the conservative attack apparatus, mainly guided by the Republican Party, surveyed in my previous two chapters. The bottom-line conclusion is that by the twenty-first century, the two had merged indistinguishably—and proudly—as epitomized by Podhoretz's enthusiasm for Sarah Palin in 2010. My main point in defense of leftists in academia and media is, once again, that condemnations of their political correctness need to be evaluated in the perspective of the coordinated, unrelenting, and often unscrupulous attack campaign against them by elements on the right, in this chapter the intellectual-journalistic right and in the next, the scholarly right. This campaign has distorted accurate proportions through a double standard in those who obsess over sins on the left while suppressing comparable sins on their own side or who even praise the same kind of attitudes and behavior on their side that they denounce on the other.

The history has been told many times over of how neoconservatism evolved out of sectarian factions in the American Old Left dating back to the Russian Revolution, most prominently in the group of "New York Intellectuals" associated with the magazines *Partisan Review* and *Commentary*.[1] Several prominent members of this group came out of circles allied with the American Communist Party and its support of Stalinism, but sooner or later rejected these circles to become Trotskyists in the late thirties and forties, then "Cold War liberals" in the fifties, and neoconservatives in the seventies. The New York Intellectuals, who included a mix of political journalists and academics, were distinguished by being both highly learned and fiercely polemical. Some such as Irving Kristol were already leaning toward conservatism by the 1950s; others, such as Norman Podhoretz, Midge Decter, and Nathan Glazer, initially sympathized with the New Left in the sixties, but reacted against its excesses over the next decade or so and joined Kristol in identifying themselves as neoconservatives.

The primal political conflict, in the thirties and forties, came out of the betrayal of socialist ideals by Stalin in the Soviet Union and by the Communist Party's international propaganda apparatus, which recruited many intellectuals, artists, and scholars into subordination of their individual integrity to a doctrinaire party line, promulgated by leftist cultural operations like those of the Popular Front. So belligerent, devious, and influential were the cultural Stalinists that many of the intellectuals who did battle with them were traumatized for the rest of their lives, thenceforth seeing a Stalinist under every bed, a slippery slope toward the Gulag, in the (mainly noncommunist) New Left protest movements in the sixties and academic and journalistic leftism from the eighties to the present. Thus Irving Kristol facilely transferred his anti-Stalinist invective tropes to allegations about the mentality of the liberal "New Class," claiming in 1975, "Like all crusades, it engenders an enthusiastic paranoia about the nature of the Enemy and the deviousness of his operations" (*Neoconservatism* 228), with no consideration of the possibility that he and other conservative culture warriors might have become mirror images of that paranoia.

A trenchant judgment of this pattern was made in 1983 by Diana Trilling, one of the central figures in the earlier *Partisan Review-Commentary* circle, writing in *The New Republic*:

> Neoconservatives such as Joseph Epstein, Norman Podhoretz, and Hilton Kramer, all of them editors of important periodicals, are not so young but that they have to be fully aware of the irreparable damage that was done to the cultural and even the political life of this country by their Stalinist forebears who, instead of honorably debating issues, poisoned the intellectual atmosphere with lies and invective. By what

process of self-hallucination do they now persuade themselves that just because they operate from an opposite premise, the anti-Communist premise, they do us any better service with such methods? (40)

The pattern resembled one of James Thurber's animal fables, "The Bear Who Let It Alone," about a bear who goes on destructive binges after drinking too much honey mead. He becomes a teetotaler, but in his anti-mead zealotry, he wreaks just as much havoc. The moral: "You might as well fall flat on your face as lean over too far backward" (253).

Intellectuals and Standards: The Case of *Commentary*

The politics of modern intellectuals and their relation to social elitism and populism are vexingly complicated subjects. Particular topics in dispute here include (1) inconsistencies on both the left and right in swings between defenses of and denunciations of intellect, especially in relation to elitism versus populism, (2) intellectuals' responsibility to uphold high critical standards and independence from ideological dogma or political partisanship, (3) the adversarial role of intellectuals toward mass society, and (4) the temptations of, and corruption by, the quest for political power by intellectuals on the left or right, particularly within the "New Class" in industrial society of technocratic managers, professionals, scientists, journalists, teachers and scholars. The dilemmas posed by these issues have led theorists on both the left and right into equivocal positions. I have addressed leftist equivocations on other occasions, some of which I will cite in passing, but will mainly try here to sort through those on the right.

An exemplary introduction to these issues can be found in *Breaking Ranks*, Norman Podhoretz's memoir of the sixties and seventies, published in 1979, which set the tone for the neoconservative critique of the academic and journalistic left that culminated in the anti-PC campaign a decade later. Podhoretz castigated the 1960s New Left and counterculture for their blurring of critical distinctions and intellectual standards. While acknowledging that the leaders and supporters of the Berkeley Free Speech Movement had committed little actual violence, he charged, "The violence that was done, in other words, was precisely to language and ideas. Everything was simplified into slogans, fit for shouting and chanting" (208–9). And:

> As an intellectual, I would have found it hard to stomach open contempt for distinctions under any circumstances and under any aegis. I

had been trained to regard such contempt as simple philistinism—an expression of hatred for intellectual values and for the pursuit of truth (which, in the words of a wonderful French epigram, always "resides in nuance")....They were willing to sacrifice intellectual values for their radicalism as against loyalty to intellectual standards, whereas I was choosing to break political ranks rather than betray what I regarded as my responsibilities to the intellectual community and the intellectual vocation. (209)

And about *Commentary*'s offensive against the New Left, he modestly observed, "I could say that the reason for our effectiveness was a high literary standard" (306).

However, the truth that resides in nuance disappeared from *Commentary*, and neoconservative discourse in general, in the 1970s when Podhoretz, Irving Kristol, and their circle embraced and were embraced by the Republican Party. In a 1991 *Commentary* retrospective by Podhoretz's wife Midge Decter, "Ronald Reagan & the Culture War," Decter asserted that the explanation for his successes in spite of intellectuals' scorn "lies in the very fact that neither Ronald Reagan's ideas nor his responses to the world ever seemed to be in the least complex." She continued, "Even as late as 1976, when he mounted a challenge to Gerald Ford for the Republican nomination, most of the ex-liberals who were to become his passionate supporters only four years later did not take Reagan seriously. Though already deeply disaffected toward the liberals—of whatever party—they were still in the early stages of the process of stripping spiritual issues down to their simplicities and possibly a bit snobbish about their reluctance to push this process through to its end" (45–46). Similarly on issue after issue, neoconservatives would praise their allies for the same traits—in this case oversimplification—that they excoriated in liberals and leftists. Four legs good, two legs bad.

The literary issues Podhoretz raised in *Breaking Ranks* were in the line of the constant disputes since at least the Russian Revolution about whether intellectuals and artists should subordinate their ideas to political parties and ideologies or remain independent, impartial upholders of critical and aesthetic standards. As late as 2001, in *My Love Affair with America*, Podhoretz condemned "critics of the Left to whom art was a 'weapon,' and who praised or damned novels and poems and plays entirely for the political or ideological positions they took" (120). But he and many of his associates had themselves changed their tune (without ever explicitly admitting it) as soon as they turned to the right. By the time of Podhoretz's 1986 book *The Bloody Crossroads: Where Literature and Politics Meet*, the erstwhile defender of supra-political literary standards condemned Camus and Kundera for being unwilling to subordinate their artistic autonomy to the cause of anticommunism. (In the famous feud between Camus and Sartre, Camus accused Sartre of subordination to the French Communist Party and the Soviet Union, but Camus's position was that of third-camp socialism equidistant from Soviet communism and Western capitalism. For a history of how American journalistic accounts of this feud falsely portrayed Camus as an ardently pro-American cold warrior, see Lazere, "American Criticism of the Sartre-Camus Dispute.") Like many other American conservatives, Podhoretz also tried to claim George Orwell as a proto-neoconservative, overlooking Orwell's unwavering commitment to socialism and his rejection of the apocalyptic anticommunism of American conservatives like James Burnham, whose ideas became a model for the depiction in *1984* of opposing ideologies as mirror images. Podhoretz failed to mention Orwell's comment, quoted in Bernard Crick's biography, "The name suggested in NINETEEN EIGHTY-FOUR is of course Ingsoc, but in practice a wide range of choices is open. In the USA the phrase 'Americanism' or 'hundred per cent Americanism' is suitable and the qualifying adjective is as totalitarian as any one could wish" (*George Orwell* 566).

In 2010, Benjamin Balint, who had been an assistant editor at *Commentary* from 2001 to 2004 and was then a fellow at the conservative Hudson Institute, published *Running Commentary*, an inside view that was harshly critical of the magazine's latter-day subordination of critical standards and political autonomy to the Republican Party line, as well as venal practices like puff-piece reviews of books by financial donors (175–76). Balint confirmed earlier accounts of the magazine's heavy-handed editing during the reign of Podhoretz and his successor Neal Kozody—as in writers' anecdotes about their amazement at seeing one of their own sentences in print. Balint says that Podhoretz even heavily edited fiction, and that he regularly breached the traditional autonomy in political journals of "the back of the book"—reviews of books and other cultural works. Balint quotes Daphne Merkin, who stopped reviewing for *Commentary* when she "became disenchanted with the editors' insistence on putting politics into every frail vessel of a book or film review that came along" (149). Balint adds that in 1980, the magazine replaced its regular fiction reviewer, Pearl K. Bell (Alfred Kazin's sister and Daniel Bell's wife) with Carol Iannone, a scourge of feminism, multiculturalism, and the academic left "who could be trusted to wage the literary fight" (149). Iannone attracted notoriety in 1991 when National Endowment for the Humanities head Lynne Cheney pressed for her to be named to the agency's advisory board, drawing a protest from the Modern Language Association because she had virtually no scholarly publications; her nomination was rejected, provoking neoconservative cries that she had been "borked" (in the manner of Reagan Supreme Court nominee judge Robert Bork, a neoconservative stalwart, who was rejected by congressional Democrats). She went onto be a founder of the National Association of Scholars and editor of its *Academic Questions*, ostensibly a scholarly periodical but in practice a journal of opinion with much the same tone as *Commentary*.

Between the 1980s and 2000s, *Commentary* featured panegyrics to the towering intellects of Republican officials from Henry Kissinger and Dan Quayle to Donald Rumsfeld, and to the aesthetic excellence of conservative actors like John Wayne and Clint Eastwood (in his Dirty Harry period). The then-conservative David Brock was commissioned to write the 1991 puff piece on Vice President Quayle, whose chief of staff was William Kristol. Brock reports that his other self-described hack pieces of the period prompted Podhoretz to laud him as "a right-wing Bob Woodward" (*Blinded* 191).

In foreign affairs, *Commentary*'s most influential article under Podhoretz was Jeane Kirkpatrick's "Dictatorships and Double Standards" in 1979 attacking American liberals, especially advocates of international human rights, for applying a harsher standard against "authoritarian" dictators, who sided with the United States against communism and whose reigns were impermanent, than against communist dictators, whose regimes were allegedly immutable, or against crypto-communist insurgents in the Third World. That article led directly to her appointment as UN ambassador by President Reagan. In retrospect, however, it appears that *Commentary* consistently applied the opposite double standard. In Podhoretz's 1983 article in *Commentary*, titled "Appeasement by Any Other Name," he wrote about liberal and leftist critics of American support of the right-wing Duarte government in El Salvador:

> In Congress and in the media, the new isolationists work to obstruct the giving of aid; they devote all their energies to attacking the elected government of El Salvador for its abuses of human rights; they ridicule the administration's judgment that these abuses are declining; and they loudly and persistently demand that the guerrillas be given a share of power. (33)

And:

> One would never guess from these words that 68 percent of the dollars we have sent to El Salvador have gone to economic rather than military aid; that what we have allied ourselves with in El Salvador is a democratically elected government; that it is trying with some success both to carry social reform forward and to cut down on the murders and other horrors that always and everywhere accompany guerilla war; that if the guerrillas came to power they would be far more repressive than the present government in El Salvador. (34)

The shrugging nonchalance of "the murders and other horrors that always and everywhere accompany guerilla war" excused particular agents and acts, particularly those of the Duarte government and Reagan administration. Podhoretz has never granted any comparable dispensation to crimes committed by leftists. There was no mention here (or anytime later in *Commentary*, to my knowledge, of the thousands of civilians murdered, before and after this article, by death squads and militias aligned with the government of both El Salvador and the United States (directly through the Army School of the Americas), led by the psychopathic Roberto D'Aubuisson, including some eight hundred peasants in El Mozote, Archbishop Romero, four American churchwomen, and six Jesuit priests. If Podhoretz believed that these victims were agents of the international communist conspiracy or that their deaths, though mildly regrettable, were just inevitable "collateral damage" in the war against communism, he was never forthright enough to say so. If he ever came to believe otherwise, he never apologized for his callousness toward those murdered and those who attempted to bring Salvadoran and other Central American right-wing atrocities to light.

In that 1983 article Podhoretz also neglected to note a conflict of interest; his and Decter's son-in-law Elliot Abrams was then assistant secretary of State for Inter-American Affairs and for Human Rights and Humanitarian Affairs. According to *Wikipedia*, "In early 1982, when reports of the El Mozote massacre of civilians by the military in El Salvador began appearing in U.S. media, Abrams told a Senate committee that the reports of hundreds of deaths at El Mozote 'were not credible,' and that 'it appears to be an incident that is at least being significantly misused, at the very best, by the guerrillas.'"

Abrams was also to become a key actor in the Iran-Contra affair in 1986, and pled guilty to two charges of providing misleading information to Congress. He was pardoned by President G. H. W. Bush on leaving office in 1992, but in 1997 the DC Court of Appeals publicly censured Abrams for having given false testimony on three occasions before congressional committees. Faithful to Roger Stone's all-purpose playbook for Republicans, "Admit nothing, deny everything, launch counterattack," neither Abrams nor the Podhoretzes ever admitted fault or even regret for his actions; in 1993 Abrams published *Undue Process: A Story of How Political Differences Are Turned into Crimes*. He also was president of the Ethics and Public Policy Center from 1996 to 2002. In 2001, President George W. Bush appointed him as special assistant to the president and senior director for democracy, human rights, and international operations at the National Security Council, serving mainly as an advisor on the Middle East. In support of her founding of the Committee for the Free World in 1981, Abrams' mother-in-law had charged about liberal intellectuals' views on foreign policy, "Anti-democratic ideas have seeped into the culture at every point, corrupting thought and debasing language almost exactly term for term, as George Orwell predicted" (quoted in Goldstein). But what would Orwell have said about Abrams' resumé of qualifications to become, in Republican parlance, Czar of Democracy, Ethics, Human Rights, and Humanitarian Affairs?

Decter's daughter and Abrams' wife, Rachel Abrams, currently writes in the *Weekly Standard* and in a blog, *Bad Rachel*, mainly about the Middle East, where on 18 Oct. 2011, following an Israel-Hamas prisoner exchange, she described Hamas as:

> the slaughtering, death-worshiping, innocent-butchering, child-sacrificing savages who dip their hands in blood and use women—those who aren't strapping bombs to their own devils' spawn and sending them out to meet their seventy-two virgins by taking the lives of the school-bus-riding, heart-drawing, Transformer-doodling, homework-losing children of Others—and their offspring—those who haven't already been pimped out by their mothers to the murder god—as shields, hiding behind their burkas and cradles like the unmanned animals they are, and throw them not into your prisons, where they can bide until they're traded by the thousands for another child of Israel, but into the sea, to float there, food for sharks, stargazers, and whatever other oceanic carnivores God has put there for the purpose.

In our present perspective, changes have occurred in the former USSR, China and Vietnam (now bases for American corporate sweatshop labor), Latin America, and Africa—if not in the intractable Middle East—that were inconceivable to the polemicists on opposing sides locked in mortal combat throughout the Cold War. Yet there have been few second thoughts expressed, especially by the neoconservatives, reconsidering the extent to which their judgment might have been distorted by the political certitudes and emotional excesses of the moment, such as the doctrine that communism was a monolithic international bloc, impregnable to internal divisions, reform, or containment short of overwhelming military force, or that consequently any and every means were justified toward the end of opposing its existence or potential rise in every remote region of the globe, rationalizing collusion with many of the world's most brutal regimes. Today the Cold-War rhetoric of high dudgeon and mortal combat has simply become a template for conservatives to upload for use not only in the Middle East but in every campaign large and small, including that against leftist PC in academe and media.

Then there was the marriage of convenience between the mostly Jewish neoconservatives around *Commentary* and the Christian right, based largely on fundamentalists' support for Israel deriving from the account in the Book of Revelation of the role of the Jews and Jerusalem in the Apocalypse. Writing in *Commentary* in 1984, Irving Kristol excused an evangelical preacher who claimed that God does not hear the prayers of Jews: "Why should Jews care about the theology of a fundamentalist preacher?...What do such theological abstractions matter as against the mundane fact that this same preacher is vigorously pro-Israel?" ("The Political Dilemma.") In a chapter of Michael Lind's *Up from Conservatism* titled "No Enemies to the Right" (a spin on the Communist Party's Popular Front slogan in the 1940s, "No enemies to the left"), Lind reviews a key episode for his defection, concerning his articles exposing anti-semitic conspiracy theories in the 1991 book *The New World Order* by Pat Robertson, then head of the Christian Coalition, a powerful lobby in the Republican Party. Conservative intellectual organs like William F. Buckley's *National Review* and Hilton Kramer's *New Criterion* defended Robertson and savaged Lind. In *Commentary*, Podhoretz conceded that Robertson purveyed lunatic conspiracy theories, yet concluded that he should still be supported because he was pro-Israel (Lind 111). Lind claims that during the same period an unnamed conservative journal editor explained to him its support for Robertson and the Christian right: "Of course they're mad, but we need their votes" (117). In other words, evangelical conservatives serve Republicans as the equivalent of what Lenin called "useful idiots" on the left.

Robertson's increasingly deranged ravings, such as his and Jerry Falwell's claim that 9/11 and Hurricane Katrina were God's punishment of America for homosexuality, abortion, and other sins, continued to be paraded in later years as a freak show in the media, with little demurral from neoconservative intellectuals. On his *700 Club* telecast on 21 Mar. 2006, and later on the Larry King show in the company of David Horowitz, Robertson waxed glowingly about Horowitz's book *The Professors: The 101 Most Dangerous Academics in America*, which Robertson said sheds light on the "thirty to forty thousand" left-wing professors who are "racists, murderers, sexual deviants and supporters of Al-Qaeda.... These guys are out and out communists, they are radicals, they are, you know, some of them killers, and they are propagandists of the first order.... You don't want your child to be brainwashed by these radicals.... Not only brainwashed but beat up, they beat these people up, cower them into submission." Horowitz, who in other settings claimed to be a responsible intellectual and scholar (he received an MA in English from Berkeley), only nodded in agreement, although Robertson's account was even more outlandish than his book's.[2] (In another appearance with Larry King, Horowitz's similar accusations against teachers' unions, including murder, were captured on You Tube (David%20 Horowitz%20Laughed%20off%20of%20Larry%20King%20-%20 YouTube.webarchive). Once again, most neoconservative intellectuals refrained from criticism of both Robertson and Horowitz.

THE TWO FACES OF IRVING KRISTOL

When Irving Kristol died at 89 in 2009, he was widely venerated for his erudition and worldliness, his prestige as a professor at NYU, editor of half-a-dozen intellectual journals, and genial personality. In his neoconservative phase, his stated ideal was to elevate the intellectual and ethical level of American corporate executives, the wealthy, and Republican-Party leadership to that of a classical, civic-republican ruling elite. In 1965, Kristol and Daniel Bell founded *The Public Interest*, a social policy journal reflecting Bell's themes in his 1960 book *The End of Ideology*. That journal's aim would be to steer clear of ideological partisanship and polemics, especially on the left, in favor of airing policies deriving from objective, empirical scholarship in social science. *The Public Interest* did, however, have an ideological predisposition toward exploring the limitations in the assumptions of the New Deal welfare state and the Johnson administration's War on Poverty, through the work of scholars such as Nathan Glazer, who would also become an editor, Daniel Patrick Moynihan, Edward Banfield, and James Q. Wilson. (Glazer's and Moynihan's conservative-leaning positions there and in *Beyond the Melting Pot* and *Affirmative Discrimination* became flashpoints on racial politics that were attacked by leftists on issues—including affirmative action and cultural versus economic influences on poverty—that have continued to set leftists against mainstream Democratic policies under presidents Clinton and Obama.) Despite this ideological predisposition, however, the journal maintained a high standard of scholarship and internal debate. In Glazer's retrospective for the final issue in 2005, where he said he was happy to see a few articles in defense of the welfare states of Europe, he noted examples such as "What Europe Does Better for Single-Parent Families," "Welfare Is Not the Problem," and an argument in 2000 between James K. Galbraith and Bruce Bartlett over abolition of the inheritance tax ("Neoconservative" 15). He added, "Liberal students of public policy did not disappear from the pages of *The Public Interest*. Many respected the commitment to reason, argument, facts, and research, even if so many articles were promoting a conservative agenda, and they continued to submit articles, some of which we published. But there can be no question where the main drift ran. I see this as a failing on our part" (16).

As Kristol moved steadily further to the right, his colleagues earlier labeled as neoconservatives like Glazer, Bell, and Moynihan broke from him and reaffirmed their liberal Democratic identity, while maintaining some scholarly collaborations. In Bell's 1978 *The Cultural Contradictions of Capitalism*, he famously declared himself "a socialist in economics, a liberal in politics, and a conservative in culture" (xi). Glazer returned to a qualified liberal position in *We Are All Multiculturalists Now* (1997). Kristol, however, had declared his shift of party in the 1972 election, when he was among the intellectuals who signed an ad stating, "Of the two major candidates we believe that Richard Nixon has demonstrated the superior capacity for prudent and responsible leadership" (quoted in Steinfels 89). (In *The Rise of the Counter-Establishmenti*, Sidney Blumenthal reported that "as the Watergate affair unfolded, Kristol tersely responded to all questions about it: 'No comment'" [153].) He quickly became a Republican polemicist—indeed a leading power broker and propagandist—the "Godfather" of the conservative counter-establishment that Lewis Powell called for in his 1971 memo, and his son William has inherited that mantle.

Kristol's intellectual prestige enabled him to get away with irresponsible rhetoric diametrically opposed to the appeals in his scholarly mode for standards of excellence and virtue, scrupulous adherence to open-mindedness and empirical evidence. (The intimidating power he and his circle came to wield in political and journalistic circles undoubtedly muted criticism of his split personality.) In venues like *Wall Street Journal* (*WSJ*) op-eds, he urged Republican leaders and business executives to apply "a dose of Machiavellian shrewdness" and "a clear sense of one's ideological agenda and the devious routes necessary for its enactment" (quoted in Dorrien, *Neoconservative* ll2). These "devious routes" were evident in his support of anti-semitic, evangelical Christians who were pro-Israel on biblical grounds, as well as in his motives for championing supply-side economics in the Reagan years; he later admitted in *The Public Interest* that he never really knew whether it would work as advertised but that it was effective in electing Republicans ("American Conservatism 1945–1995"). As Thomas Frank argued in *The Wrecking Crew*, supply-side was also effective in the larger, Norquistian strategy of demolishing liberal government programs and defunding the left.

Kristol's other devious routes included his advice to executives in corporations and foundations to defund the left in media and academia, to go on the attack through invective and attack advertising with rebuttals that were "detailed, polemical, and sharply phrased so as to challenge the reporter's (or newscaster's) professional integrity," like a defense attorney undermining witnesses' credibility, because liberal journalists "have to be hit over the head a few times before they pay attention" ("On Economic Education"). The ostensible tone of such pieces may have been wryly humorous, but whimsical metaphor was beyond the wave length of more crude-minded conservative constituants who pushed such verbal violence much closer to literalness, in the manner of the Knoxville man described in chapter 2 who went on a killing spree in a Unitarian church in the belief that "all liberals should be killed...because they had ruined every institution in America with the aid of major media outlets." Kristol urged university trustees to stop acquiescing to the academic left, remaining willfully ignorant about ideological issues, and being afraid of "getting involved with highly ideological types on the faculty" ("Conservatives' Greatest Enemy"). These provocations were seldom qualified by concern for maintaining the freedom of journalists and scholars to take positions opposed to those who hold their purse strings.

Kristol's polemical modes became the sweeping generalization, the oversimplification, the strident exaggeration, the "systematically one-sided attitude" (Huxley). His 1993 essay "My Cold War," the conclusion to *Neoconservatism: The Autobiography of an Idea*, ends with a famous rant on "the rot and decadence" that was "the actual agenda of contemporary liberalism.... There is no 'after the Cold War' for me. So far from having ended, my cold war has increased in intensity, as sector after sector of American life has been ruthlessly corrupted by the liberal ethos. It is an ethos that aims simultaneously at political and social collectivism on the one hand and moral anarchy on the other" (486). OK, I confess, I taught for 40 years in order to gain power and riches, and to instill rot, decadence, collectivism, and moral anarchy in students.

Kristol's columns disguised dogmatic, unsupported opinions with tropes like "the American people know that...," "the simple truth is...," or "the obvious truth is...." In 1985 he sympathized with "populist anger" against the liberal elites in law schools, courts, and legislatures who coddle violent criminals. He charged about these elites:

> They become indignant at crimes committed against property committed by the relatively affluent, rather than crimes against the person committed by the relatively poor. But it is murder and robbery and rape that the average American is mostly concerned about, not financial fraud. And his unwise common sense tells him that our unwise elites do not share his beliefs. ("The New Populism," *Neoconservatism* 363)

This level of writing would merit a "D" in Freshman English. Isn't "the average American" a fleshless abstraction? On what empirical evidence was this chimera or these other claims based? Mightn't the major premise pose an either-or fallacy? What sources of information on this issue are readily available to most Americans, and how extensively have most studied the facts and opposing views on it? Do journalistic sources like the *WSJ* give ample voice to a contrary line of argument positing a causal relationship or moral judgment about crimes by the rich versus those of the poor? Does most American secondary and college education centrally teach these topics and debates, and do neoconservatives (who at other times decry the civic illiteracy of "the average American") agree that it should?

Thus Kristol, along with and Podhoretz and Decter, in the seventies established the paradigm for what, ever since, has become the constant equivocation on the right between claims to intellectual high-mindedness and indulgence in crude invective in the cause of "stripping spiritual issues down to their simplicities"—the credo in ever more vulgarized forms of today's Republican right wing. Could even Podhoretz or Kristol deny that the likes of Rush Limbaugh, Ann Coulter, Sarah Palin, Glenn Beck, and the Tea Party became far more influential than the New Left ever was in reducing everything to "slogans, fit for shouting and chanting"? The only reference to Limbaugh that I find in Kristol is one in 1993 praising him and other conservative talk radio for spreading populist opinion through the free market of ideas as a counterforce to liberal media (*Neoconservatism* 383). There and elsewhere he and other neocons failed to consider seriously that the free market of ideas might be a prime cause of the "rot and decadence" of a culture devoted to maximizing profits, and of the Republican Party winning elections, by appealing to the lowest common denominator of knowledge, reasoning, and ethics.

As neoconservatives regularly shifted ground from defending to denouncing intellectualism, they were equivocal about whether or not their criticisms also applied to conservative intellectuals or only liberal ones. Thus Podhoretz on several occasions approved of William Buckley's fatuous crack that he would rather be governed by the first two thousand names in the Manhattan phonebook than by the faculties of Harvard and MIT. Would that include Nathan Glazer, Daniel Bell, Daniel Patrick Moynihan, Edward Banfield, James Q. Wilson, Seymour Martin Lipset, Richard Herrnstein, Richard Pipes, Harvey Mansfield, Stephen Thernstrom, faculties of the Harvard School of Business and MIT weapons labs, or Harvard graduates Mitt Romney, William Kristol, William J. Bennett, Daniel Pipes, Elliot Abrams, Grover Norquist, and Alan Keyes—or are conservative academics and politicians magically exempt from this anti-intellectualism? Buckley, Podhoretz, the Kristols, David Horowitz, and other conservative intellectuals boast of being champions of Middle American populism, but their lives have been conveniently insulated from much extensive contact with it. (An exception was Kristol's military service in World War II, which he attests cured him of left-wing illusions about the noble proletariat. Podhoretz in *Making It* presented an equally elitist put-down of his proletarian comrades in service after being drafted in the peacetime army.) I suspect that their smugness would be shaken at the results of an empirical study of the governance qualifications of the first two thousand names in the Manhattan phonebook, or those in communities where I have lived most of my life, like Des Moines, San Luis Obispo, Knoxville, and Springfield (Missouri), where college humanities faculties provide one of the few counterbalances to the mind-deadening combination of parochial prejudices and mass-cultural regimentation.

NEOCONSERVATIVES IN POWER

In the conclusion of *Breaking Ranks* in 1979, Podhoretz said sarcastically of sixties cultural leftists, "To be an intellectual—a scholar, a thinker, an artist, a writer—was not enough. Not even 'the production of literary masterpieces' was good enough. Nor was it even good enough to be, as Shelley had said, the unacknowledged legislators of the world: they had to be acknowledged, they had to exercise actual political power" (362). And elsewhere, about the New Left, "The least one might hope is that its apologists will deny themselves the note of pathos with which they habitually talk when it suits their propagandistic purposes to describe it as a powerless minority" ("New Hypocrisies" 9). Podhoretz and other neocons were masters of that note of pathos, which they continued to harp on throughout the years of their own rise to power.

The neoconservatives' shift of ground about intellectual autonomy and standards, discussed above, followed hard upon their political ascendancy from the seventies to the present. Recounting his interview with Irving Kristol in 1990, Dorrien says he raised the point that "the supreme irony of [Kristol's] attacks on the self-promoting opportunism of New Class intellectuals was that they were most convincing as descriptions of the career he knew best." "'I am, admittedly, part of the same New Class,' Kristol remarked. He acknowledged that neoconservatives wanted power no less than their liberal enemies and that neoconservatives enjoyed considerable advantages over them in applying for corporate funding. The crucial difference was that neoconservatives were dissidents within the New Class.... 'The liberalism of the New Class was nothing but a vehicle for gaining power for themselves. That is the strategem we have unmasked, while admittedly being part of the New Class ourselves'" (102). Dorrien unfortunately failed to ask the follow-up questions to Kristol: What empirical proof is there that this sweeping claim about New Class liberals' motives was valid, or that neoconservatism was anything more than a vehicle for those like the Kristols and Podhoretzes to gain power?

As the neoconservatives embraced and were embraced by the Republican Party, beginning with the 1972 election, Podhoretz and Kristol were praised and awarded honors by the administrations of each succeeding Republican president. Ronald Reagan blurbed

Podhoretz's *The Present Danger* in 1980. Dorrien lists a score of their family members and other associates of *Commentary* and the *Public Interest* who acquired posts in the Reagan administration. In another of his inimitable flip-flops, Podhoretz exulted at a 1983 conference of Midge Decter's Committee for the Free World: "We are the dominant faction within the world of ideas—the most influential—the most powerful.... People like us made Reagan's victory, which had been considered unthinkable" (quoted in Balint 163). Nowhere in Podhoretz's voluminous autobiographical writings did he acknowledge these "down the memory hole" reversals of position or address the obvious question of whether neoconservative intellectuals were subject to the same loss of independence and corruption by power that he and Kristol had repeatedly condemned on the left. Aside from occasional slips like Podhoretz's here, the rhetorical stance of the whole movement, even up to the present, continued to be playing up the power of the left while depicting neocons as "a powerless minority." *Hell of a Ride*, John Podhoretz's 1993 memoir of his jobs in the Reagan and Bush administrations (where he was a speechwriter) and of his friend Bill Kristol's embarrassing term as chief of staff to Vice President Dan Quayle, was more candid about neocons' own ventures into the halls of power than anything that has ever appeared in the official family publications.

John and Bill Kristol would go on in 1995 to become the founding editors (initially with David Brooks) of the *Weekly Standard*, financed by Rupert Murdoch. John also became an editor at the *Washington Times* (financed by right-wing Korean billionaire Reverend Moon of "Moony" fame) and editorial page editor for Murdoch's tabloid *New York Post*, for which both he and Norman were columnists, while both became frequent talking heads on Murdoch's Fox News, along with Bill. Scarcely a word of criticism of Murdoch's worldwide contributions to the "moral anarchy" of mass culture and politics was to be found in any neoconservative intellectual organ, even after the British scandals over hacking and corrupt political influence by Murdoch publications erupted in 2011. In 2009, John succeeded his father as editor of *Commentary* (following an interregnum by Neil Kozody), on which occasion Norman coyly declared, "I was absolutely amazed. It would never have occurred to me in a million years" (Balint 199). *Commentary* had long had a reputation as being a "family business," and the Podhoretzes and Kristols were notorious for their promotion of family members and associates into governmental, journalistic, and think tank positions. What families on the academic or journalistic left have attained this kind of dynastic power—to the left, that is, of the Kennedys or mainstream media family enterprises such as the *New York Times*, *Washington Post*, and *Los Angeles Times*?

The apotheosis of neoconservative power came in the administration of President George W. Bush, whose foreign policy derived directly from the program of the Project for a New American Century (PNAC), founded in 1997 with William Kristol and other leading second-generation neocon intellectuals as theoreticians, like Paul Wolfowitz and Lewis "Scooter" Libby, a student of Wolfowitz when the latter taught political science at Yale, in alliance with Richard Cheney and Donald Rumsfeld before the 2000 election, and with Midge Decter and Norman Podhoretz also listed among the supporters. (Libby would become chief of staff to Vice President Cheney and legal fall guy in the Joe Wilson-Valerie Plame scandal). The very term "neoconservative" morphed in public usage from its earlier associations into PNAC's post–cold war vision of a worldwide, diplomatic and military *pax americana*, foremost among whose goals was control of the Middle East and defense of Israel. Thus in PNAC's ardor to overthrow Saddam Hussein—predating 11 Sept. 2001, but then turning it into a pretext for the 2003 Iraq War—a byword was that the road to Jerusalem runs through Baghdad. Some neoconservatives were sobered by their own "law of unintended consequences" when the Iraq and Afghanistan wars did not conform to their rosy scenarios, but those in the *Weekly Standard* and *Commentary* inner circles never budged from their cheerleading roles as the wars sank in quicksand for over a decade; the *Weekly Standard*'s cover crowed "VICTORY!" over President Bush's infamous "Mission Accomplished" photo op after the initial assault on Baghdad. (Among many accounts of the PNAC circle, see Heilbrunn's *They Knew They Were Right*, James Mann's *The Rise of the Vulcans*, and Gary Dorrien's *Imperial Designs*.) By this time, the laudable breadth of neoconservative vision, regardless of its moral or intellectual tenability, often seemed to have narrowed to, "Is it good for Israel?" And many neoconservative defenses of Israel, like Rachel Abrams' quoted above, merged with the Islamophobia that seamlessly replaced the anticommunist crusade on the right after 9/11. Once again, what grouping of liberal intellectuals, let alone leftist ones, has in recent decades attained anything like the power of what became widely known as "the neoconservative cabal"?

Bill Kristol's inheritance of his father's "dose of Machiavellian shrewdness" and "devious routes" included writing Dan Quayle's "Murphy Brown" speech bashing single mothers, directing Republicans' scuttling of health care reform under Clinton only because its passage would make the Democrats popular, and financing astroturf rallies among Southern blacks in support of Clarence Thomas' nomination to the Supreme Court, with never an acknowledgment of the later-revealed truth of Anita Hill's charges against Thomas (see Easton; Mayer and Abramson). The *Weekly Standard* under Kristol waffled between a semblance of intellectual independence and the Republican Party line. Its back of the book did feature some lively cultural criticism like John Podhoretz's film reviews, and was not always politically doctrinaire; this was also the case with *Commentary* under John's editorship.

Allan Bloom as Neoconservative

With all the critical accolades that have elevated *The Closing of the American Mind*, Allan Bloom's 1987 assault on academic and cultural liberalism, to the status of a classic, surprisingly little has been written about Bloom's direct ties to the neoconservatives or about the role of their propaganda machine in establishing his fame. In Bloom's introductory chapter to his 1990 collection of essays *Giants and Dwarfs*, titled "Western Civ" and originally delivered as an address at Harvard, then published in *Commentary*, Bloom, responded to the reception of *The Closing* in liberal circles as a conservative tract by claiming that he was neither a conservative ("my teachers—Socrates, Machiavelli, Rousseau, and Nietzsche—could hardly be called conservatives") nor a liberal, "although the preservation of liberal society is of central concern to me." He saw himself, rather, as an impartial Socratic philosopher, above political engagement or "attachment to a party" and denying, against leftist theory, that "the mind itself must be dominated by the spirit of party" (*Giants* 17). (Note the irony of this passage in the context of *Commentary*'s shift away from this position by that time.) A close rereading of his books, however, confirms that they are lofty-sounding ideological rationalizations for the policies of the Reagan-Bush-era Republican Party.[3] Bloom raged against the movements of the sixties—anti–Vietnam War protests, black power, feminism, affirmative action, multiculturalism, and the counterculture—while glossing over every injustice in American society and foreign policy (he scarcely mentioned the Vietnam War itself).

A contrary view to mine on Bloom was voiced by Jim Sleeper in a 2005 reconsideration in the *New York Times* in which he highlighted the more liberal aspects of Bloom's thought; among other points,

Sleeper argued that the intellectual elitist (and atheist) Bloom would have been no less horrified by the manifestations of Republican-allied, antiacademic populism in our time than he was by those on the left in the sixties. I agree, although my judgment is that Bloom's writing, while generally erudite, insightful, and witty, is filled with the same inconsistencies and evasions that critics have pointed out in the other neocons, particularly in minimizing the role of corporate capitalism in the degradation of politics, culture, and morality. Bloom's famous diatribe against rock-and-roll culture resembles no other works so much as Herbert Marcuse's *One-Dimensional Man* and other classics of Frankfurt School marxism. Bloom and other conservatives like Irving Kristol simply co-opted the Frankfurt critique for the political right by detaching mass culture from its role as an arm of corporate capitalism (with the essential role of ceaseless stimulation of desires and consumption to hype up profits) and presenting it as an autonomous entity serving only "liberal" moral relativism. Bloom's tendentiousness, however, precluded his acknowledging any merit in the Frankfurt authors, whom he simplistically derided with little indication that he had read them. *One-Dimensional Man* is "trashy cultural criticism with a heavy sex interest" (226). (Was he maybe thinking of *Eros and Civilization?*) Erich Fromm's *Escape from Freedom* "is just Dale Carnegie with a bit of middle-European cultural whipped cream on top" (147). (Was he maybe thinking of Fromm's later books in popular psychology, not his definitive study of the psychology of fascism?) Theodor Adorno's "meretricious fabrication of the authoritarian and democratic personality types has exactly the same sources as the inner-directed-other-directed typology, and the same sinister implications" (225). (This sounds like a nod to Bloom's Chicago colleague Edward Shils, who shared Bloom's disdain for empirical social science research.) But what were glib judgments like these and the rest of *The Closing* other than Bloom's, and the right's, own competition in trashy cultural criticism?

Bloom's personal affiliations also belied his boast of being above "attachment to a party" and captivity to "the spirit of party." *The Closing* grew out of an article in *National Review.* Prior to *The Closing,* he was for years codirector of the John M. Olin Center for Inquiry into the Theory and Practice of Democracy at the University of Chicago, and he wrote for the journal of the Institute for Educational Affairs (IEA), codirected by William Simon and Irving Kristol. When IEA morphed into the Madison Center for Educational Affairs, also an Olin project, in 1990, Bloom became codirector with William J. Bennett—former head of the Republican National Committee. William Kristol wrote a rave review of *The Closing* in *The Wall Street Journal* (where his father was on the editorial board), which is quoted on the paperback jacket. The other most influential review, in *The New York Times Book Review*—"HITS WITH THE APPROXIMATE FORCE AND EFFECT OF ELECTROSHOCK THERAPY" is quoted in the jacket blurb—was written by Roger Kimball of *The New Criterion*, yet another Olin beneficiary. So much for the *Times'* insistence on vetting of reviewers for conflicts of interest. Yet neoconservatives have the chutzpah to accuse liberal academics and journalists of cronyism.

More significant historically was Bloom's influence as mediator between the ideas of his mentor at the University of Chicago, Leo Strauss, and what became known as the "cabal of Straussians" behind the Iraq War in the administration of George W. Bush. Perhaps the most revealing account here has been the fictional one in Saul Bellow's 2000 novel *Ravelstein*, whose title character Bellow vowed was a true-to-life portrait of his close friend Bloom. Among the other characters is one modeled on Paul Wolfowitz, who was, as Jacob Heilbrunn confirmed in *They Knew They Were Right*, among several of Bloom's students whom he steered into Republican foreign policy circles. (So much for conservatives', and Bloom's, advocacy of political neutrality by professors.) Bellow's *Ravelstein* says of Wolfowitz's fictitious counterpart, "It's only a matter of time before Phil Gorman has cabinet rank, and a damn good thing for the country" (59). *Ravelstein* depicts Ravelstein's apartment as a high-tech communications center with a Wolfowitz-like disciple in Washington and other movers and shakers in international affairs during the Reagan and first Bush administrations, including the 1991 Gulf War—in which Ravelstein and his protégés (few of whose real-life counterparts ever served in the military) privately condemn President Bush for a failure of nerve in not taking Baghdad and toppling Saddam Hussein. Bellow portrays Ravelstein reveling in the money, celebrity, and influence in Republican politics that ironically resulted from his best-selling book that decried such vulgar distractions from the life of the mind. He is thrilled at being feted by President Reagan and Prime Minister Thatcher, as Bloom was.

Another affinity between Bloom and the neocons was his tendency toward exaggerations about the evils of the cultural, campus, and racial left that, especially in retrospect, verged on hysteria: "Whether it be Nuremberg or Woodstock, the principle is the same" (*Closing* 314). Jacob Heilbrunn, himself a conservative, comments about Bloom's famous clash with armed black protestors when he was teaching at Cornell in 1969:

> This wasn't really a totalitarian takeover, much as Bloom might have wished it were, so much as a short-lived (and dangerous) ebullition of hatred from black radicals. The bandolier-wearing leader of the Cornell rebellion, Thomas Jones, would end up as a prosperous Wall Street pension fund manager. The neoconservatives, by contrast, never left the claustrophobic mental world that they began to inhabit in the 1960s. (89)[4]

Bloom's and many other conservatives' overheated equation of radical American blacks with Nazi Brownshirts and Heidegger's *Rekoratstrede* surrender of universities to Hitler does appear in retrospect to have been an overreaction, by scholars and journalists theretofore sheltered from real-world armed conflict, to what may have been delusions of revolution by some elements of the black power movement, born out of justified desperation over violent white reactionism in the late sixties; the uprising at Cornell occurred the year after Martin Luther King was murdered. But did that movement ever really represent a revolutionary force on the scale of Nazism? The Black Panthers and Symbionese Liberation Army have long faded from the view of Americans other than those neoconservatives who indeed have never left the claustrophobic mental world that they have inhabited since the sixties, and whose distorted vision has been passed on to Fox News and the Tea Party.

A final topic concerning Bloom that continues to attract critical debate, his promiscuous homosexuality, is pertinent here as one more instance of neoconservatives' double standard in moral judgments on their allies versus their opponents on the left. In a 2000 article in the *New York Times Magazine* about Bellow's lurid depiction of the subject in *Ravelstein*, D. T. Max quoted Wolfowitz saying that in Bloom's Chicago circle when he was alive, "It was sort of, Don't ask, don't tell" ("With Friends"). According to James Atlas's biography of Bellow, "A frequenter of the sex emporiums of North Clark Street, Bloom confessed to Edward Shils that he 'couldn't keep away from boys'" (*Bellow* 564). Bellow's narrator graphically describes Ravelstein having the symptoms and medical treatment for HIV. Ravelstein himself says, "I'm fatally polluted. I think a lot about those pretty boys in Paris. If they catch the disease, they go back to their mothers, who care for them" (138). After galley proofs circulated, pressure was put on Bellow to revise, and he backed down to the extent of telling D. T. Max, "I don't know that [Bloom] died of AIDS, really. It was just my impression that he may have." Yet Bellow subsequently made only minor revisions in the passages about HIV for the final book. Many of Bloom's allies had long denied that he had AIDS. When I described Bellow's account in a column for *Inside Higher Education*, I was reproached by conservative commentators for slander against Bloom. I replied that they should have reproached Bellow, not me; but Bellow's own conservative credentials seemed to shelter him from criticism on this matter. It would seem that the subject was finally settled, in a strikingly offhand aside, in Andrew Ferguson's 2012 preface to the twenty-fifth-anniversary edition of *The Closing*, also published in the *Weekly Standard*: "Ravelstein endured a tortured death from AIDS, as did Bloom" (1).

These questions might not be worth dwelling on if Bloom and his book had not been canonized by social conservatives and Straussians, both of whom anathematize homosexuality and sexual promiscuity of all kinds and who champion "manliness." If Bloom's private life was indeed louche, doesn't that render suspect the encomiums in *The Closing* to Platonic love, especially in *The Symposium*, and Bloom's denunciation of modern sexual license? And might the stonewalling by Bloom's allies be an instance of the Straussian "noble lie"? In his *Commentary* review of *Ravelstein* (24 Dec. 2001), Norman Podhoretz, who elsewhere raged endlessly against homosexual promiscuous "buggery" as the almost-deserved cause of the AIDS epidemic, displayed his trademark double standard in ignoring the more tawdry details to give Bloom dispensation for keeping his homosexuality discreetly closeted, and in accepting at face value Bellow's late disclaimer about being certain that Bloom had AIDS.

The Deflection of Responsibility

To reiterate the relation of this chapter to my central themes, much in the initial validity of the neoconservative intellectual movement became compromised as it increasingly turned into a branch of the Republican attack machine against the academic and cultural left, in the process grossly exaggerating and distorting the power and corruption of the left as a red herring to distract public attention from the far greater power attained by neocons themselves and the corruptions of capitalistic business as usual. One of the most succinct formulations of the case I am making was by Gary Dorrien in the conclusion to *The Neoconservative Mind*:

> Neoconservatives gave a free ride to the business and financial elites who controlled America's investment process. They justified the corporate class's leveraged buy-outs and greenmail, and defended the managerial prerogatives of technocratic elites no longer bound to community, cultural, or even national loyalties.... They deflected responsibility for America's social and economic decay onto America's cultural elites.... The moral corruption and narcissism that neoconservatives condemned in American society... owed more to commercial imperatives than to the failures of some fictionally autonomous "culture."... They insisted that America's moral and cultural deformities were separable from its economic system. Most neoconservatives condemned what they described as an erosion of moral values under modernity.... It was primarily under the pressure of the business civilization they celebrated, however, that the communities of memory that once sustained these values were being eviscerated. (382–83)

It is a legitimate responsibility of those of us on the academic and journalistic left, then, to evaluate conservative and neoconservative arguments versus the contradictory leftist arguments suppressed or distorted in them, and to attempt to engage conservatives in honest responses to our critique.

7

Conservative Scholarship: Seeing the Object as It Really Isn't

From the late 1970s to the present, the conservative attack machine has also included organizations of students, faculty members, trustees, and alumni, along with outside groups like Accuracy in Academia and David Horowitz's personal crusades against campus PC. There is little to be added to the many thorough accounts of these organizations' histories.[1] All I want to highlight is their convergence with the branches surveyed in my three previous chapters, in terms of their (often concealed) direct connections with the Republican attack apparatus, their rhetorical deviousness, and logical inconsistencies—culminating in their becoming virtually identical ideologically to the Tea Party right wing dominating the Republican Party and conservative media like Fox News today. In each instance, as noted in chapter 5, the justification has been that these organizations are only providing needed balance against the biases of liberal-to-leftist forces that are more powerful, and that they are providing evidence and arguments that are intellectually superior. In many of these instances, I again argue that the forces of the right falsely present themselves as analogous to those of the left, blurring the difference between ideas that are arrived at through individuals' independent thought—whatever those individuals' biases may be—and those arrived at through individuals and organizations serving more or less directly the interests of sponsors and parties. Thus there are few counterparts on the academic left that bear the same, direct relation to the Democratic Party apparatus that these organizations on the right have borne in relation to the Republican central command. Behind the high-minded rhetoric of "evening the scales," the overriding goal of operations on the right appears to have been calculated, as Grover Norquist baldly put it, "to crush the structures of the left." Again granting the integrity of many cultural conservatives, isn't it coy of them to get indignant over any suggestion that the rewards of party service and multi-million-dollar patronage by special interests taints the independence of scholars and journalists and is likely to attract opportunists?

Irving Kristol was yet again a central figure in building these organizations, and the self-contradictions in their operations have reflected his own. Kristol's initial academic enterprise was the Institute for Educational Affairs, which he founded in 1978 with support from the John M. Olin Foundation, headed by William J. Simon, "Forbes 400" leveraged-buyout specialist and Secretary of the Treasury under President Ford. Olin at its peak spent some $55 million a year on grants "intended to strengthen the economic, political, and cultural institutions upon which...private enterprise is based." (Olin ceased operation at the end of its original charter in 2005.) A prime example of the Kristol-esque contradictions between such high-minded ideals and more vulgar practices was IEA's sponsorship of a network of conservative campus journals including the infamous *Dartmouth Review*, whose antics included tearing down shanties built by campus antiapartheid groups on Martin Luther King's birthday. I coined the adjective "Olinite" in my *College English* article on Lynne Cheney in reference to culture-wars works funded by that foundation like Cheney's and others by Bloom, Bennett, Robert Bork, Roger Kimball, Dinesh D'Souza, Carol Iannone, Christina Hoff Sommers, Robert Lichter et al., and John Ellis. In Cheney's book *Telling the Truth*, she made the standard argument about the conservative foundations being outspent by liberal ones, but a footnote was revealing:

> In the interests of full disclosure...two organizations whose boards I chair, the National Alumni Forum [later to become the American Council of Trustees and Alumni] and the Committee to Review National Standards, have received Olin grants, as has the Madison Center, on whose board I serve. The Aspen Institute, on the board of which I served in 1993 and 1994, has received funding from both the Ford and MacArthur foundations. (225, fn. 50)

Considering that Ford and MacArthur were two of the larger foundations that Cheney claimed have a liberal bias, she weakened her own argument here.

Since the late seventies, the conservative foundations have heavily funded college student, faculty, and trustee organizations that regularly launch attack campaigns against the left. It is a telling sign that these offensives by groups and individuals who vaunt their allegiance to high scholarly standards have not been waged within scholarly or serious journalistic circles, but have been calculated, with the help of public relations agents like those employed by conservative think tanks, to grab headlines in mass media little inclined to verify their accuracy and to play to a public that is both ill-informed about and unsympathetic to the academic humanities. Most recently, National Association of Scholars (NAS) president Peter Wood, crowed in his blog in the *Chronicle of Higher Education* (4 Apr. 2012), about a new NAS report on leftist faculty bias at the University of California, "My main role was to move the document to publication and to secure as much national attention for it as possible. That's a success story. Peter Berkowitz (who serves on the NAS board of directors) wrote about the report in *The Wall Street Journal* weekend edition, and we've had a good run of stories in both the California and the national papers, including stories in the *Washington Post*, the *San Francisco Chronicle*, and the *Los Angeles Times*" ("Politics, Education"). Neither the individual faculty members under attack, teacher advocacy groups like NEA and American Federation of Teachers (AFT), nor professional associations like American Association of University Professors (AAUP) and (in my field) Modern Language Assocation (MLA) and National Council of Teachers of English (NCTE) have the machinery for launching such offensives against or even responding to their conservative critics, in mainstream media. By the time it takes to verify errors in these attacks, the media are inclined to dismiss requests to correct them as "old news."

Concerning student organizations sponsored by conservative foundations, *Time* magazine's online edition in 2004 featured a lengthy, informative article by John Cloud about relative funding of the campus left and right, titled "The Right's New Wing." Cloud reported that Young America's Foundation annual budget was $13 million:

> Today the left can claim no youth organization as powerful as Young America's Foundation, ISI, or the Leadership Institute. One of the biggest young-liberal groups, the Sierra Student Coalition (an arm of the Sierra Club), has a budget of just $350,000 for 150 college chapters.... Last school year, the 38-year-old National Association for Women spent twice the amount it usually does on campus in order to publicize April's feminist march on Washington, but the total, $5000, was just 4% of Young America's budget.

Cloud also noted, "The College Republican National Committee, which atrophied to just 409 chapters in 1998, now lists active members on 1,148 campuses. The College Democrats of America say they have members on 903 campuses, 20% fewer." (Also see chapter 4 on the role of Jack Abramoff, Grover Norquist, and Ralph Reed in College Republicans history.) The Washington Post reported in 1999 that Richard Mellon Scaife through his foundations had given some $146 million to these conservative organizations (Kaiser and Chinoy). The *Chronicle of Higher Education* reported that T. Kenneth Cribb, Jr., president of ISI, which issues periodic reports blaming civic illiteracy on leftist college faculties, earned nearly $700,000 in 2009. In two comparisons, "Mr. Cribb's compensation is about $20,000 higher than that of the head of the Cato Institute, a libertarian group with a budget about twice the size of the Intercollegiate Studies Institute's. The leader of the Center for American Progress, a liberal institution with a budget about twice as big as ISI's, made $270,000" (Laster).

Over the years I was teaching, I had about a dozen students who identified themselves as members of these conservative organizations, plus several who belonged to groups like Campus Crusade for Christ. Some of them were serious students happy to meet the challenge of weighing conservative versus left views in a scholarly manner, and I valued their presence for providing sources and enlivening class dynamics. Others simply parroted the scripts and talking points provided by their organizations, and were unwilling or unable to go beyond them with research weighing their claims against opposing ones. I believe that, in general, at least some students who complain about being intimidated by leftist professors are really just unhappy about the whole academic enterprise of having to expose one's preconceived notions to critical questioning and opposing views. In any case, I bent over backward to be respectful and fair to conservative students, and most ended up saying they liked my courses. I always told students that if any thought I was biased in a grade, I would cheerfully raise it, but I never had a taker and never received a formal complaint about a grade.

A 2005 report in the *Chronicle* titled "What Makes David Run," by Jennifer Jacobson, was prompted by David Horowitz's 15 minutes of fame promoting his Academic Bill of Rights in state legislatures. According to Jacobson, Horowitz was making upward of half-a-million a year in personal income from foundation grants and college lectures, at $5,000 each, largely paid for by the same foundations subsidizing conservative student groups. Between 1999 and 2005, the Scaife and Bradley foundations contributed about $3.5 million to Horowitz's Center for the Study of Popular Center in Los Angeles. Jacobson quoted Horowitz, protesting against allegations that he might be out for money and publicity, "I am less well funded than the American Association of University Professors, far less well funded than the ACLU" (6). I have long been perplexed by this statement, which seems almost a parody of conservative false equivalences. Was he thinking of the total dues of these large membership organizations or their executives' salary—also funded by dues, not outside patrons?

In my email correspondence with Horowitz, I mentioned to him that Kevin Mattson in the *Nation* (18 Apr. 2005) quoted him describing professors as "a privileged elite that work between six and nine hours a week, eight months a year, for an annual salary of about $150,000," and I asked if that quotation was accurate. He replied, "The Mattson quote is out of context. I was referring to Ward Churchill's 115,000 salary plus benefits (say about 125,000 plus speaking gigs at 4k a pop, which makes it about 150,000). [Cf. Horowitz's own $5,000 'a pop.'] Of course Cornel West and Skip Gates make several hundred thousand in salary and probably exceed 1 mil. with speaking fees and their book factories. I also said that they are in class 6–9 hours a week, eight months a year and every 7 years get a 10 months paid vacation" (email 11 Apr. 2006). However, C-SPAN had broadcast a speech by Horowitz at Duke in March 2006 that repeated exactly the same claims quoted by Mattson about unnamed "professors," implying all professors. I emailed him a lengthy correction of his facts, including the research and publication obligations in professors' workloads and sabbaticals, as well as my own top salary of about $65,000 at Cal Poly for 12 hours of classes, three quarters a year, grading all of my own papers, in about a 60-hour workweek. In reply, Horowitz allowed, "Of course I am willing to refine statements I made in the course of a speech. I wasn't writing an encyclopedia article, I was making a speech. You have a problem understanding context" (email 11 Apr. 2006). I guess I also didn't understand the context of Horowitz's TV appearances before millions with Pat Robertson, in which they claimed that professors and teachers' unions murder and abuse children—though Horowitz later helpfully explained that context to me: "I was promoting my book."

Horowitz saw himself as the David battling the Goliath of the academic and civil-liberties establishment, with liberal-to-left biases as its unmarked norm. That might be a defensible position, but in his case it was tainted by equivocation between his personae as an independent critic of academe and as a Republican operative. One of Horowitz's books was titled *How to Beat the Democrats* and was blurbed by Tom DeLay. Another, *The Art of Political War*, was used as a playbook in the 2000 election by Karl Rove and George W. Bush, who later literally embraced Horowitz at the White House. It included advice to Republicans like the earlier-cited epigraphs, "Aggression is advantageous because politics is a war of position, which is defined by images that stick" (12), and "In politics, television is reality.... With these audiences, you will never have time for real arguments or proper analyses. Images—symbols and sound bites—will always prevail." (Could Horowitz cite any instance of officials of AAUP or ACLU, their organizations as a whole, or Gates and West—to say nothing of Ward Churchill—thus directly serving the Democratic Party apparatus, and in such a cynical manner? Again, note the contempt for "these audiences" among Republican polemicists who pretend to champion ordinary Americans against snobbish liberal intellectuals.[2] Incidentally, I am inclined to agree about Henry Louis Gates and Cornel West that it is among the cultural contradictions of capitalism that at least a small number of cultural leftists, including an even smaller number of blacks, can become rich and famous, though one might think Horowitz would admire such kindred entrepreneurs, neither of whom, to their credit, is subservient to patrons like Scaife or to a political party; West consistently criticizes the Democrats, and especially President Obama, from the socialist left. Gates's closest affiliation with the Democrats was being invited to the White House for a beer with President Obama after a run-in with a white policeman who arrested him entering his own house in Cambridge.

Reasoned Scholarship and Civil Debate?

The usual conservative foundations funded the National Association of Scholars (NAS) and kindred groups like the American Council of Trustees and Alumni (ACTA) and Manhattan Institute's Center for the American University. From the founding of NAS in 1987 by Stephen Balch and Herbert London, its longtime heads, to its present operations under president Peter Wood, I have constantly found NAS, along with ACTA and Manhattan Institute, to be the most bewildering cases of the inconsistencies on the right that I have traced throughout this book. Some of their members are distinguished scholars, but their officers have generally had meager scholarly accomplishments, and their public stances, journals, and periodic "research reports" have tended to echo the more vulgar operations of the conservative attack machine. (Its officials' short-tempered intolerance of criticism or corrections, which I have personally encountered on several occasions, recalls John Dean's account of the psychology of authoritarian dominators, "Not surprisingly, the very conservatives who love to hurl invective against the ranks of their enemies prove to have the thinnest of skins when the same is done to them.")

NAS claims to oppose what it considers excessive politicization and partisan advocacy in education, and it declares itself to be wholly independent of party affiliation, indeed not even conservative, except to the extent of supporting traditional curricula and pedagogy. This stance has always been equivocal. The organization grew out of the Campus Coalition for Democracy in 1982, headed by Balch, a professor of government at CUNY's John Jay College. In 1983 this group sponsored a conference at Long Island University on the political conflicts in Central America, which consisted of a platform for the Committee for the Free World (CFW), founded by *Commentary*'s Midge Decter, and which featured Reagan foreign policy officials including Jeane Kirkpatrick, Elliot Abrams, and Michael Ledeen, along with Nicaraguan Contra leader Arturo Cruz. CFW also provided a liaison for formation of NAS with the support of Kristol's and Simon's Institute for Educational Affairs and the familiar array of conservative foundations like Olin, Scaife, and Smith-Richardson—the latter of which, according to Sara Diamond in *Facing the Wrath*, had published a confidential memo in 1984 titled "The Report on the Universities," outlining a program for countering the academic left through strategies like "deterrence activism," "idea marketing," and a project to "mimic left-wing organization" with a national faculty organization and local chapters—which became NAS (118–20). NAS's advisory board included Kirkpatrick and Kristol. London, most recently president of the conservative Hudson Institute, ran as a Republican for mayor of New York City and as the Conservative Party candidate for governor of New York. Did NAS ever investigate Balch's and London's possible partisan advocacy in their courses, or that of Kristol, Kirkpatrick, and its more recent officials?

In 2010, the online *Chronicle of Higher Education* started a blog by Wood, successor to the line of hotheaded presidents of NAS, who posted frequent, long-winded opinions on subjects in cultural politics far afield from his own subject of anthropology. In recent *Chronicle* blogs, Wood has stated, "A decent civics curriculum would eschew political advocacy in favor of teaching students the essentials of the subject itself. This would necessarily include acquainting students with the controversies—but not just one side from one point of view" ("Civics Lessons"). And, "Since its founding in 1987, NAS has championed academic freedom. Not, to be sure, the strange inversion of academic freedom—freedom academic—that triumphantly defends the right of faculty members to propagandize their students and to treat scholarship as a subspecies of politics. Rather, NAS has defended the academic freedom of faculty members and students to think and to express their own thoughts in situations where they are pressured to conform to someone else's political standard" ("Gay Marriage"). Yet again, one can endorse these high-minded aims while noting that in NAS's tirades, pressures to conform to someone else's political standards virtually always come from the left, rarely from the right, that college education and academic freedom have increasingly been confined within the institution of the corporatized university, that vast areas of higher education outside the liberal arts pressure students and faculty to conform to the corporate and military-industrial agenda, and that the whole conservative obsession with leftist political conformity in the liberal arts disingenuously isolates the manifest content of college courses from the entire larger gestalt of "unmarked" conservative social pressures that I have described as "business as usual," which I have proposed as a legitimate subject for critical inquiry in liberal education.

Wood continues in the same blog to repeat tropes like, "NAS has taken no position on gay marriage or global warming and by its nature can't. It is an organization that deals with academic standards, the governance of colleges and universities, higher education finance, and public policies that affect scholarship and learning. And it has a membership of some 3,000 mostly academics whose personal views on substantive social and political issues are all over the map" ("Gay Marriage"). His point here is that *academic study* of issues like gay marriage and global warming has a Democratic bias, justifying NAS correction of this bias. Perhaps, but the pronouncements of NAS academics like Wood on these issues likewise have a Republican bias, and the organization has always received funding from Republican-aligned foundations representing some corporations with conflicts of interests in sponsoring research on issues like global warming. Moreover, I have never heard NAS officials attempt to explain how their defense of high academic standards can be reconciled with all their indirect affiliations to a political party that has become synonymous with anti-intellectualism, defunding of liberal education at the K-12 and postsecondary levels in favor of vocational training, imposition on education of the managerial model of accountability, and support for the for-profit school industry that slights liberal education. I will again be accused here of guilt by association, but that is a fallacious line of argument only if an association does not actually exist, not if it is openly boasted of, in the manner of longtime NAS activist John Ellis acknowledging in his book *Literature Lost* that he was "proud and grateful to have had this work generously supported" by the Bradley, Carthage, Olin, and Smith-Richardson foundations (Ellis vii).

Similarly, the stated mission of ACTA, founded in 1994 as the National Alumni Forum, was to "support liberal arts education, uphold high academic standards, safeguard the free exchange of ideas on campus, and ensure that the next generation receives a philosophically rich, high-quality college education at an affordable price" (*goacta.org*). Again, these avowedly nonpartisan goals were wholly admirable—but the organization was founded by Lynne Cheney, with funding from Olin and other conservative foundations and with a familiar cast of Republican partisans like Irving Kristol, William J. Bennett, and judge Lawrence Silberman as national council members. The council included a few token Democrats like Senator Joseph Lieberman and Martin Peretz—prototypical conservative Democrats of the kind that leftists love to hate, and Lieberman resigned when the organization became controversial.

In these cases and countless others, conservatives invoke nonpartisanship and disinterestedness to condemn academic or journalistic leftists' betrayals of these virtues—while they themselves, in their pose of Olympian impartiality, tend to assume that objective truth, nonpartisanship, disinterestedness, and civility are simply synonymous with Republican-Party positions, which are thus immune from charges of bias. One of the niftiest pieces of rhetorical sleight of hand by such conservative polemicists has been to attack the academic left for politicizing education and for rhetorical shrillness, while hiding the tracks of their own tacit affiliation with the strident Republican right; after all, the Republican Party has been the home to well-known hotheads like Newt Gingrich, Robert Bork, John Bolton, Bill Bennett, and Norman Podhoretz, along with allies in mass media like Rush Limbaugh, Ann Coulter, and Bill O'Reilly. (Conservative journalists like David Brooks and Ross Douthat have become favorites of mainstream media like PBS and the *New York Times* exactly because they avoid this bombastic prototype.)

The NAS home page states, "NAS is an independent membership association of academics working to foster intellectual freedom and to sustain the tradition of reasoned scholarship and civil debate in America's colleges and universities. The NAS advocates for excellence by encouraging commitment to high intellectual standards, individual merit, institutional integrity, good governance, and sound public policy." The mission statement of the Manhattan Institute's online journal *Minding the Campus*, similarly claims, "We hope to foster a new climate of opinion that favors civil and honest engagement of all sides, offering an engaged debate for readers concerned with the state of the modern university." In 1996, Sanford Pinsker, then editor of NAS's journal *Academic Questions*, wrote in an opinion column titled "Cooling the Polemics of the Culture Warriors" for the *Chronicle of Higher Education*, "A glance at the uncivil world around us should be enough to convince academics that pursuing rhetorical strategies that rely on anger and insult has done us no more good than it has politicians and talk-show hosts" (A56).

I wholly endorse these goals, along with these and kindred groups' other stated ideals such as encouraging study of the liberal arts, especially history, in both secondary and postsecondary education, although these groups tend to approach historical knowledge as a matter of undisputed truths rather than as a contested subject for "reasoned scholarship and civil debate" or "civil and honest engagement of all sides." Similarly, NAS's webpage originally stated that the organization "was founded in 1987, soon after Allan Bloom's surprise best-seller, *The Closing of the American Mind*, alerted Americans to the ravages wrought by illiberal ideologies on campus." Here and elsewhere in NAS, ACTA, Manhattan Institute, and other conservative sites, statements about such "ravages" are assumed to be uncontestable, objective facts, not subjective opinions whose factuality might be challenged through reasoned scholarship and civil debate, as I and many other scholars have tried to do.

Consider this part of NAS's long list of issues that it "is concerned about":

ACADEMIC CONTENT
- Hollowing out of liberal education
- Politicization of the classroom
- Trivialization of scholarship and teaching
- Disappearance of core curricula
- Neglect of important books
- Marginalization of key subjects

- Declining study of Western civilization
- Overemphasis on the current, popular, marginal, ephemeral
- Overemphasis on issues of race, gender, class, sexual orientation

Once again, the implication in the phrasing is not that these are highly varied, complex matters for open debate among those of different ideological views, but universally agreed on, monolithically interrelated, evils, most if not all perpetrated by the academic left. Little debate on them is in fact allowed in these groups' venues, which are as one-sided as the most PC leftist enclaves.

Shortly after 9/11, ACTA issued a highly publicized report, *Defending Civilization*, attacking the alleged anti-Americanism of university faculties.[3] Likewise, in his 2002 book *Why We Fight: Moral Clarity and the War on Terrorism*, Bennett said of "the educational establishment" that "those who are unpatriotic are, culturally, the most influential" (141), and he called for "reinstatement of a thorough and honest study of our history, undistorted by the lens of political correctness and pseudo-sophisticated relativism" (149–50). Bennett also wrote in the *Los Angeles Times* after 9/11, "America's support for human rights and democracy is our noblest export to the world....America was not punished because we are bad, but because we are good." Beyond debatable matters of factual accuracy here, there was a self-contradiction in ACTA and Bennett that has run through many conservative salvos in the culture wars. On the one hand, they defend educational objectivity, avoidance of partisan advocacy, "thorough and honest study"; on the other hand, they sometimes seem to want history and current events to be "distorted by the lens" of unilateral, simplistic advocacy for American patriotism, exempt from thorough and honest disputation. Could the causes of September 11 be determined without a thorough and honest consideration of evidence for the less-than-total innocence of American foreign policies in the Middle East and elsewhere? Neither ACTA nor Bennett, in his 170-page book, presented any substantive refutation of dissenters about America's virtuousness like Noam Chomsky, Edward Said, Howard Zinn, and James Loewen. Wasn't some intellectual counterforce warranted against the one-sided propaganda that was produced by the Bush administration, as by every administration in every war? Surely it is as simplistic never to blame America as to blame America first.

After 9/11, a patriot might well have been horrified by the terrorist attacks and supported retaliatory action in Afghanistan, but at the same time have been wary of blanket endorsement of every American military action like the subsequent one in Iraq, especially those hidden by censorship and jingoistic propaganda. A patriot might have been equally wary of government officials' possible conflicts of interest in multibillion-dollar military and construction contracts in these military actions, or of the danger of the administration taking advantage of the wartime suspension of a loyal opposition to suppress civil liberties and railroad partisan foreign and domestic policies through Congress and the courts. Was it qualms like these that Bennett derided as "pseudo-sophisticated relativism"? (For further response to Bennett, see chapter 10.)

Conservatives regularly invoke appeals for "reasoned scholarship and civil debate" selectively to bash leftist abuses of these qualities, while exempting their own uncivil attacks on leftists, who are not deemed worthy of civil consideration. The characteristic style of these assaults has once again been rhetorical overkill, filled with sweeping overgeneralizations, straw man villains, and unremitting high dudgeon. In a *Chronicle* blog, "The Curriculum of Forgetting" (21 Nov. 2011), Wood wrote, "The stance of generalized antagonism to the whole of Western civilization and the elevation of 'critical thinking' in the sense of facile reductionism (everything at bottom is about race-gender-class hierarchy) makes the university function more and more as our society's chief source of anti-intellectualism." Facile reductionism, anyone? No quotations or sources cited, no evidence adduced, for any of these three inflammatory exaggerations. In an exchange in the blog's comments section, I asked Wood to cite some empirical evidence rank-ordering "the university" and critical thinking in particular as sources of our society's anti-intellectualism, in comparison to other forces like mass-cultural stupefaction and the right wing of the Republican Party, whose prominent figures at that time like Glenn Beck, Sarah Palin, Herman Cain, and Rick Santorium were competing to be most demagogically anti-intellectual and disdainful of education. He did not respond, but by the standard of NAS's habitual claim that it does not address political issues other than those directly dealing with higher education, his claim about "our society's chief source of anti-intellectualism" was prima facie not only unverifiable but a breach of NAS's realm. Nor did Wood respond to my guest column for *RAIL*, "A Blog About Reasoning, Argumentation, and Critical Thinking," tracing the history of distortion of critical-thinking scholarship in NAS publications ("Why is the National").

Further acrimonious criticism by critical-thinking scholars following Wood's *Chronicle* blog did lead to conciliation on one point of misunderstanding. Those of us speaking for the Association for Informal Logic and Critical Thinking (AILACT) conceded to Wood that in the years following the 1980 mandate for critical-thinking courses in the California State University, originally defined as informal logic and argumentation and taught in the disciplines of philosophy, English, or speech-communication, diverse other departments grabbed for funding by claiming, without support, that whatever they taught was also critical thinking. With the rise of leftist critical race, gender, and class studies, as well as critical studies in professions like law and science, such courses also sometimes passed muster as filling critical-thinking requirements. My own judgment is that these courses have varied widely in their quality and adherence to the original criteria of critical thinking; some undoubtedly have deviated enough to warrant criticisms like Wood's. I agree that administrative overseers have tended to default on the responsibility to insist that any such courses, politically oriented or not, adhere to explicit instruction in fundamentals of informal logic and argumentation. Here is one of many points where scholars on the left and right should be collaborating in common cause rather than remaining stuck in polarization. Wood grudgingly conceded that his quarrel was not with critical thinking as study of informal logic and argumentation, but with deviations from that meaning. However, neither he, NAS, ACTA, or Manhattan Institute, to my knowledge, has ever extensively addressed the role of courses in critical thinking or argumentative rhetoric in their concept of a traditionally based core curriculum; nor have they considered what the legitimate applications of those disciplines might be to study of political rhetoric—a central topic in classical studies and in American higher education into the nineteenth century, as definitively traced by historian of rhetoric Michael Halloran. In ways like these, conservatives have devised red herrings to distract attention from vital issues that those on the left and right should be negotiating in good faith. I tried to make these points, in a collegial manner, to Wood and Iannone in an email exchange a few years ago, but they expressed no interest in dialogue and angrily refused even to consider my proposal for an article in *Academic Questions* or blog on their web page addressing these issues. After a series of evasions filled with huffy faux-indignation, Wood's last message was, "Go away, little man" (email 30 June 2009, available on request). So goes "reasoned scholarship and civil debate."

Another instance of conservative scholars not practicing what they preach about reasoned scholarship and civil debate was David

Gelernter's article "A World Without Public Schools" in The *Weekly Standard* of 4 June 2007, which attacked *The Official SAT Study Guide,* published in 2006 by the College Board, as one of "many ways to see the school establishment's bias." Gelernter is a computer science professor at Yale and frequent contributor to *TWS, Commentary,* and other neoconservative periodicals, who like Wood pontificates on political issues entirely outside his academic field, a practice savaged by conservatives when liberals are the culprits. (He *is* an impressive polymath who can write eloquently about art and other humanistic topics when he is not grinding a political ax.) As evidence of this bias in the study guide, he wrote, "Here's a sentence from a passage that students are quizzed on. 'The First World War is a classic case of the dissonance between official, male-centered history and unofficial female history.' You might object that the idea of 'official history' is a sham and a crock, unless you refer specifically to accounts commissioned by the combatant governments themselves. But this silly assertion is presented as if it were fact." Gelernter next quoted a passage criticizing "the Eurocentric conviction that the West holds a monopoly on science, logic, and clear thinking." After ranting for a long paragraph about this "breathtakingly absurd, breathtakingly offensive" passage, he asked, "What kind of imbecile could write such a passage?—and offer it to unwitting high school students as *fact?*" (Gelernter's italics).

The fact is that the study guide clearly does not present either of these passages as "fact" or as the opinion of its authors. The first is quoted directly (on p. 544) from one of two books on World War I presented for comparison-and-contrast. The second (on p. 392) is introduced, "The following passage appeared in an essay written in 1987, in which the author, who is of Native American descent, examines the representation of Native Americans during the course of United States history."[4] (Gelernter did not punctuate either as a quotation-within-quotation.) I wonder whether, if Gelernter had acknowledged the source, he would have still described its author as an imbecile and whether the editors would have let it stand.

Furthermore, both texts were quoted simply as a basis for reading comprehension tests. The sample test questions following the texts were aimed solely at interpretation of what particular words and phrases mean (and in the first, of how the two commentaries differ)—without any implication that they are factual or that students are asked to agree or disagree with them. Minimal journalistic ethics and competency would have compelled either Gelernter or his editor to make this distinction. Such shoddiness is doubly ironic in an article (and journal) purporting to uphold rigorous standards against their debasement by biased liberal scholars and educators. I wrote to Gelernter, suggesting that he acknowledge these errors, and to *TWS* suggesting that they publish a correction, but neither responded. (*TWS* dropped their regular correspondence section years ago.)

I grant that Gelernter might more legitimately have quoted the passages in order to raise the question of why such views were chosen by the study guide's authors simply for testing reading comprehension. We would need to hear their own explanation before drawing any conclusions. It is plausible, however, that the vast majority of sample test questions in this study guide and actual SAT-type examinations in the present—and even more so in the past—have been based on texts by white males and do undoubtedly perpetuate Eurocentric ideological assumptions (whether defensible, as Gelernter argues, or not). So occasional inclusion of differing samples of texts for comprehension could be considered as an innocuous, minimal acknowledgment of the existence of diverse viewpoints—not as dire proof of the tyranny of the liberal educational establishment that Gelernter and other conservative culture warriors get so apoplectic about.

Quotation out of context has also been a staple of the decades-long effort by conservatives to discredit the work of Noam Chomsky and Edward Herman through red-baiting of these democratic socialists and allegations of anti-semitism against these two Jews. *The Anti-Chomsky Reader*, edited by Peter Collier and David Horowitz in 2004, was rich with examples, but I will present only one classic case, concerning two adjacent articles there by Paul Bogdanor and Werner Cohn critiquing an article by Chomksy about Israel in Herman's short-lived journal *Lies of Our Times* in January 1990. Cohn's "Chomsky and Holocaust Denial" presented the fuller context of Chomsky's piece, which criticized A. M. Rosenthal's argument in the *New York Times* that since a Palestinian state already existed in Jordan, another was not warranted in the Israeli-occupied territories. Chomsky's way of identifying the anti-Palestinian prejudice in Rosenthal and other mainstream American journalists was to reverse roles and caricature an anti-semitic view that would be equally bigoted, as Cohn quotes him: "'We might ask how the *Times* would react to an Arab claim that the Jews do not merit 'a second homeland' because they already have New York, with a huge Jewish population, Jewish-run media, a Jewish mayor, and domination of cultural and economic life.'" (Cohn 117). Cohn did not pursue the substantive issue of a

Palestinian state, but for three paragraphs jumped on "Chomsky's sneering tone about the Jews of New York" and his further alleged anti-semitism here, as though Chomsky's caricature expressed his own beliefs. Three paragraphs later Cohn did get around to acknowledging that the views here *may* not be Chomsky's own but those of "an unnamed anti-Semitic Arab." Nevertheless, Cohn concluded that "he endorses and justifies the anti-Semitic assertions without taking direct responsibility for them" (117–18). This was an unconscionable misrepresentation; Chomsky's caricature may have been in dubious taste, but it is nonsense to insinuate that he endorsed this or any other variety of anti-semitism, as distinguished from criticism of Israel's policies and lobbying. (There is no trace in the massive works on media by Chomsky and/or Herman of "Jewish-run media" and such.). The distortion in Cohn's account was exceeded in the preceding article by Bognador, "Chomsky's War Against Israel," whose account of the same Chomsky passage reduced it to, "Elsewhere he felt compelled to mention New York, with its 'huge Jewish population, Jewish-run media, a Jewish mayor, and domination of cultural and economic life,'" with no more context than that, as evidence of "the unadulterated bile that Chomsky has seen fit to pour upon his fellow American Jews" (107).

As though Cohn and Bognador weren't bad enough, Alan Dershowitz's later book *The Case for Peace* contained this indirect quotation of Chomsky: "The Jews do not merit 'a second homeland' because they already have New York, with a huge Jewish population, Jewish-run media, a Jewish mayor, and domination of cultural and economic life" (172). The sentence was not cited directly from Chomsky's own article but as "quoted in" *Cohn*! What was one to make of all of this dishonesty and editorial sloppiness in the midst of endless tirades by Chomsky's attackers about his "massive falsification of facts, sources, evidence, and statistics, conducted in the service of a bigoted and extremist ideological agenda" (Bognador) and about his resorting "to misrepresent the writing of others" (Cohn)?

The fall 2002 issue of *Partisan Review* was devoted to a symposium titled "Our Country, Our Culture," which was occasioned by the fiftieth anniversary of another, celebrated *Partisan Review* symposium titled "Our Country and Our Culture." The idea of the 2002 symposium held the promise of a fruitful retrospective on the shifts in the American intellectual and cultural scene over this half-century. The result, however, was disappointing, mainly because the scope of participants and viewpoints was limited almost entirely to the conservative circles that dominated *Partisan Review*'s later years as its one surviving, original editor William Phillips (who died shortly after this issue appeared) became a neoconservative—in contrast to the 1952 symposium, in which liberals clashed with leftists like C. Wright Mills, Irving Howe, and Norman Mailer. The symposium consisted largely of a chorus of attacks on the current academic and cultural left, typified by novelist, literary critic, and *Commentary* regular Cynthia Ozick:

> If we are to worry about conformism, now is the hour. What does conformism mean if not one side, one argument, one solution? And no one is more conformist than the self-defined alienated. In the universities, a literary conformism rules, equating literature with fashionable leftist themes. And beyond this, literature departments also promote the conformism that paradoxically goes under the pluralist-sounding yet absolutist name of "multiculturalism" or "diversity": a system of classification that reduces literary culture to the venomous rivalries of group grievance. Postcolonialist courses offer a study in specified villainies. Certain texts—ah, how I have come to loathe the word *texts!*—certain texts are presented uncritically, as gospel, without opposing or dissenting or contextual matter. (620–21)

None of the other participants remarked that Ozick's straw man stereotypes here exemplified the same intellectual crudeness that she and the others attributed to the academic left, with no documented examples cited in support and no minimal qualification that among the thousands of scholars she indicted, any might have produced work of integrity and intelligence. And Ozick's examples came exclusively from the left, without a hint of self-examination by her or any of the other panelists of the one-sided, "fashionable" conformity on the right that pervaded this symposium, as it does current conservative intellectual circles generally. I must say that I sometimes have the same reaction as Ozick to groupthink and jargon in the academic left; in a conversation I once had with a graduate student at Duke, she described the history of her marriage as a "text." And I agree that advocacy of multiculturalism and diversity can itself paradoxically become a dogma, excluding mainstream culture from study, and thus exempting it from critical interrogation. But such thinking is neither universal, unopposed, nor the menace to civilization that it is blown up into by the right.

Fair and Balanced Scholarship?

Conservative intellectuals are fond of invoking Matthew Arnold's ideal of the function of cultural criticism, to "see the object as in itself it really is." Yet they seem utterly unable or unwilling to see the ideas of leftists as they really are. In my gatherings with left and feminist authors, we have read aloud conservative accounts of our works and gasped, "Is THAT what I said?" Like Fox News claiming to be "fair and balanced," conservatives' rhetorical stance defending "traditional standards of accuracy and evidence" against leftist abuses (Cheney, *Telling the Truth: Why* 61) was reminiscent of the line from *Once Upon a Mattress*, a musical-comedy version of the fairy tale about the princess and the pea, in which the possessive queen is looking for a test that any female candidate for the hand of her son is certain to fail: "We need a test that looks fair, and sounds fair, and seems fair, and isn't fair" (Barer and Rodgers).

Perhaps the epitome of this Arnoldian rhetorical stance was Cheney's 1995 book *Telling the Truth: Why Our Culture and Our Country Have Stopped Making Sense—and What We Can Do about It*, written when she was a fellow at American Enterprise Institute. (Cheney wrote her doctoral dissertation at Wisconsin on Arnold). The book was developed from a booklet that she had written as head of National Endowment for the Humanities (NEH) from 1986 to 1993, at the time when her husband was secretary of defense. Cheney provoked controversy at NEH through staff appointments, like that of Carol Iannone, and through policies opposing perceived instances of left PC in grant applications. Her associate director there and research assistant for *Telling*, Lynne Munson, continued in later years to be a prominent culture warrior at NEH and elsewhere. In a column about Cheney's provocations at NEH, George Will wrote, "In this low-visibility, high-intensity war, Lynne Cheney is secretary of domestic defense. The foreign adversaries her husband, Dick, must keep at bay are less dangerous, in the long run, than the domestic forces with which she must deal" ("Literary").

In the preface to her book, Cheney wrote, "The challenge is hereby offered: Try to show I am mistaken if you wish, but do so with sound evidence and sound reasoning. Invective and accusation will merely serve as evidence of the low status into which truth has fallen in our time" (6). But she no sooner set this fair-minded tone than she herself launched into two hundred pages of invective and accusation, factual errors, slipshod documentation, semantic slanting, quotations out of context, and other distortion of leftists' positions—occasionally sinking to the level of Newt Gingrich's demagogy in blaming the 1960s counterculture for every contemporary crime, as when she implied that French postmodernist philosophy inspired not only the increasing distortion of truth by American public figures (mainly Democrats, of course) but the Philadelphia inner-city youths who made fun of the murder of an ice-cream vendor (204–5).

In my *College English* review of her book, I documented a score of such examples as abuses of my ground rules for polemicists. Here are just a few of the more glaring ones. After criticizing various liberally slanted reports on gender bias by the American Association of University Women (AAUW), Cheney claimed:

> The research efforts of the AAUW illustrate well a point made by Cynthia Crossen in her book *Tainted Truth* about how postmodern thinking has affected the research enterprise. "Researchers have almost given up on the quaint notion that there is any such thing as 'fact' or 'objectivity,'" Crossen writes. Instead, the point has become to amass data in order to support an agenda, in the case of the AAUW, an agenda that is moving sharply left. (*Telling the Truth: Why* 35)

In Crossen's book, however, the quoted sentence appeared between these two: "Many researchers' ethical standards have drifted from the scientist's toward the lobbyist's.... The path to truth is blocked by a financial obstacle—the escalating funding power of private interests" (*Tainted* 17–18). Crossen, then a *Wall Street Journal* reporter and editor, said nothing about either AAUW, as Cheney implied, or postmodernism; her main target was the corruption of research, journalism, and polling by conservative corporations and their subsidized political lobbies, foundations, and think tanks. It is fascinating to speculate on the state of mind of an author who laments, about left scholars, "how debased argument can be when one discounts, as so many academic activists do, traditional standards of accuracy and evidence" (*Telling the Truth: Why* 61), while she deliberately sets out to distort a passage criticizing her allies for doing exactly that into one criticizing her opponents for doing it, and in the process accuses *them* of Orwellian doublethink.

My article also recounted my own eerie experience of finding myself nodding in agreement with Cheney's criticism of a doctrinaire English professor—until I realized that it was *me*. She had come across a then-recent article of mine, also in *College English*, titled "Back to Basics: A Force for Oppression or Liberation," which actually made some of the same criticisms she does of leftist teachers, but she pulled a few phrases out of context to charge, "This faculty member is determined to convert his students to his point of view. He has no intention of introducing them to other perspectives" (*Telling the Truth: Why* 13). She had somehow missed my following passage: "Conservatives are correct in insisting that it is illegitimate for teachers to advocate a revolutionary or any other ideological position in a one-sided way and to force that position on students—and despite the tendentious exaggerations of conservative critics about the tyranny of left political correctness, this sometimes does occur" ("Back to Basics" 11). The editor of *College English* and I both brought this unconscionable distortion to her attention, but she refused to retract it and continued to repeat it in at least one subsequent speech, at a Republican Issues Conference broadcast on C-SPAN. The episode was incomprehensible to me, and became even more so in light of Cheney's subsequent rise to Second Lady, because of the incommensurability of her life situation, as a high-ranking Republican whose husband was one of that party's most powerful, partisan, and wealthy officials—then CEO of Halliburtan Industries, with estimated net worth of $100 million—and mine as a teacher of undergraduate composition to technology and business majors at a rural state college, living modestly on about $65,000 a year. For her and other powerful Republicans to search out small fry like me and many other objects of their ire as menaces to Western civilization would seem a prime case of rhetorical overkill.

Here is how Sanford Pinsker, who had earlier denounced "rhetorical strategies that rely on anger and insult," practiced what he preached in his *College English* response to my article on Cheney, while evading any substantive rebuttal of my catalogue of her distortions: "One of the earmarks of the contemporary ideologue is the sheer amount of prose he or she will mount up to 'prove' a partisan point....As my grandfather used to put it, a fool can throw a stone into a lake where even six sages could not find it" ("Comment" 85). Pinsker neglected to consider that this insult might just as accurately describe Cheney's own sheer amount of prose, or that numerous articles in *Academic Questions* contained a high component of rhetorical strategies that rely on anger and insult.

One gets the sense that Cheney and her allied critics approach left texts with malice aforethought, scanning them like a heat-seeking missile tracking lurid sentence fragments to blast out of context. Another case in point is attacks on Marxist literary theorist Fredric Jameson by conservatives like Roger Kimball and John

Ellis, which consisted of grotesque distortions of Jameson's ideas and those of the Frankfurt School critics whose work he continued, supported by dishonestly taking out of context a few sentence fragments to make Jameson sound like a unreconstructed Stalinist or Maoist, while ignoring the overall lines of his painstakingly nuanced thought developed in many volumes. Ellis, a German professor at the University of California, Santa Cruz, and NAS regular, mixed several cogent arguments with the familiar array of unsupported, sweeping allegations and unverified citations from questionable secondhand sources. He showed fuller familiarity with Jameson's work than Kimball, but he lost credibility because of his apoplectic tone and compulsion to put the worst light on everything Jameson says, never giving the benefit of the doubt. (He and Jameson were once colleagues at Santa Cruz, and he was probably nettled, understandably, that Jameson helped turn the literature program there into a bastion of left theory.) Both Kimball, in a critique of Jameson in Hilton Kramer's and his journal the *New Criterion* ("Fredric Jameson" 13), and Ellis in *Literature Lost* (121) cited a phrase by Jameson referring to "Maoism, richest of all the great new ideologies of the 60s," without acknowledging the next sentence: "One understands, of course, why left militants here and abroad, fatigued by Maoist dogmatisms, must have heaved a collective sigh of relief when the Chinese in turn consigned 'Maoism' itself to the ashcan of history" (*Ideologies* 188)-89).

Ellis distorted not only Jameson but Gerald Graff in defense of Jameson. In *Beyond the Culture Wars*, Graff wrote:

> [O]ne reason for the notorious difficulty of today's politically oriented criticism is its habit of going out of its way *not* to repeat the crudities perpetrated by the Marxists of the 1930s and the New Leftists of the 1960s [...]. Jameson bends so far backward to avoid predictably reducing ideas to expressions of social class interest that he finds even in fascism a certain "utopian" dimension, monstrously perverted.
>
> In this respect Jameson is not as far as he may seem from Orwell, who sought to negotiate a middle ground between those who refused to see that art is political and those who refused to see that it is anything else. (*Beyond* 159)

In Ellis's decontextualized account, Graff's "silliest assertion is the claim that Fredric Jameson is 'not as far as he may seem from Orwell.' A man who must persuade himself that an unreconstructed apologist for Stalin and Mao is not far from Orwell is clearly under strain" (*Literature* 256). Kimball and Ellis were determined to make Jameson into a vulgar Marxist, but their caricature of a scholar who has developed the most scrupulous critique of Marxism and communism simply made *them* into vulgar anti-Marxists.

For a scholar of German literature, Ellis also presented a shamefully reductive account of the Frankfurt School, saying of Jameson's *Late Marxism*, "The thinkers to whom he returns again and again are from the first half of the twentieth century, for example, Georg Lukács and the Frankfurt school figures Theodor Adorno and Max Horkheimer, all men whose ideas were formed before Marxists had to face what Stalin had done. *Late Marxism* even offers us Adorno as the thinker for the 1990s—surely an improbable notion when so much that is critical has happened since Adorno's outlook was formed" (*Literature* 124). Never mind that Jameson's book was based on Adorno's *Negative Dialectic* of 1966, *Minima Moralia* of 1951, and (with Horkheimer) *Dialectic of Enlightenment* of 1944 (revised in 1947 and 1969), supplemented by an encyclopedic survey of contemporary Marxist scholars, most of them anticommunist, with whom Ellis showed no acquaintance. Ellis also ignored other major Frankfurt works from the forties through the seventies like Adorno's "Television and the Patterns of Mass Culture," Marcuse's *One-Dimensional Man* (which turns Marxism *against* Stalinism, as Jameson does), Leo Lowenthal's *Literature, Popular Culture, and Society*, and Erich Fromm's *Escape From Freedom* and *The Sane Society*. If any of these works endorsed Stalinism, Ellis failed to enlighten us as to where. About Ellis's attack on feminist scholarship, feminist critic Rita Felski remarked in *Literature After Feminism*, "Nowhere does Ellis seriously engage the work of a feminist literary scholar or show any knowledge of the main trends in the field. Indeed, many of his comments reveal an astonishing level of ignorance.... Again and again, Ellis claims to refute feminism by repeating what are commonplace ideas of feminist scholarship" (7).

Ellis returned to the fray in 2012, as the coauthor, with Peter Wood, of yet another "research report" for NAS alleging to show the persistence of leftist political bias in the faculties of the University of California, titled *A Crisis of Competence: The Corrupting Effect of Political Activism in the University of California* (Wood "Politics, Education"), replaying the same tunes NAS has harped on for three decades. By this time, the past efforts of the authors and organization have been so discredited that there was no good reason for anyone to waste further time on them, other than the credulous mass media to which Wood admits they were pitched, as noted earlier, and Republican Party demagogues like Rick Santorum. The report implied, by all it omitted, that tenured radicals pose a greater danger to UC than four decades of Republican-driven tax and budget cuts that have destroyed its once-proud national ranking. Neither Ellis, Wood, nor any previous author of such reports, to my knowledge, has presented empirical evidence in support of their claims that faculty PC has been a major cause of the decline in students majoring in the liberal arts, in comparison, say, to the financial squeeze forcing them into more job-oriented majors. Nor has Ellis or Wood addressed the corporatization of university governance (with corporate-executive administrators enforcing cost-costing efficiency and accountability measures), the for-profit-colleges lobby, the conservatizing effects of student loan debt, or the know-nothing attacks on the content and financing of higher education by Republican officeholders and candidates. Conservatives continue to fixate exclusively on the academic left as the pool table that is the source of all the TROUBLE right here in River City.

Solidarity in Aberration and Error

In sum, conservatives have perpetuated a series of distortions that evade good faith deliberation about the ideas of leftists. Many valuable critical works on the left since the 1960s, in the humanities, social science, and even natural science, have documented specific instances in which established authorities' claims to be objective, rational, and nonpolitical are belied by their practices, or in which the biases of dominant groups are assumed to embody indisputable truths. In so doing, left critics are merely following the rich humanistic canon of works that expose hypocrisy, self-deception, or failure to practice what one preaches (see chapter 10). Rather than evaluating these instances on a case-by-case basis, conservatives typically make an inductive leap to caricature such critics as denying "the possibility of human beings doing anything nonpolitical—such as encouraging the search for truth" (Cheney, *Telling the Truth: Why* 15–16).

Peter Wood denounces multiculturalism as "the stance of generalized antagonism to the whole of Western civilization and the elevation of 'critical thinking' in the sense of facile reductionism (everything at bottom is about race-gender-class hierarchy)." And Cheney affirms "truths that pass beyond time and circumstance, truths that, transcending accidents of class, race, and gender, speak to us all" (*Telling*, 14). Contrast their account with that of John K. Wilson in *The Myth of Political Correctness*:

> Multiculturalists do not claim that race, class, and gender determine everything, but they accurately observe that these categories have been neglected by traditional analysis. Certainly, race, gender, and class are not the sole determinant of a person's beliefs. But it would be wrong to claim that race, gender, and class have absolutely no influence, or to ignore the fact that members of oppressed groups (and their views) have historically been omitted from academia. (81)

Wilson's account, which might also have included revisions of conventional historical views of capitalism, colonialism, militarism, and non-Western cultures, opens the door to a wealth of legitimate scholarship and teaching of conflicting views, while Wood's and Cheney's in effect slams that door shut, by implying that these different schools of study are mutually exclusive rather than fruitfully complementary.

In the end, the most glaring offense of conservative polemicists is the absence of self-questioning among them as individuals and organizations, in the manner of my ground rules #2, "Identify your own ideological viewpoint and how it might bias your arguments," and #3, "Be willing to acknowledge misconduct, errors, and fallacious arguments by your own allies.... Do not play up the other side's forms of power while downplaying your own." In Cheney's book, she acknowledged, "If we cannot get outside ourselves to be objective, where are we to find a standard by which to judge if we are fair?" (*Telling the Truth: Why* 180). Yet Cheney never once tried to get outside herself to address her own possible biases as a powerful, wealthy member of the Republican establishment or to weigh the biases of that establishment evenhandedly against those of Democrats and leftists, especially in education and the media. Conservative insiders have often remarked that their movement has made a conscious effort to paper over internal dissension or self-criticism, in order to present a united front and avoid the faction fights that have always cursed the left (even though conservatives still resort publicly to lurid depictions of a monolithic left). This lack of self-criticism also extends to conservatives' general refusal, as in ground rule #2, to "concede the other side's valid arguments" and to "acknowledge points on which you agree at least partially and might be able to cooperate."

As if it were not exasperating enough for critical teachers to try to convey to students (or for left journalists to convey to their audiences) the myriad ways in which they have been inundated with conservative biases throughout their lives, the effort to convey to them the deviousness of much of the massive body of plausible-looking information put out by conservative forces like these trashing liberal and left ideas presents a nearly insurmountable added burden. For both student and scholarly or journalistic researchers, the time and energy needed to swim against the endless flood of offensives by the conservative counter-intelligentsia can end in drowning—which may be precisely its intention.

Everything I have written here is open to disagreement, and I welcome correction of errors. I have not been attempting to "whitewash" the entire academic or cultural left. One can always zero in on isolated passages in leftist sources that sound extreme out of context, and even reputable scholars or journalists on the left occasionally go overboard, as in the notorious case of the high-powered theorists who edited *Social Text* being taken in by Alan Sokal's hoax article denying that there is any objective scientific truth. There also will always be those in the ranks of the left who trumpet their own confused, vulgarized versions of complex ideas and mirror the false dichotomies of conservatives—I have battled with them among English faculties and graduate students, in *The Retreat* and in person. To single them out to tar more creditable thinkers and ideas, though, is to break my ground rule #3, to present the other side's case "through its most reputable spokespeople and strongest formulations, (not through the most outlandish statements of its lunatic fringe)." (I would hope conservative readers will concede that I have presented their case in my last two chapters mostly through its most reputable and influential spokespeople.) Rather than just responding with tu quoque arguments piling up more examples of leftist abuses, I urge conservative polemicists to join in a meta-polemical effort by both sides to weigh abuses on both in the larger perspectives on American politics and education that I have tried to establish here.

High among the humanistic "truths that pass beyond time and circumstance" (Cheney) is that the certitude of one's own party being the exclusive guardian of truth and virtue constitutes hubris, the pride that goeth before a fall. Ought not Judeo-Christian humility and charity compel us all to admit, as the nonbeliever Albert Camus said in the tradition of secular-humanistic skepticism, that "there is a solidarity of all men in error and aberration" (*Resistance* 217)?

Part III

Responsible Leftist Teaching

8

BALANCING COMMITMENT AND OPENNESS IN TEACHING: GIVING CONSERVATIVES THEIR BEST SHOT

My method of coping with these problems facing critical pedagogy entails an effort on the teacher's part to balance a rationally established, politically committed position (some would say "a bias") with open-ended challenges to it. This method aspires—haltingly, to be sure—to William's Perry's highest stage of development in moral reasoning, that of committed relativism. I apply this method mainly within the context of an advanced composition course in argumentative rhetoric and writing from sources, first formulated in my 1992 "Teaching the Political Conflicts: A Rhetorical Schema," then developed in textbook form in *Reading and Writing for Civic Literacy*.

The first aim of the course is cognitive and ideological coherence, through continuity of assignments from the first to the last day. This can be a more daunting challenge than the political dimension, entailing stressful reconditioning of students to maintain continuity through recursion and cumulation of assignments, rather than jumping, as they are accustomed to, from one reading topic and writing assignment or exam to the next while forgetting all the previous ones. (I similarly try to retain continuity in my literature courses through straight-line thematic development and a final essay exam that synthesizes the entire course.) The course is structured cumulatively through a single, extensively developed topic of controversy that all of the students focus on together—in recent years, liberal and left versus conservative views on economic policies—in place of the conventional atomization resulting from each student choosing individual, diverse topics from one paper to another, which impairs the capacity to understand or construct an extended line of argument. Despite some students' initial unhappiness about not having their accustomed freedom to choose topics and about being obliged to stick with a single, extended thematic development, this process usually ends up creating much more sense of a scholarly community in the class and broadening of intellectual capacities in each student. In anonymous course evaluations and messages after grades are in, many students affirmed that the cumulative and recursive structure increased their ability to read for critical understanding and to synthesize material in writing, to a level far beyond any other course they had taken; several have gone on to do independent study with me continuing the explorations they began in the course.

This approach involves another point of difference that I have with most practitioners of critical pedagogy and student-centered teaching in general. For them, the most effective pedagogical practice is for students to engage in dialogue or debate with their peers at whatever their common level of knowledge and rhetorical sophistication is, and only to go as far as their own back-and-forth leads them with minimal intervention by the teacher. While I acknowledge the advantages in it, I find it unsatisfactory when students end up with positions that I know can easily be superseded, as a result of my having been around the block on these arguments for many more years.

So I always try to advance the argument further, to my own stage of knowledge and beyond, and to raise its level of discourse from that of popular media easily accessible to them, to that of scholarship or more serious journalism in journals of opinion, books, and research reports. I also intervene whenever the dialectic gets stalled at a point where I can provide a pertinent line of argument or sources that the students haven't found, and often to challenge a too-facile consensus among them, whether liberal, leftist, or conservative. And I sometimes use the endpoint of one semester's studies of a particular dispute as the starting point for the next semester and pool of students, or for continued independent study by previous students. This process enlists students in what I believe to be an essential mission of scholarship: constantly to be building on the body of knowledge and elevating the level of thought on subjects of public importance. Improbable as it may sound, enough of my undergraduates have come to understand and become committed, skilled participants in this mission to convince me that it is worth continuing its pursuit, in spite of what is lost in other worthy goals of critical pedagogy.

In course structure, about half the semester is spent on exposition of principles of argumentative rhetoric and writing, in application to readings I have assigned that serve to introduce key rhetorical and political themes. Then a unit on political rhetoric and semantics begins with an elementary survey of political terminology (including its complexities, ambiguities, and confusions), issues that divide the left and right, and predictable patterns of left-wing and right-wing rhetoric—all of which are applied recursively to the previous readings, revealing added dimensions to them.

To apply this unit, I assign for the rest of the semester daily comparative analysis (in student notes to be turned in and discussed at the beginning of each class) of the *New York Times* versus *Wall Street Journal* news and opinion pages, and weekly analysis of the *Weekly Standard* versus the *Nation*. I explain that this exercise, along with the rest of the course, is designed to prime the pump toward their habituation in the inductive process of continually accumulating new information and applying analytic skills to it that is a defining trait of Alvin Gouldner's "culture of critical discourse" and the basis of advanced scholarly study.

Next, I survey the problems summarized in the previous chapters and present as a hypothesis (not as dogmatic assertion) that most students are more likely to be familiar with the conservative agenda and framing than with liberal or certainly, leftist, counterparts, especially exposed in a systematic manner. To test this hypothesis, I present them with an outline of conservative versus liberal and left arguments on economic issues, reproduced below. Then I assign them several sources that I think make the left case on these issues in a well-reasoned, comprehensive manner. Most come to agree, provisionally, that they were more familiar with conservative views on these issues than with the arguments and data in these sources.

Giving Conservatives Their Best Shot

At that point, I say, "OK, but don't let lefties have the last word here. There's a whole library and Internet full of conservative sources, and if they have good rebuttals, you should easily be able to find them and demonstrate how their arguments are better reasoned and supported." So, far from monolithically imposing leftist views, I REQUIRE that students spend what at that stage is about the last third of the semester researching, individually and in teams, the best conservative rebuttals, then writing a point-by-point evaluation of them against left arguments, including comparative analysis of their reasoning and verifying their documentation. I direct them to conservative Websites like intellectualtakeout.com, townhall.com, and David Horowitz's discoverthenetworks.com, which feature menus of conservative sources and lines of argument on current controversies, and I encourage them to bring in conservative speakers from outside. I will, however, assert professional authority to identify a source whose obvious bias I am familiar with and they are not, such as "some cockamamy pollster" and "world-famous laboratory" that tobacco lobbyist Victor Crawford concocted in defense of smoking.

My approach owes a great deal to Gerald Graff's concept of teaching the conflicts. I think some of Graff's critics have been unfair in claiming he advocates that the teacher just acts like a referee, maintaining a pose of false neutrality between conflicting viewpoints that are assumed to be equally credible when they may not be, or that he presumes a false parity or level playing field between opposing forces that are in fact incommensurate in power. In my understanding, Graff's approach is just a safeguard against teachers monolithically forcing their side of an issue a priori on students who may not even understand what the issue is or how opposing sides differ on it. So our responsibility is to convey at the outset an evenhanded, factual and rhetorical understanding of where and how the opposing sides disagree. Then we are justified to say something like, "Look, I am a leftist because my experience and academic studies have led me to the conclusions that liberal and left sources in general tend to be more independent, better reasoned and documented, than conservative ones (especially those funded by corporations), and that there is not a level playing field in America between the left and right on the level of mass discourse. So it would be dishonest of me to pretend that I think both sides are equally credible. But, hey, I may be biased or lying, and there are plenty of sources on the opposing side who take issue with everything I have said here and with everything that left sources write, so you need to read them and learn to judge for yourself who makes the better case—and to keep me honest." Teachers with conservative viewpoints can certainly take the same approach in their courses, and the best of all possible courses might be team-taught by a leftist and rightist, or a liberal and a socialist, airing their disagreements in class.

The sequence of assignments at this point includes small-group discussions and research teams, full-class debates, and several short papers and daily notes that serve as drafts toward an argumentative term paper. So about two-thirds of the course is teacher-centered and banking-method, which I judge to be necessary for introduction to the rhetorical and critical-thinking components, political vocabulary, and partisan lines of opposition that few students have been familiar with, but students increasingly take over in the last third, culminating in debates in the final few weeks, between teams that they organize that create an atmosphere of sports-like competition.

Through the open-ended sequence of assignments, it is virtually impossible for me or any other teacher to stack the deck toward predetermined outcomes, since students are always coming up with new sources and arguments that I am unfamiliar with. If the conservative sources students that find are not as well argued as leftist ones, students benefit from the exercise in spotting fallacious reasoning and conflicts of interest on their own. If they find conservative arguments that appear superior, that serves the healthy purpose of obliging leftist classmates to see if they can find effective counter-rebuttals, in an ongoing dialectic in which no one has "the last word," and in which any apparent last word in one course can become the first word the next time the course is offered. I have benefited myself from being introduced by students to conservative sources and arguments I hadn't heard before, and from being obliged to ratchet up the level of response to them in my own writing.

In grading, this course design really frees the teacher from any inclination, even unconscious, toward bias in favor of political views she/he agrees with, since it becomes easy to grade solely on the basis of students' ingenuity in researching sources, their astuteness in identifying and evaluating opposing lines of argument, and their skill in synthesizing their studies into a well-organized term paper. Their ultimate judgment about which side makes the better arguments on balance seems to me incidental and a private matter, so I discourage them from even making it, to save them from the temptation of sucking up to the teacher.

Mine is not a foolproof method for guarding against teachers' biases on controversial issues or in grading. Others can undoubtedly suggest good ways of improving on or replacing it. But it does have the advantage of foregrounding the issue of such bias and controlling for it by guaranteeing student access to views opposed to the teacher's. (I always announce at the outset that conservative students, and their disagreement with my views, are especially welcome in the class to liven it up; and I say that if any of them think I ever grade them down on the basis of political views differing from mine, I will cheerfully raise their grade without haggling. Despite the temptation this might pose for cynical exploitation of it, I have never had a taker.) Even this method, of course—like any other one—ultimately depends on the individual teacher's integrity. It is a constant test of that integrity, which can be abused by the irresponsible, and its success depends on establishing students' trust and an atmosphere of open, courteous, good-humored give-and-take. So its results can only be judged in the practice of every particular course, and after the fact by students once a course is over. (I keep a file of evaluations and messages from former students, which I make available by email to anyone who inquires.) Google is filled with conservative attacks on my articles and speeches discussing my method that just assume my teaching practices must be devious without the vaguest direct knowledge of them. Likewise, Lynne Cheney charged about my article "Back to Basics," which described the same position I express here, "This professor is determined to convert his students to his point of view. He has no intention of introducing them to other perspectives" (*Telling the Truth: A Report* 13). Not only did my article contradict her, but she had no direct knowledge of my classes, and when I mailed her my syllabus and assignments further contradicting her, she ignored them and continued to repeat the same charge in other venues.

To reiterate, I try in my argumentative writing course to strike a difficult balance: Teaching students to give the fullest, fairest hearing to liberal/left and conservative views, while also conveying forthrightly to them why I have, over decades of study, found the liberal/left arguments on these issues generally stronger—with the caveats of my possible biases and the open-endedness of these arguments. I have devised a model for use in my course that attempts to incorporate these balanced aims in an "Outline of Conservative and Left Arguments on Economic Issues," following this chapter. I distribute this as an introduction to the part of the course on the research paper and critical analysis of opposing sources. This outline gives the last word to left refutations of conservative arguments, reflecting the conclusion from my own studies over the years that conservatives generally are better at propagating their own agenda and attacking straw leftists than at responding to concrete left rebuttals; but it also indicates that the last words here can be regarded as the first words toward further back-and-forth. Indeed, at that point I provide students with a reading list of leading conservative sources on these economic issues, including those recommended by Cheney in *Telling the Truth*.

An Outline of Conservative and Left Arguments on Economic Issues

The following is an outline of the broad points of opposition between conservatives and liberals or leftists on economic issues. (On some points noted, liberals and leftists disagree.) In keeping with the principles of General Semantics, the outline is meant to be open-ended. The facts that the leftist arguments get the last word here and are more numerous simply serve as a challenge to students to use this as a point of departure, seeing what effective conservative rebuttals they can find. So "the last" words in this outline could be ETC., ETC., ETC.

I. The Conservative Position

The basic position of President Reagan, both President Bush, and the Republican Party is that American government has been overloaded trying to provide for the public welfare in programs like education, Social Security, Medicare, welfare, unemployment insurance, minimum-wage laws, and so on. Moreover, excessive taxation and bureaucratic government regulation of business (especially for environmental protection) have stifled the productive power of free enterprise. This overload on government has led to inflation, deficit spending, and dependency of beneficiaries of programs like welfare on "handouts." Therefore, if government spending on domestic programs is reduced and taxes cut by equal percentage rates across all income lines (with the largest savings going to wealthy individuals and corporations), private enterprise will be freed to function more effectively; it will be more efficient than government and the public sector of the economy in generating jobs, producing more tax revenue, and filling other public needs. The reason these beneficial "Reaganomic" policies haven't been fully effective is that they haven't been given an adequate chance to work, their full implementation having been blocked by Democrats in Congress and other leftist bureaucrats and special-interest groups purely because of their partisan and selfish motives. Deficit spending has increased only because Democrats in Congress rejected every effort by presidents Reagan and both Bushes to reduce the budget.

Additional Conservative Arguments

1. Budget and tax cuts in the federal government under presidents Reagan and both Bushes, and in states like California

since Proposition 13, have just trimmed the fat of unnecessary programs and administrative waste, leaving intact essential programs and the "safety net" of support for the truly needy.
2. Flat-rate taxes and tax cuts are fairer than progressive taxes because all income levels pay and benefit from cuts at the same rate.
3. Government spending in many areas such as education and welfare can be more properly and efficiently handled by states and localities than by the federal government; the funding burden should be shifted to them.
4. Much of the overload on government has resulted from selfish, excessive demands for "entitlements" from special interests like welfare recipients, minorities, the elderly, veterans, teachers, and students. These groups have become dependent on handouts and have lost their incentive to work.
5. Individual initiative, not government programs, is the best solution to social problems. Conservatives believe in equality of opportunity, not an inaccessible equality of outcome as liberals do, and believe that all Americans do have equal opportunity to succeed. Anyone can get a good job and be financially successful if they try hard enough. It is usually people's own fault if they are poor or unemployed. They should just try harder and be more virtuous.
6. Spending on national defense is an exception to the need for cutting government costs because increases in the eighties were necessary to defeat Russia in the arms race (Communism's collapse vindicated Reagan's hardline policies); maintaining strong defense is still necessary because of terrorism and other potential threats, like Saddam Hussein, Al-Qaeda, and Iran, to American security.
7. The most effective way to reduce poverty and unemployment is to permit the rich to get richer—the trickle-down theory or "supply-side economics"—because their increased spending trickles down to benefit all other segments of society proportionately. The concentration of wealth at the top is not a zero-sum game, in which the gains of the rich come at the expense of the middle class or poor.
8. Wealthy individuals and corporate executives can be entrusted to use their increased benefits for the public welfare because in order to attain and maintain their position they have to be exceptionally intelligent, hardworking, honest, and civic-minded.

9. Most rich people have worked hard for their money and have risked their investments, so they shouldn't be penalized by high taxes and government regulations that stifle their incentive to work and to invest. Executives' high salaries are proportionate to the profits they have produced for their companies.
10. Minimum-wage laws, high corporate or individual taxes, and excessive regulations—especially in environmental, safety and health issues—force industries to move their operations to other locations in the United States or other countries. Such increased expenses are also passed on to consumers in higher prices, so they are self-defeating.
11. The rich are generous in sharing their wealth; the more money they are allowed to keep, the more they give to charities.
12. Wealth is compatible with religious, and especially Christian, morality. Many wealthy people use their wealth to support religious organizations and causes.
13. Leftist criticisms of presidents Reagan or George W. Bush and the rich often consist of "sour grapes" rationalizations by government bureaucrats, intellectuals, teachers, journalists, or public employees who are just unwilling or unable to make it themselves in the private sector and who are jealous of those who do. These "bleeding hearts" sentimentalize the poor.
14. Leftist teachers' and other public employees' arguments may reflect ethnocentric bias, conflict of interest, or special pleading, since these sources benefit personally from higher taxation and the resulting increases in government spending. Likewise, arguments by leftist intellectuals may be self-interested, concealing their drive to replace the rich as the new ruling class.
15. In spite of all its faults, history has shown that that capitalism or free enterprise is a more efficient and humane economic system than any form of socialism or mixed economy.
16. Statistically based arguments: Empirical evidence that Reaganomics worked includes the facts that the 1980s saw a reduction in inflation and the longest period of steady growth in the American economy since World War II; millions of new jobs were created; the rich paid higher dollar amounts and an increased percentage of tax revenues, and total tax revenues increased. Liberal-leftist claims of a growing gap between the rich and the middle class and poor are based on faulty statistical analyses. There has been much more socioeconomic mobility in recent decades than liberals want to admit, with many people moving out of poverty into the middle class, and many others dropping out of the upper income brackets.

II. The Liberal/Leftist Position

Democracy in America is being destroyed and replaced by plutocracy—rule by and for the rich. In the left-of-liberal view, presidents Reagan and both Bushes have been agents of plutocratic special interests, as are most Republican and Democratic politicians, including presidents Clinton, and Obama, who appeal to liberal constituencies to get elected, but then sell them out on many if not most issues. Reaganomic policies have had the effect, intentionally or unintentionally, of entrenching plutocracy, by making the rich richer, the middle class and poor poorer, and eliminating needed welfare programs and productive areas of public spending and employment. Government spending serves to prime the pump when the economy slumps and to provide services the private sector fails to, while progressive taxation (progressively higher percentage as income or property value increases) serves to reduce the gap of wealth and power between the rich and the rest of the population (Keynesian economics). The conservative line of argument against Keynesian economics is largely a propaganda program engineered by wealthy special interests to rationalize their own greed. In fact, Reagan and both Bushes consistently proposed budgets that were higher (mainly because of defense increases) than those passed by Congress, but their budget increases amounted to "Keynesian" socialism for the rich, free enterprise for the poor.

Additional Leftist Arguments (refuted conservative arguments appear in parentheses):

1. American cultural conditioning favors the rich by fostering common blocks to clear thinking like authoritarian awe and sentimentality toward the rich, the ethnocentrism and wishful thinking of middle-class people hoping to become rich, favorable stereotypes of the rich and prejudiced ones of the working class and poor.
2. (9) There is often little correlation between how hard people work or how much risk they take and how much money they make. Many of those who make the most money don't make it through work at all but through investments (often inherited) and speculation, while many of those who work the hardest and under the greatest risk (e.g., farmworkers, coalminers, police, firefighters) make the least. Corporate executive salaries have gotten totally out of proportion to performance—in many cases, CEOs have gotten vast increases of income even when their companies have

lost money—partly because of conflicts of interest between CEOs and boards of directors who determine their compensation.
3. (5) Conservative "try harder" arguments fail to recognize the basic inequities structured into a capitalist economy and the external economic forces—national and worldwide economic trends, inflation, recession, and so on —that often make individual effort futile. In a free enterprise economy, there is no certainty of full employment, of a job being available for everyone who needs one, or of a minimum wage above poverty level. Conservatives have constructed a straw man leftist who demands nothing less than total equality of outcome from social policies, but most liberals and leftists simply believe that present-day American is far from presenting equal opportunity for all, so that their policies are only aimed at bringing that opportunity about.
4. (7) There is no conclusive evidence that the trickle-down theory has ever worked in practice or ever will. Contrary to conservative claims that supply-side tax cuts would actually increase tax revenues, federal and local revenues have been lower than they would have been under previous progressive rates, and huge deficits have resulted at both the national and local levels. Much of what the rich get back in tax cuts is often invested not in job-producing enterprises but in personal luxuries, tax dodges, hedges against inflation, speculation, corporate takeovers resulting in monopoly and inflated prices for consumers and lost jobs for workers, or investments in foreign countries exploiting cheap labor there while taking jobs and money out of the United States.
5. (7, 8, 10) Outlandish corporate profits and gaps between executives and employees in recent decades belie conservatives' claims that the rich getting richer benefits everyone, as well as their appeals to pity for overtaxed, overregulated corporations. Businesses often use these appeals to pity and the appeal to fear of their relocating from localities or the United States as blackmail to get their way. Globalization and outsourcing of jobs simply exploit the absence in poorer countries of minimum-wage laws, labor unions, and environmental, safety, and health regulations. Corporate relocation abroad has devastated the situation of American workers in a greedy manner that contradicts conservative claims about how virtuous and patriotic capitalists are.
6. In contrast to the private sector, where much money spent does not trickle down to the rest of society, virtually all money spent in the public sector "trickles up" back into the private sector. Spending on education, public health, welfare, and so on, is a

good investment by society that pays off in higher productivity. Spending by tax-funded public agencies (e.g., universities) creates jobs and subsidizes private-sector contractors for construction, equipment, and services. Corporate interests want (and depend on) these subsidies without wanting to pay the taxes needed to fund them.

7. The private sector is just as wasteful and inefficient as the public sector, and the most waste in both occurs at the executive levels, where spending is administered (primarily in administrators' own interests). Thus budget cuts resulting from laws like Proposition 13 in California have left governmental administrative "fat" intact while bankrupting local governments, causing layoffs of rank-and-file public employees and harmful cuts in essential services like education and law enforcement. The conservative belief that there is a vast amount of fat that can be trimmed from government agencies at the rank-and-file level is often just wishful thinking or rationalization of conservatives' politically motivated desire to squeeze out liberal constituencies served by government spending.
8. (3) As a result of local tax cuts like Proposition 13, state and local governments are even more hard-pressed financially than the federal government, so conservative claims that funding responsibilities are better handled at the local level are simply rationalizations or passing the buck.
9. (9) Those who can afford to pay the most taxes and who benefit most from a prosperous society—that is, the rich—should be expected to pay the most. Flat-rate tax cuts disproportionately benefit the rich and widen the gap in wealth and ownership of incoming—producing holdings like stocks, bonds, real estate, and farms, enabling the rich to increase their power in all of the following ways.
10. The rich can buy political influence with both the Republican and Democratic parties and government officials, causing legislation to be passed in their interest and against that of the middle class and poor, particularly in tax policies, such as regressive cuts in income, corporation, inheritance, and property taxes that in recent decades have sharply reduced the burden on the rich.
11. As a result of #10, above the tax burden has shifted increasingly from the rich to the middle class, especially in tax increases for Social Security, Medicare, and sales; as a further result, the overtaxed middle-class votes to support cuts in public services that harm themselves and society as a whole but that don't harm the

rich because they don't depend on these services—services like education, Social Security, public health insurance, welfare, law enforcement, libraries, and public transportation. The middle class rationalizes these cuts by turning the poor, "big government," and public employees into scapegoats, blaming them instead of the rich for the financial squeeze on themselves.

12. The rich can use the power of hiring and firing to force workers and students (as future workers) into compliance with pro-rich attitudes; because we have to cater to them to get or keep a job, we tend to fall into doublethink compartmentalized thinking to rationalize our servitude to them.

13. The rich are able to create a favorable public image of themselves through ownership or sponsorship of news and entertainment media, advertising, and public relations. They exert a large degree of control over education through positions as donors or university trustees and through sponsoring research in both universities and private "think tanks" that supports their interests.

14. (8) Many rich people and corporations get away with criminal or unethical activity that causes relatively little public indignation or opposition from law enforcement agencies, compared to lower-class criminals or "leeches." The middle class tends to have a double standard or selective vision in playing down misconduct by the rich and playing up that by the poor. How can we expect poor people to respect the law or act morally when those at the top of society set such a poor example?

15. It is often affluent conservative businesspeople who benefit most from the government subsidies that conservatives claim they oppose (compartmentalized thinking): subsidies to farmers (including for food stamps); to insurance companies, doctors and pharmaceutical manufacturers and sellers for health insurance; to bankers for student loans; to bondholders for government debts, and so on.

16. (6) Wealthy people and corporations control the defense industry, which is the biggest government subsidy of all, whose only customer is the government and whose spending on weapons that are only intended to be destroyed or replaced by more advanced ones is disastrous for the national economy. (But the defense industry is exempt from conservative attacks on government bureaucracy and waste, because it produces big corporate profits and campaign contributions.) More and more of our national income has been eaten up on this wasteful spending that is a major cause of inflation and deficit spending and that has squeezed out spending on

more productive domestic programs like education and employment for public works. During the Cold War, the military-industrial complex and its wealthy executives became the tail that wagged the dog of defense policy in their own self-interest, artificially perpetuating tensions with Russia to bolster their profits and power (mirroring the military establishment in Russia that was similarly self-interested). The main reason Communism collapsed was not the American arms buildup but inept, dictatorial bureaucrats running the government and economy. But because American conservatives are always partial to militarism, they tend to be blind to the military as a special interest and to fraud and waste in military spending, which have accelerated again after September 11 and the Iraq War, rationalized by appeals to fear of terrorism.
17. The rich can influence foreign policy to protect their foreign investments, markets, and sources of natural resources and cheap labor. International competition for markets has frequently been the cause of wars throughout history.
18. The wealthy profit from wars conducted in their class interests and consuming weapons that they produce, but they and their children rarely risk their own lives fighting in those wars. Any business interest that profits from a war should be expected to pay increased taxes to finance it.
19. (11) Rich people on the whole do not give a great amount to charity, relative to their income or net worth, and they benefit from what they give through tax deductions, trusteeships, and a favorable public image as philanthropists or supporters of religion.
20. (12) Attempts to reconcile wealth with Christianity amount to hypocritical rationalizations, since they are completely contrary to the teachings of Jesus Christ.
21. (15) Some semi-socialist countries (e.g., Denmark, Sweden) have surpassed America in per capita income, quality of life, and well-functioning democracy, while some capitalist countries (e.g., Saudi Arabia, Egypt, South Africa under Apartheid, Chile under Pinochet, El Salvador under Duarte, the Philippines under Marcos) are plutocratic, right-wing dictatorships, and Americans' prosperity and freedom are paid for at the expense of poor people in those countries, which are in effect colonies of American corporations.
22. Statistically based arguments (16): Since the 1980s, the income of the richest 1 percent of Americans has skyrocketed, and the

gap between the rich, middle class, and poor has become greater than at any time since the 1920s. The rich obviously are paying more in taxes because their income is greater in relation to everyone else's, thanks to Reaganomic subsidies, and their after-tax savings have increasingly outstripped everyone else's. Inflation has been reduced mainly through reduction of real income for the majority of workers, largely through outsourcing of jobs to Third-World sweatshops. Economic growth since the eighties has been slower than that in previous decades, and the jobs created have been mostly low-wage ones. The main reason more people are working is that two or more people in the same households have been forced to work in order to make the real income previously earned by one; most Americans now have to work more hours to make the same real income they did 30 years ago.

9

A Case Study: Leftist versus Conservative Arguments on College Costs

To indicate the way the approach outlined in chapter 8 plays out in my courses, I bring in the outline of opposing arguments on economic issues about two-thirds into the course. But it has been anticipated by reading and writing assignments back to the first weeks on pertinent topics and sources in current events, including the debates on rising college costs and student debt. The perspective on these topics and sources continues to widen and deepen throughout the term, in a series of short paper and notes assignments, which cumulate in a term paper. The oppositions between sources here on college costs neatly exemplify the lines summarized in the outline—especially Conservative #1, 3, 4, 5, 14, and Left #6, 7, 8, 9, 15.

Between about 2004 and 2008 (the last time I taught this class), the point of departure, setting the agenda, was a 2004 column by Adolph Reed, "Majoring In Debt," in *The Progressive*. (The developmental sequence of study in my argumentation courses is to begin with rhetorical analysis of relatively "easy" journalistic sources, then to advance to more scholarly ones—in both cases, balancing sources from the left and right.) Reed identified himself here as a member of the socialistic Labor Party, and his position was clearly to the left of any mainstream Democratic politician except perhaps Dennis Kucinich and Bernie Sanders, so his column was a useful example of the differences between liberals and leftists. From the viewpoint of a black Chicago native, Reed has written several articles critical of Barack Obama from the left, before and since his election as president. Reed is also a political science professor at the University of Pennsylvania, a private, Ivy League university, so my students generally have agreed that his arguments for making tuition free at all universities did not seem to be special pleading, and were even perhaps against his direct interests. As typical of opinion columns, his did not fully document sources, although it did identify several such as congressional committee studies, and it referred to the website of the Campaign for Free Higher Education, which included a long, fully documented article on which his was based, "Why Political Scientists Should Support Free Higher Education," by professors Preston H. Smith II and Sharon Szymanski, which had also appeared in the journal of the American Political Science Association.

Reed's argument began:

> The crisis in public education is intensifying. As almost every state reels from the effects of recession and tax cuts, legislatures slash funding for higher education, the largest discretionary item in most state budgets. Colleges respond with hefty tuition increases, reduced financial assistance, and new fees. These measures put an extra burden on the average family, whose net worth has declined over the last two years for the first time in half a century.

He continued with data showing the decline in financial aid, especially Pell grants, over the previous three decades., In 1975, the maximum Pell grant covered 84 percent of costs at a four-year public college. By 2004, the grant covered only 42 percent. Meanwhile, colleges were shifting away from grants and toward loans. A decade earlier, 50 percent of student aid was in the form of grants and 47 percent was in the form of loans. By the time Reed was writing, grants were down to 39 percent of total aid; loans had increased to 54 percent. Reed added that in the increased reliance on loans, eligibility shifted from poorer students to richer ones, though he failed to note a more widely recognized recent shift from need-based to merit-based scholarships, which has also favored wealthier students.

Reed added that a report by the Congressional Advisory Committee on Student Financial Assistance indicating that by the 2010s, as many as 4.4 million college-qualified high school graduates will be unable to enroll in a four-year college, and two million will not go to college at all because they can't afford it. He noted:

> Many students who do go to college have to work long hours, which adversely affects their education. A whopping 53 percent of low-income freshmen who work more than thirty-five hours per week drop out and do not receive a degree. Contrast this with low-income freshmen

who work fewer hours: Of those who work one-to-fourteen hours per week, only 20 percent do not receive a degree, according to the Congressional Advisory Committee on Student Financial Assistance.

Those who graduate carry an enormous debt. The majority of students (64 percent) graduate with an average debt of almost $17,000, up significantly from $8,200 in 1989. Faced with repaying huge loans, students often reconsider their career plans. Our society suffers if students abandon lower paying occupations in teaching, social services, and health care in order to seek courses of study that lead to higher income jobs that speed loan repayment.

Reed then proposed as a solution that the federal government subsidize free tuition at all universities, for all students who meet admission standards. He supported this proposal on several grounds, beginning with the assertion, "Higher education is a basic social good," or a benefit, not only to students but to contemporary society as a whole, in meeting crucial economic, scientific, and civil needs—an investment by taxpayers that is repaid many times over in countless ways. He used several analogies—in the past with the history of little or no tuition at American public universities, and with the G. I. Bill after World War II—and in the present, with free K-12 public schools and with other democratic countries that have free higher education at all levels, or long had it prior to recent worldwide financial setbacks.

The further exacerbation since 2004 of the negative trends identified by Reed, Smith, and Szymanski has been widely documented. In a 2012 column in the *New York Times* titled "Ignorance Is Strength," prompted by denigrations of higher education by Republicans like Rick Santorum, Paul Krugman wrote, "These days, public higher education is very much under siege, facing even harsher budget cuts than the rest of the public sector. Adjusted for inflation, state support for higher education has fallen 12 percent over the past five years, even as the number of students has continued to rise; in California, support is down by 20 percent. One result has been soaring fees. Inflation-adjusted tuition at public four-year colleges has risen by more than 70 percent over the past decade." And, "Another result is that cash-strapped educational institutions have been cutting back in areas that are expensive to teach—which also happen to be precisely the areas the economy needs. For example, public colleges in a number of states, including Florida and Texas, have eliminated entire departments in engineering and computer science." On the recent economic effects of Republican assaults on public K-12 education and on teachers' unions, see "Prolonged Attack on Public Education and Unions Leaves Teaching Profession Woeful" (Common Dreams Staff 8 Mar. 2012).

At this writing, in June 2013, the major political dispute over college costs concerned a standoff between President Obama and Republicans in Congress about different sources for funding of loans to avert a scheduled doubling of interest rates to 6.8 percent on federally subsidized Stafford loans. So by this time, the constant increase in student loan debt has been accepted as a given by both parties and the mass media, eclipsing attention to the main underlying cause, long-term cuts in both state and federal taxes and budgets for higher education that have decimated support to universities to control tuition costs and provide financial aid other than loans, like Pell Grants. There was at this time, however, also some momentum in California and other states to reverse tax cuts and cuts to funding of public higher and secondary education.

Conservative Rebuttals

I then assigned students to see what conservative counterstatements they could find to these liberal and left arguments, on the journalistic and scholarly levels. The first was a column, also published in 2004, in *National Review* (*NR*), and posted on *Town Hall*, by *NR* editor Rich Lowry, titled "Where's the Misery?" About claims like Reed's of sharp increases in tuition, Lowry asserted:

> Almost no one pays official tuition rates, and college tuition has become more affordable in recent years, not less. A report in *USA Today* found that the amount students pay public universities has fallen by a third since 1998. "In fact," according to the paper, "today's students have enjoyed the greatest improvement in college affordability since the GI Bill provided benefits for returning World War II veterans."

He continued, "It is positively raining college aid, meaning students are in a tight competition with the elderly over who can be more pampered by government.... Total federal and state financial aid hit a record $49 billion in 2003."

Lowry's causal analysis was almost the opposite of Reed's attributing tuition increases to reductions in revenue from government: "The game for universities is obvious—hike official tuition rates ever higher. Then everyone thinks students cannot afford college and plies them with more aid, which ends up lining the pockets of the schools. It's one of the great scams of our time."

Lowry concluded:

> The problem isn't that students hungry for knowledge are being frozen out from college, but the opposite. Marginal students take their generous aid and go to colleges that don't teach them. Eighty percent of universities aren't selective, e.g. more or less happy to accept anyone who shows up with a check. Only 37 percent of first-time freshmen graduate in four years, and only 60 percent graduate in six years. Universities are happy to take money from unprepared students and fail them right back out, or dumb down their standards to stay on the government-aid gravy train.

About half the students found Lowry's line of argument absurd and his tone offensive, in relation to their own situation (as well as to that of the "pampered" elderly), in which many have to work virtually full time to afford college. But the other half agreed with Lowry against Reed. This response puzzled me the first time I taught this material, until several such students admitted that they were from affluent families and on full, merit-based scholarships or loans, so their arguments amounted to, "I'm all right, Jack." Some also agreed with Lowry's account of slacker students, recounting stories of all those they knew who were just partying their way through college; but others took issue with this anecdotal evidence, arguing that such foolish students are the exception rather than the rule and that it is unfair to use them as a pretext for cutting access or financial aid to more motivated students who are poorer and unable to afford partying.

These discussions were another instance of the tendency of students to address issues in an egocentric manner, as well as of the tendency in American culture to reduce all social issues to personal ones. Most of the students could only view the issues here in terms of the individual experience and attitudes—largely self-interested—of themselves or those they knew, with little awareness of national economic and public policy exigencies. So we discussed the possible element of subjective bias in their responses, both conservative and liberal (as well as in my own as one whose income depends on the system that Lowry labels a scam), and I advised them to bend over backward to consider what elements of truth there may be in the other side's arguments, as well as to study broader and more impersonal social perspectives.

The next topic became what evidence Lowry presented to support his claims, in comparison to Reed's citation of sources like congressional committee studies and Smith and Szymanski's fully documented article. Lowry's only, vaguely cited, source was an article in *USA Today*. Some students were able to identify that, through Google, as "Tuition Burden Falls by a Third," by Rich Cauchon (28 June 2004). Here is one student's analysis of Lowry and Cauchon:

> Cauchon's article is less opinionated but not much better documented than Lowry's, citing only "a USA Today analysis," which I have not been able to locate on the Internet. Cauchon claims that students only pay 27% of the listed tuition prices ("Tuition Burden Falls by a Third"). As a college student who pays far more than 27% of the listed tuition price, I think the only way that this statistic is plausible is if it is an average in which athletic and other full-ride scholarships are considered.
>
> Lowry claims that financial aid is at all time high. However, he may be committing the half-truth fallacy, because this statistic does not consider a possible increase in numbers of students enrolled that would cause the total amount of aid to escalate, or the possibilities that financial aid (other than loans) has not risen in tandem with overall college costs—not only tuition but housing, food, clothing. and transportation—or that aid has lagged behind declining family income.
>
> Lowry and Cauchon do not say whether they include loans in financial aid and in the portion of nominal tuition that students do not directly pay. If loans *are* included, it is deceitful on their part not to say so, since liberals like Reed argue that students are graduating in a great amount of debt. In any case, both authors completely downplay the problem of student debt.
>
> In searching for Cauchon's article, I also found another article in *USA Today* two years later, by Mary Beth Marklein (25 Oct. 2006), which happens to flatly contradict much of what Cauchon and Lowry say, at least for the later two years, and which is based on a College Board report that was easy to locate. In contrast to Lowry and Cauchon, Marklein writes, "Median debt levels are 'almost certain' to have increased in recent years, the [College Board] report says, because neither grant aid nor family incomes have kept pace with cost hikes."
>
> Cauchon cites "new federal tax breaks and a massive increase in federal and state grants." But he later acknowledges the shift from Pell grants and other need-based scholarships to merit-based scholarships, which mainly benefit students from wealthier families. He notes that most of these increased breaks have benefited families earning $40,000 to $100,000 a year, but downplays the obvious decline in college access for families below that level, many of whose income is too low to be eligible for these tax breaks, and often too low to afford college at all.

Other topics in Lowry and Cauchon that my students identified as requiring verification through research include:

- What hard evidence is there that universities have unnecessarily raised tuition rates to solicit increased government funding to "line their pockets," presumably for the personal enrichment of administrators or faculty? (Leftists agree that much administrative waste and even fraud do occur, but the issues here are whether this is a specific source of it, and what share does not trickle down to students.)
- How much do universities profit from commissions from student loan agencies, and is there evidence that this is a common motive in their raising tuition?
- If only 37 percent of first-time freshmen graduate in four years, and only 60 percent graduate in six years, in how many cases are the primary causes student lassitude and faculty failure to teach them, rather than factors like financial hardship that Reed cites? (Do both Reed and Lowry commit the reductive fallacy?)
- What is the source and evidence for Lowry's figure of 80 percent of universities that "aren't selective" or for his claim that venality is the only or main reason that they "dumb down their standards"? If secondary schools are failing to prepare students for college, what choices do the colleges have?

Some support for Lowry might be found if there is evidence that colleges have dumbed down their standards in this period to attract more students to compensate for reduced government funds. Some leftists agree that universities "scam" students, but for the purpose of shortchanging undergraduates in favor of graduate education, faculty research (also a source of revenue from corporate and government grants, patents, etc.), and beefing up endowments invested on Wall Street—a revenue source universities have been forced increasingly to depend to further compensate for cuts in government funding, with disastrous consequences in the crash of 2008. So while conservatives play up universities' ties to government bureaucracies, leftists play up universities' increasing emulation of corporate managerial structure and practices.

Conservative Scholarship: Richard Vedder on College Costs

The next phase of the course was giving conservatives their best shot, at a more scholarly level of discuss than Lowry or Cauchon. I first referred students to a classic conservative elitist position opposed to equal social opportunity, as voiced by Allan Bloom in *The Closing of the American Mind*: "The university is, willy-nilly, in some sense aristocratic in both the conventional and natural senses of the term. It cannot, within broad limits, avoid being somewhat more accessible to the parents of means than to the children of the poor" (291). Few conservative sources are as forthrightly exclusionary as Bloom, though many seem tacitly to share his view.

The best-documented source that my students were able to find was Richard Vedder, an economics professor and director of the Center for College Affordability and Productivity at Ohio University in Athens. He is the author of *Going Broke By Degree: Why College Costs So Much*, funded and published by American Enterprise Institute's National Research Initiative (2004), and is a fellow at Heritage, which posted his lecture "The Real Costs of Federal Aid to Higher Education" on 12 Jan. 2007. He was also a member of the Spellings Commission on the Future of Higher Education in the administration of George W. Bush. He acknowledges mentors like Milton Friedman, William J. Bennett, and Charles Murray (coauthor of *The Bell Curve*, with its controversial views on racially inherited IQ). He has recently been a regular blogger on the economics of higher education for the *Chronicle of Higher Education*. So his work is a prototype of the products of the conservative counter-intelligentsia discussed previously.

Vedder's findings are, predictably, mirror opposites of leftist scholars', on key issues like this, in his Heritage Lecture: "There is little doubt in my mind—and I've run regressions to verify it—that the soaring financial aid, in part federally financed, has contributed somewhat to the escalation in college tuition costs." His work has the appearance of objective, scientific research, devoted to studying empirical data and drawing measured conclusions from it. But he, no less than Reed, has a partisan agenda, that of Reaganomic free market ideology, which students quickly perceived without prompting from me. Several of his arguments are substantial and their conclusions uncontroversial; some coincide with liberal or left ones, though he doesn't acknowledge that. Rather than exploring ways that the faults of universities might be corrected, however, he draws conclusions like this in his Heritage lecture: "As a long-term objective, the federal government should largely exit the higher education business. Shorter-term, lawmakers should oppose vast increases in student-aid programs." And, about his study on higher education in Michigan for a conservative think tank there, the Mackinac Center for Public

Policy: "It calls into question a growth strategy based on expansion of higher education. Indeed, other results included in the econometric estimation suggest that a better growth strategy would be to put the entire Michigan state government on a starvation diet in order to finance a reduction in the overall tax burden. While higher education expenditures are not growth-inducing, the evidence shows that tax reductions are." (Another paper published by this center is titled "Privatize the University of Michigan.")

An initial survey of Vedder's work in our class left most students bewildered about which side could be believed, though the more conservative students were inclined to declare Vedder the clear-cut winner because of all his facts and figures, while some liberals voiced skepticism about his research and reasoning. In the concluding month of class that was allocated to this study, those who wrote term papers on the topic (they had other options, on related topics) were able to get little further than summing up the opposing lines of argument and bodies of evidence supporting them, without going into extended evaluation of them. I settled for saying only that I hoped this topic of study helped to acquaint them with the dilemmas of opposing views and predictable rhetorical moves on the left and right. I refrained in class, out of fear of poisoning the well, from voicing my growing sense of the flaws in Vedder's work that started to emerge out of students' analyses. Since the last time I taught this class, I have undertaken this closer study as a prime exhibit of the scholarly and pedagogical problems I address in this book. One such problem is how far we can or should go in evaluating work like his with only lay economic knowledge, but with the basic tools of critical thinking and rhetorical analysis. (His public lectures and op-eds in papers like the *Wall Street Journal* are, after all, available online to undergraduates; the Heritage piece is made media-friendly with bulleted "talking points," while most of his book is accessible to general readers, aside from sections of economic jargon and data.) In other problems, I ask my readers whether my analysis and the conclusions I draw from it are adequately supported and fair-minded, or a premeditated hatchet job? Would it be prudent to use this as a point of departure in this unit of class study if I teach it again, or would it indeed be accurately perceived as poisoning the well? Would it be intellectually responsible *not* to make this analysis available to students as a point of departure, rather than leaving them at their own analytic level as an endpoint, in the interest of student-centered learning?

To begin with, to Vedder's credit, I and other liberals and leftists agree with many of his criticisms of university management. He is certainly right that universities deploy PR puffery to sell the public on their socioeconomic benefits, so that a degree of hype is to be expected in their reports, and that a good share of the funding they gain through poor-mouthing never gets to undergraduates in aid or instruction. He agrees with leftists in criticizing the rise of administrative bloat, self-perpetuating bureaucracy, and superstar faculty salaries upward of $250,000. (He does, however, play up faculty salaries more than the far higher ones of top administrators, whom he may be reluctant to criticize because their rationalization is that they deserve pay comparable to private-sector executives. And few professors in the humanities, at least in public universities, make anywhere near $250,000. My top salary was around $65,000, which is closer to the norm.) I obviously agree with his criticism of the rewards accruing to proliferation and specialization of faculty research in academic fields other than science, including "the five-hundredth article on *King Lear*," at the expense of civic education (*Going* 58). Other areas of agreement include criticism of the multiple corruptions of intercollegiate sports, the beefing up of endowments (which he interestingly proposes as a source for student loans in place of governmental ones), grade inflation, and the shift from need-based to merit-based financial aid, which he suggests is partly motivated by colleges' desire for prestige in mass media top-college rankings. This is the kind of common ground between conservative and liberal or leftist scholars that should serve as the basis for constructive dialogue, rather than perpetual polarization.

The biggest gap in Vedder's work, as in most of the other conservative critics of higher education, is his virtual silence on, in Lawrence Soley's title phrase, *The Leasing of the University: The Corporate Takeover of Academia*, also the subject of many recent books such as those by Aronowitz, Newfield, Readings, Schreker, and Washburn. My other criticisms of Vedder include a pattern throughout his work of lurching between purportedly scientific analysis of data and unsupported, politically partisan interjections, which even my conservative students perceived as biased. In this respect, his work is another example of my earlier suggestion that conservative culture warriors tend to confuse their own partisan opinions, if not dogmas, with objective truth. As a prime example, Vedder goes to great lengths to play up every possible cause for universities' economic decline and for rising tuition in recent decades, other than government budget cuts, which sharpened from 2000 to 2008 under Bushonomics and plunged even more after the crash of 2008—all presumably to his approval. In a chapter of *Going Broke* surveying these causes, budget cuts are reduced to one brief paragraph at the end, and he doesn't rank-order these statistically with the other causes. He plays up areas of wastefulness in university management, many of which are indisputable, but offers no evidence that they have exceeded the lag between unavoidable increases in operating costs and the declining level of government funding, for which a great deal of evidence is available. (See Sacks, *Tearing Down the Gates*; Newfield, *Unmaking the Public University*; Biemiller, "Over 20 Years, State Support for Public Higher Education Fell More than 25%"; according to Stan Katz's "Can We Afford State Colleges?" in the *Chronicle* in 2010, "Over the past generation we have moved from an environment in which states paid for 70 percent of cost and students paid 30 percent, to a situation in which those numbers have exactly reversed.") Nor does Vedder consider the extent to which some of public universities' questionable financial practices, like runaway expansion of subsidized research and speculative investments of endowments, may have been driven by this shortfall in government budgets, rather than being a justification for the latter as he argues.

The broader difference between Vedder and liberals on the causes of universities' growing financial problems lies in his Reaganomic core belief that nonprofit institutions simply are not motivated toward the cost-effectiveness and fiscal accountability of businesses. His book was published in 2004, so it is telling that he fails to mention the periodic cycles of business collapses and scandals like those in the savings and loan industry in the eighties or the Bacchanalian extravagances and creative accounting of Enron and other corporate giants that fell in the early 2000s. Have there been any scandals in American universities or any other public institutions remotely comparable to those cases, or to the even worse disasters of unaccountability in the top ranks of American business since then? His selective vision here is a nice instance of the item in my "Ground Rules for Polemicists" warning against weighing an ideal model of your own side against the worst actual practices of your opponents.

Vedder's most provocative thesis is that "soaring financial aid, in part federally financed, has contributed somewhat to the escalation in college tuition costs." (This phrase in his Heritage lecture comes a few pages after another version in which the adverb is not "somewhat" but "mightily.") In a 2005 *Wall Street Journal* op-ed, "Why Does College Cost So Much?" Vedder wrote, "Since 1994, financial-aid payments (mostly federal loans and grants) have risen by an extraordinary 11% a year. When someone else pays the bills, we become less sensitive to price." And in his Heritage lecture, he added, "The so-called student debt crisis would not exist if the federal government had not made it easy for 18-year-old students to borrow." These claims angered some of my students, who thought lumping loans together with grants was deceptive and pointed to Adoph Reed's data, in "Majoring in Debt," about the shift from government grants to high-interest loans; they argued that it is *they* who will be paying the bills for their loans long after they graduate, and they are having to work almost full time to get through school in addition—a point that Vedder neglects. He also neglects the shift from loans funded directly by government to private ones administered by banks, which amounts to a subsidy to those banks' profits in exchange for a reduction in government administrative costs. So banks too have acquired a stake in tuition increases.

In the *WSJ* op-ed he acknowledged, contrary to Lowry and Cauchon, "Tuition charges are rising faster than family income, an unsustainable trend in the long run.... Price-sensitive groups like low-income students and minorities are missing out." Apparently it is not so easy for *those* 18-year-olds to borrow, but Vedder does not dwell on this inconsistency or the one between his saying the rise of tuition is unsustainable and saying it's no problem because of ample financial aid. Such inconsistencies also recur throughout *Going Broke*, where at one point he acknowledges, "Much financial aid received by students from families of modest means comes in the form of loans, often putting the student in substantial debt early in life" (8). To be fair to Vedder, one of his points here is that the shift from need-based to merit-based scholarships and subsidized loans has made rich students richer and enabled them to pay higher tuition. To the extent that this shift has contributed to tuition increases, at the expense of poorer students, leftists would be quick to agree with him, but they are more inclined than he to investigate the political machinations behind this shift and seek ways to reverse it, rather than jettisoning public funding altogether. In any case, some conservatives jump from Vedder's point that subsidizing wealthier students drives up costs to the conclusion that there is no cost problem at all, in the manner of Rick Lowry crowing, "It is positively raining college aid."

In *Going Broke*, Vedder reiterates the claim that government has made too much easy money available to students, then he goes on to argue that the demand created by all that money has exceeded the supply of higher educational facilities; therefore, rising tuitions result through the law of supply and demand. I do not have the expertise to evaluate all of Vedder's statistical data and modes of economic analysis, but my lay impression is that he presents this analysis as an abstract hypothesis, with inadequate empirical evidence to support it. It seems to me, first, that he would need to present statistics showing cases where the level of financial aid has exceeded that of tuition and has outstripped it in growth rate, rather than vice versa, and, second, that he would need to present evidence of publicly funded universities explicitly raising tuition in response either to increases in financial aid or to shortage of facilities. I have found so such evidence in his works, in comparison to the flood of evidence showing tuition increases, cuts in financial aid, and shortage of facilities resulting directly from government budget cuts.

More importantly, it appears to me that a private-sector model of supply and demand is inapplicable to government-funded services, especially education. In principle, if student demand increases, say, for state universities, voters can approve of tax increases authorizing legislators to increase allocations to meet it, expanding and even creating new facilities as needed, as was commonplace in the two or three decades following World War II. Vedder apparently cannot acknowledge this option because it is anathema to the general tenets of supply-side economics that undergird his entire work and that play out in all his arguments about the waste of taxpayers' money on public education, versus his preferred option of cutting taxes and all government spending to stimulate spending in the private sector. So this line of argument leads back to the pros and cons of the basic liberal-left "trickle-up" line, that the more we spend, within judicious limits, on public-sector services like education or public health care, the more everyone benefits (the inverse of the conservative argument that the more money rich people make, the more trickles down to everyone else). In none of his work that I have seen does Vedder systematically weigh the evidence in support of these opposing views.

One of Vedder's most extensive arguments is that neither the teaching nor the research function of today's universities is economically or socially efficient, and that both might better be shifted to the private sector. His case here is skewed by some puzzling omissions. For example, he says little about professional graduate schools like medicine, law, public policy, business, and engineering—in their irreplaceable roles of credentialing, research and consulting, conferences, and multiple other services to professional corporations, government, and the military. A related lapse is in his account of the overall university research function, which is scarcely mentioned in his shorter pieces. In his book he minimizes its benefits to society and business, in the course of arguing for its privatization. His account gives little hint of the fact that is obvious from a glance at reports issued by any university's research and development office: that applied scientific and business research have become the tail that wags the dog of higher education. To the extent that federal and state governments fund that research, it is a giant taxpayer subsidy to the businesses that profit from it and the faculty entrepreneurs who can make millions from their research, as well as being a cash cow to universities that get their cut in "overhead" charges, on which they have been increasingly dependent as government budgets have been cut.

Vedder's argument for shifting the funding burden to the private sector disingenuously ignores what a bargain for businesses it is for taxpayers to be sharing their research expenditures, from which those businesses receive hefty returns. If they didn't, does Vedder think they would incur this expense? (During the Free Speech Movement at Berkeley in 1965, the Independent Socialist Club, to which I belonged, published a report on University of California regents' multiple conflicts of interest in campus research directly profiting their businesses; see *The Regents*). Some leftists would agree that this research should be taken over by businesses themselves and would further argue, as noted in the outline in chapter 8, that under the present system wealthy corporations and individuals should be happy to shoulder more of the tax burden for higher education, along with other public services, as minimal investment for high returns. One more odd twist is in Vedder's data showing that university research only accounts for a small percentage of national investment in research (thus, he argues, it is largely dispensable). In support he says, "Interestingly, federal funding of research by for-profit private sector organizations exceeded that of universities," and "much (nearly 20 percent) of basic research was done by nonprofit research institutes other than universities...or by the federal government" (*Going 121*). Whoa—is he arguing for directly giving the federal government and nonprofits even *more* money and power?

The thesis of Vedder's Michigan study, also developed in his book, is that "there is compelling and strong econometric evidence nationally that state appropriations for higher education do not have positive effects on economic growth as claimed by many university presidents." His paper and book, however, only provide two, extremely limited, supporting arguments. The first is that "roughly half the students entering four-year degree programs fail to graduate within six years. More appropriations may merely lead to small increases in enrollments among marginally qualified students who then fail to graduate." The unproven implications in this argument are (1) that appropriations spent on these students are wasted (without considering the money these students pay into the college and community as long as they are in school, or the intellectual benefits they may have derived from general education courses) and (2) as with Lowry, that failure to graduate is mainly attributable to lassitude rather than, as suggested above, inadequate secondary schools or financial obstacles like loan debt and having to work long hours at jobs.

In his Heritage lecture, he goes so far as to opine, "I think many of the kids going to college are innately superior to begin with, so the differential may have very little to do with what the college is doing," so presumably these superior students could gain access to professions and high-tech jobs without going to college. Aside from the hypothesis in the last clause (which is intriguing but probably not testable), "innate" means genetic, but nowhere does Vedder seriously consider the socioeconomic factors that discriminate in college access against poor students whose innate intelligence might equal that of wealthier ones. (Another unit of study in my course and textbook involves the conflicting arguments of Jonathan Kozol and William J. Bennett on the "savage inequalities," in Kozol's term, between property tax–based funding of wealthy, mainly white high schools and poor, mainly black ones—a topic that would seem pertinent to Vedder's study of higher education in Michigan, with its extensive poverty in inner cities and industrial suburbs like Flint impairing college preparation.)

Vedder's second line of argument in support of his sweeping claim that "state appropriations for higher education do not have positive effects on economic growth" was based on his studies that first showed no positive correlation between several states' expenditures on higher education and per capita personal income within those states, and that also showed a "brain drain" of out-migration by college graduates from some of the states he studied. A report on these studies by Andy Guess in *Inside Higher Education* (22 June 2007) was followed by critical comments about its methodology and reductionist causal analysis. In addition, these two correlations were an inadequate measure of all the economic *and civic* benefits of public universities that liberals claim in the lines of argument in chapter 8, few of whose points Vedder systematically factors in anywhere in his work.

All his tables and graphs here fly in the face of the commonsense experience of living anyplace in America where the local and state economy are wholly dependant on tax-funded universities, often by far the largest source of employment, business revenue, and taxes. Tennessee is among the poorer states and ones with lowest taxes (there is no state income tax), and antitax rants are the surest means to elected office and popularity in media like talk radio. But what would happen to the economy of Knoxville and Appalachian east Tennessee without the University, to say nothing of the three other largest enterprises—all government-funded—Smoky Mountain National Park, Tennessee Valley Authority, and Oak Ridge Nuclear Laboratory? According to a 2010 report in the *Knoxville News Sentinel* on a study of the economic impact of UT statewide, all the UT campuses bring in "at least $2.5 billion annually in income to the state and support more than 53,600 jobs." The study also shows the university generates "an estimated $237.7 million in state and local tax revenue." Moreover, "The figures are a conservative estimate because the study didn't take into consideration the benefits from creating an educated workforce, its research projects, and community outreach" (Harrington). Evidence like this has not prevented the state legislature from gutting the University's budget in the past decade, thereby in the liberal view killing the golden goose.

Vedder stacks the deck on several other key issues. In his *WSJ* column, he endorses some states' solutions for fiscal problems along free market lines, including "cutting down on the use of expensive tenured faculty." However, he says nothing there about the most grievous actual consequence of this policy, the shift of the teaching burden to adjuncts, with all its injustices to teachers and students alike. In his book, this problem is reduced to two brief "to be sure" asides. Vedder would seem to be caught here and elsewhere between his stated concern for undergraduate education and his belief in running universities even more like corporations than they already are, with an efficiency-expert eye on the bottom line. Like other conservatives, he denigrates current undergraduate curricula as a waste of taxpayers' money, but he has few recommendations for improving them, particularly toward civic literacy, rather than just pulling the plug on government funding altogether.

In his Heritage lecture, he said, "The notion that the government must provide funds to students to promote college attendance was not widely accepted before 1970, the era of greatest university growth. In the 1990s, the proportion of the American population going to college fell by one measure for the first time in well over a century.... Yet the federal financial aid programs for college students grew dramatically during this period." In startling contrast, Wesleyan University president William M. Chace claimed,

"During the most recent period for which good figures are available [from 1972 to 2005], more young people entered the world of higher education than at any time in American history" (1). And Sam Tanenhaus wrote in the *New York Times Book Review* in 2010, "Between 1970 and 2000, the percentage of college graduates in the population at large had more than doubled" (27). Glaring omissions here by Vedder include, in contradiction to his first sentence above, the G. I. Bill in 1944 (which he reduces to a brief "to be sure" clause) and the National Defense Education Act in 1958, which he doesn't mention at all. Another omission is the low cost of tuition in public universities prior to 1970. In one of the first implementations of Reaganomics, as governor from 1967–1975, Ronald Reagan imposed tuition at the University of California for the first time in its century of existence, while slowing increases in funding for universities and financial aid; he also made it clear that this was a punitive measure against those ungrateful students who waged the Free Speech Movement at Berkeley—see Schrag, *Paradise Lost*, and more recently, "From Master Plan to No Plan: The Slow Death of Public Higher Education," by Bady and Konczal.

These are among the many indications of Vedder's dubious use of history. His Heritage lecture asserts, "Literacy was high in the United States in 1850 even though the majority of schooling was still privately funded. The notion that government funding was somehow necessary to promote high levels of educational access is historically untrue." But he says nothing here about the Morrill Act of 1862 establishing land-grant universities nationwide, and he only mentions it once, glancingly, in *Going Broke*.

In the introduction to *Going Broke*, Vedder considers the liberal argument that "universities have possible 'spillover' effects, benefits that accrue to people other than the providers or recipients of university services. A well-educated population, for example, will likely make more informed decisions about public policies, individuals to elect to public office, and so forth, leading to better governance." But this is followed by, "Yet it can be argued that colleges have negative spillover effects as well. Campus riots and disorders harm innocent third parties. 'Politically correct' efforts by universities to stifle free expression can actually reduce discourse and disrupt the orderly communications that make democracy work" (xx). Later he adds, "Some of the well-publicized problems of universities, such as the repression of free speech, alcohol-induced campus riots, and excesses of college athletics, almost certainly weaken public political support for higher education funding" (37).

But he presents no evidence in support of any of these "almost-certain" assertions, nor does he try to factor them into his cost-benefit statistics.

He often makes the common rhetorical move (I probably do it at times in this book too) of conceding a possible point to the opposition, in a "to be sure" or "it can be argued, of course" aside—as in Vedder's nods to the benefits of higher education or to the adjunct problem—prior to presenting your side's contrary position, which is obviously the privileged one, but then never coming back to make a balanced judgment between the two. In the above passage we are left with the implication that "alcohol-induced" riots and PC (somehow linked by innuendo) are so widespread as to justify draconian cuts in government funding of college education, including for civic literacy. He also tosses in, among the "diminishing returns" of public investment: "The emphasis in the humanities and social sciences on race, class, and gender issues has led to a disproportionate amount of interest in these topics relative to others" (*Going* 58). But he again offers no econometric study of expenditures on or curricular prevalence of these issues relative to universities' overall fiscal outlays. He similarly criticizes what he considers wasteful affirmative action and diversity programs "that exist to ensure a politically correct racial and ethnic mix to the student body," commenting, "To the extent that elimination of affirmative action police [*sic*] in university communities leads to a reduction in minority admissions, it might well also lead to improved retention rates and a decline in the highly inefficient practice of admitting unqualified students who then fail to make the academic grade" (*Going* 184). Does this suggest a hidden racial agenda in the "slacker student" arguments of other conservatives like Lowry—a bait-and-switch strategy in which sentiment against middle-class "Animal House" types can be turned covertly toward excluding the poor and minorities? An article in 2010 by Jacques Steinberg in the *New York Times* about the arguments of Vedder and allied economists like Robert Lerman, notes, "At the very least, they could be accused of lowering expectations for some students. Some critics go further, suggesting that the approach amounts to educational redlining, since many of the students who drop out of college are black or non-white Hispanics." Charles Murray and some other conservatives have documented a case for this line of argument explicitly in regard to race, but Vedder does not, nor does he cite other sources that do.

Nowhere does Vedder consider the case that the function of liberal education as a Socratic gadfly to a business-dominated society merits public funding precisely because of its bottom-line impracticality. In another to-be-sure concession, he acknowledges "universities' legitimate role as refuges for unpopular ideas and heretical thought." But his on-the-other-hand example is the alleged abuse of that role by politically correct leftists, presumably suppressing the heretical thoughts of capitalist economics and American patriotism—for which his only evidence is two fragments from letters to the editor in the *Wall Street Journal* (*Going* 213). Again, his implication here is that the crimes of the academic left are so vast as to justify defunding public higher education altogether—surely a gross example of throwing out the baby with the bathwater.

Vedder's bottom-line argument, in two senses, supports businesses taking over university teaching and research, but he fails to ask whether businesses would be motivated to fund liberal and civic education at colleges other than the elite ones that their executives' children attend. His only passage touching on this point is an account of his conversations with William J. Bennett, who is a privatization advocate (and corporate consultant) in K-12 education but who does worry about the fate of college departments like classics under privatization, and Milton Friedman, who assured Vedder, "I think we can say that if the market won't support a classics department, I have very little doubt that private beneficence would do so" (*Going* 200–1). More importantly, Vedder never considers that "beneficent" businesses paying the piper would have the power to call the tune in suppressing "unpopular ideas and heretical thought" against business interests by teachers, students, and researchers. Is it overly cynical to surmise that such suppression is in fact part of the conservative agenda? Isn't it conservatives themselves who insist that businesses shouldn't finance activities opposed to their interests in government, education, media, or elsewhere? Conservative ideologues like Grover Norquist are quite explicit about their strategy to "crush the structures of the left" by dismantling government and public employment. Vedder's final solution is to privatize all higher education and fund it through a student voucher system, and my arguments against his position here are equally applicable to conservatives' motives for pushing privatization and vouchers in K-12 education. (For more negative accounts of the social costs of privatization in the entire economy of the United States and England since the 1980s, see Judt, *Ill Fares*, and Frank, *The Wrecking Crew*.)

In conclusion, Vedder's body of work is admirably wide-ranging and challenging, but it ultimately amounts to a smokescreen obscuring any acknowledgment of the case that supply-side economics has been a prime factor in the decline of American higher education, which in turn has contributed to the decline of the entire American economy in the wake of three decades of Reaganomics. Vedder's disproportionate fixation on the pernicious influence of the academic left and his general inability to restrain his unsupported, partisan opinions cast doubt on his statistical methodology and findings that purport to demonstrate objectively the deficiencies of public higher education. At one point, he says, "At the very minimum, more research by truly objective scientists into these questions is needed" (*Going* 143). You said it!

To be sure, I used the "to be sure" move in the last paragraph in concluding that the positive aspects of Vedder's work are outweighed by the negative ones, but I hope I have adequately supported that conclusion, not just asserted it. And I hope readers will grant that I have avoided what Lynne Cheney termed "name-calling and invective," on the level of David Horowitz deriding Michael Lind's *Up from Conservatism* as "a pathetic rant," and a "reprehensible, gutter-sniping book." I invite Vedder and his allies to respond to my analysis or, better yet, to engage in extended personal dialogue about these conflicts. And if I have the opportunity to teach this material again, I might use my critique of Vedder as a point of departure for students to find the best conservative counterarguments they can.

In 2011, Vedder became a regular blogger for the *Chronicle of Higher Education*. The *Chronicle* permitted me to write a blog in response to some of his positions that I have addressed here, titled: Higher Education: Golden Goose or Dead Duck?" Before it posted, I emailed him saying that I hoped my posting would prompt a continuing dialogue between us. He replied favorably and posted a courteous response on 19 Apr. 2011. However, neither the *Chronicle* nor Vedder complied with my request for further online exchanges. Here is his reply.

UNIVERSITIES IN AMERICA: A REPLY TO A CRITIC
Richard Vedder

> As a rule, I don't respond to critics. I do my blogs, and let the audience carry on a dialogue, while I move on to new topics. But last week, before posting on this site, Prof. Donald Lazere of Cal Poly, San Luis Obispo, wrote a nice e-mail saying he was writing a critical piece on my work and asking that I comment. It was a respectful and kind e-mail, and upon reading his piece I thought I would try to delineate some areas of where persons of good will can seriously differ on issues.

I will comment on seven statements in Prof. Lazere's well written post.

Talking first about questions that both Frank Donoghue and I have been blogging about, Lazere says "such questions show a typical American tendency to restrict discussion of large social issues to the level of personal attitudes and options... rather than directing attention to the needs of society at large." To me, for the most part our "society" is the sum of its parts. The notion that there are collective goals independent of individual needs is prominent in Prof. Lazere's way of thinking, less so in mine. If there are large "spillover effects" of higher education, the emphasis on the macro picture has some validity; despite conventional wisdom, I think those spillover effects tend to be exaggerated, and some of them are negative, not positive.

"I see a strange disconnect between Vedder's views and... reports like Karin Fischer's... indicating that the U.S. will 'soon face an acute shortage of scientists... which could undermine the country's global lead'" Fischer's report reflects conventional wisdom, but does that make it correct? If we had huge job shortages in the STEM disciplines, pay in those areas would be soaring relative to others—but on the whole, it is not. While the term "STEM scam" may be a bit strong, the alleged STEM shortage is minimally exaggerated in terms of causing economic problems for our nation.

"[O]verwhelming evidence shows that taxes spent in support of public higher education are one of the most profitable investments society can make." Again, conventional wisdom. Where is the rigorous evidence? Running regressions trying to explain interstate variations in economic growth in terms of public higher education spending, I get either negative or neutral results—higher spending is not associated with higher growth. This may be incorrect, but prove it rigorously using empirical evidence.

"As individuals, most college graduates earn more, pay more taxes, and are healthier, better informed citizens." The statement is true. But the issue is: Does going to college make people healthier? Are they enough healthier to justify the costs associated with going to college and foregoing work in the real world for several years? My guess is that most persons who go to college would have been healthier than most high-school graduates if they dropped out of college after one day—because of different personal traits.

"Americans increasingly need a college degree to get a job at a middle-class level of income." Two points here. First, an increasing proportion of college grads appear to be taking relatively low-paying jobs historically held by high-school graduates, for similar or modestly enhanced amounts of pay. Second, the vast growth in college graduates has created an applicant pool that allows employers to exclude noncollege aspirants. The growing supply of college grads has created the higher credentials now required for many jobs, not a vast increase in the skills required in many of the jobs.

"Vedder and many...conservative polemicists seem little interested in access for all to education in citizenship...thinking it should be exclusive to the innately superior aristocratic elite." I am not sure what 'education in citizenship' is, but the notion that there is a body of knowledge that binds citizens together and promotes national unity and purpose I can broadly accept. I wonder, however, whether colleges teach that body of knowledge much any more (and I am not alone in wondering about that). Even if colleges do adequately teach this, I wonder whether the non-college attendees would benefit much from it if they were in college. A vast portion of the increments to the college population in modern time do not even graduate, because "higher" education is just that—it implies a level of rigor, cognitive skill, and discipline that not all Americans have. If that makes me an elitist, so be it. I prefer the term "realist."

"Recognition of the myriad benefits to society of public higher education lay behind its long-standing, tuition-free status in European and other countries." High-tuition America, I suspect, has on the whole a higher quality of life than no-tuition Europe (look at immigration statistics). The great spillover effects of public education have not brought greater wealth or well-being to the countries of Europe, I suspect (to be sure, there are many other factors that impact on life's quality).

Enough is enough. Variety is the spice of life. Each of us has a different take on things. I think I am right, Prof. Lazere thinks he is. It is great we can both freely express our views, and let our audiences decide which they prefer.

10

THE RADICAL HUMANISTIC CANON

> This is what you shall do: Love the earth and the sun and the animals, despise riches, give alms to every one that asks, stand up for the stupid and crazy, devote your income and labor to others, hate tyrants, argue not concerning God.... Re-examine all you have been told at school or church or in any book, dismiss whatever insults your own soul, and your very flesh shall be a great poem.
>
> Walt Whitman, "Preface to 1855 Edition of *Leaves of Grass*" (*Complete Poetry* 415–16)

> Ideals are good, but people are sometimes not so good. You must try to look up at the big picture.
>
> Yossarian rejected the advice with a skeptical shake of his head. "When I look up, I see people cashing in. I don't see heaven or saints or angels. I see people cashing in on every decent human impulse and every human tragedy."
>
> Joseph Heller, *Catch-22* (455)

In the polarizations of the American culture wars since the 1960s, leftists have become positioned as critics of the established canon of literary and humanistic classics, and conservatives as its defenders. Many on both sides are ridiculously simplistic—leftists who would ban the very words "classic" and "great" in the cause of multicultural egalitarianism or poststructuralist anti-foundationalism; conservatives who are convinced that the classics are ageless monuments of political and moral propriety, and that everyone on the left is either a mindless moral relativist or a Stalinist commissar. My focus here is countering conservative accounts, although it can also be reversed to counter leftist ones that show ignorance of the oppositional elements in the humanistic tradition or are too quick to charge that they are eclipsed by the hegemonic ones. I reiterate that this is not meant to diminish the value of judicious canon revision—especially in recognition of groups that have been shut out of conventional histories—or of critique of the biases in the classics, but only to compensate for the gaps in some revisionist accounts.

In 2002 William J. Bennett published *Why We Fight: Moral Clarity in the War on Terrorism,* in rebuttal to liberal critics of American responses to the 9/11 attacks. He recited the familiar litany of current American high school and college students' civic illiteracy, then charged:

> The problem...is that those who are *un*patriotic are, culturally, the most influential among us....[They are] the diversity-mongers, the multiculturalists, the relativists, and the plain old anti-Americans....[They are] sustained by a cultural and moral relativism that, in place of teaching students to love their country and be prepared to make sacrifices for it, overlays their abysmal ignorance of its history with a "sophisticated" understanding of America as but one cultural option among many of equal worth, and then replaces the impulse to love and defend it with detachment, indifference, or shame. (141–46 passim)

My book has made clear that I share Bennett's concern over civic illiteracy, as well as his criticism of the excessive insistence by many progressives on diversity; so I would hope to gain his and other conservatives' cooperation in addressing our common goals. However, his rhetoric was symptomatic of the way that conservatives have framed these issues in ways calculated to preclude bipartisan cooperation. The appearance of high-minded appeal to reason and common values is belied in the wording of nearly every phrase, in ways I have analyzed in my critique of Bennett's allies in earlier chapters. Like them, Bennett suppresses consideration of other obvious factors in civic illiteracy like the financial pressures generated by corporate America and tax-cutting Republicans, defunding public education and forcing students to forego critical liberal education in favor of job training and to get through school as quickly as possible to minimize skyrocketing costs and debt. (Bennett also coyly avoids mentioning a conflict of interest in the millions he has made as a promoter of for-profit school corporations.)

As for patriotism, I believe that I and most of the academic leftists I know love our country as much as Bennett and his allies in the Republican elite, few of whom have ever made any visible sacrifice for their country, and many of whom, as Heller puts it, are well-practiced in "cashing in on every decent human impulse and every human tragedy," including corporate and political profiteering from 9/11 and the wars in Iraq and Afghanistan. We are just more inclined toward Camus's view, "I love my country too much to be a nationalist" (*Resistance* 4), and Mark Twain's denunciation of the slogan "Our Country, Right or Wrong" in the Spanish-American War: "In a republic, who is 'the Country'?... Is it the Government which is for the moment in the saddle? It cannot be its prerogative to determine what is right and what is wrong, and decide who is a patriot and who isn't.... It is in the thousand [individual citizens] that command is lodged; *they* must determine what is right and what is wrong; they must decide who is a patriot and who isn't" (*Letters* 108–9).

As Louis Menand said in his review of Bennett's book in the *New Yorker*, "When people start talking about moral clarity, you know that mystification has set in. The world is never clear, and to reduce it to binaries—good and evil, right and wrong, with us or against us—is to promote blind faith over understanding" ("Faith" 103). Conservatives like Bennett, Cheney, and ACTA assert that the failure to indoctrinate the young with patriotic zeal and belief in the superiority of our country over all others leads toward apathy, anarchy, and capitulation to foreign enemies. But aren't there also many historical instances in which an excess of national chauvinism, as in "*Deutschland Über Alles*," has caused those nations' demise? Even many of my conservative students say that what turned them off in high school was the infantilizing, goody-goody view of America in history and civics classes that was clearly at odds with their sense of reality. They are far more responsive to Graffian pedagogy that fosters debate between conservative and progressive viewpoints on history and politics, and that teaches the virtue of questioning authority. The University of Tennessee has a mission statement reading, "Whatever your academic interests, whatever your degree, you have been taught to think for yourself, reflect for yourself, and reason for yourself." When I show students this statement, they shake their head incredulously at its inconsistency with the conservatively conformist course matter and pedagogy most have encountered.

Bennett's *Why We Fight* continued:

> Many of our children... are taught from the earliest grades that there are no differences among cultures and that ours deserves no preference. They're lucky; older children learn that Americans have much to apologize for, having stolen the land from its native inhabitants, despoiled the environment, enslaved an entire population, made off with territory belonging to Mexico, mistreated women, exploited the laboring classes for the benefit of robber barons, discriminated against immigrants and people of color, and wantonly sent young men to die in imperialist wars against the defenseless and poor of the third world.

At the college level, one looks mostly in vain for correctives to this teaching. (147)

Yet Bennett never gets around to refuting any of these charges, most of which by now are beyond much dispute. A provocative book might well be written in refutation, and I hoped that Bennett's venture into writing history in *America: The Last Best Hope* would provide it, through a point-by-point response to left scholars like Howard Zinn, Noam Chomsky, William Appleman Williams, and James Loewen. But that book was a disappointment even as a conservative polemic. Bennett actually tried so gingerly to be evenhanded that he granted more to liberal views than conservative ones on the above issues.

Bennett did acknowledge in *Why We Fight*, "We have certainly had our failures, some of them shameful. But never once, I think, have we lost sight of our moral ideals, which is why, time and time again, we have succeeded in confronting, overcoming, and transcending the stains on our record, the stain of slavery foremost among them. Who among the nations can enter a similar claim?" This is rich in what Ohmann, in "Doublespeak and Ideology in Advertising," calls the homogenizing "we," recalling the joke about the Lone Ranger and Tonto whose punch line is, "What you mean 'we,' Paleface?" These are also meaningless formulations in terms of any evenhanded, comprehensive weighing of the historical record, which is never this final but always in contention. By the way, is ours the only country that abolished slavery, didn't several do so before us (most significantly Mexico, provoking Texas slaveholders into the Mexican American War), and haven't the ongoing consequences of slavery been more severe here?

Bennett's conclusion addressed "educators, and at every level. The defect can only be redressed by the reinstatement of a thorough and honest study of our history, undistorted by the lens of political correctness and pseudosophisticated relativism. This is not jingoism; it is a call to repudiate the mind-set that has encased the teaching of our history in relativist and anti-American myth and to replace it with a genuine inquiry into fact and a genuine openness to debate. I, for one, am hardly in doubt as to the outcome" (149–50). Well, I, for one, and many leftist educators I know would be delighted to join in that genuine inquiry and debate, but we have encountered no willingness by Bennett or the leading conservative organizations to cooperate in any such project. So in response to his call for genuine debate, I offer the following counterpart to Bennett's accounts here and in his best-known work, *The Book of Virtues*, and invite him to respond in kind, ideally in a symposium sponsored by one of the foundations that finance his enterprises. Many of the works I cite—most by dead white males—are standards in traditional Western Civilization courses, literary history surveys, and textbook anthologies that I taught, with delight, for many years.

THE BOOK OF SKEPTICAL VIRTUES

From this same sheet of paper on which he has just written the sentence against an adulterer, the judge steals a piece for a love letter to his colleague's wife.... This is the way men behave. We let laws and precepts go their way, we keep to another.... Human wisdom never yet came up to the duties that it had prescribed for itself, and if it had come up to them, it would prescribe itself others beyond which it would ever aspire and pretend, so hostile to consistency is our human condition.

Michel de Montaigne (1533–1592), *Essays* 493–95

I believe in the development of a critical, skeptical, humorous habit of mind, the development of a liberally educated consciousness, a sensitivity to nuances and unstated implications, an ability to read between the lines and to hear undertones and overtones, for the sake of political and social enlightenment and for the sake of our personal enlightenment and pleasure as individuals.

J. Mitchell Morse, *The Irrelevant English Teacher*

Education is the process of moving from cocksure ignorance to thoughtful uncertainty. Proverb

The trouble ain't that people are ignorant, it's just that they "know" so much that just ain't so.

Josh Billings, 19th Century American humorist.

Everything spiritual and valuable has a gross, revolting parody, which looks exactly like it. Only unremitting judgment can distinguish between them.

Jonathan Swift, paraphrased by William Empson

Question with boldness even the existence of a God; because, if there is one, He must more approve of the homage of reason, than that of blindfolded fear.... Read the Bible, then, as you would read Livy or Tacitus.

Thomas Jefferson, "Letter to Peter Carr" (*Writings* 903)

In 1938, Virginia Woolf [in *Three Guineas*] proposed one of the most exacting definitions I know. Asked what kind of freedom would advance the fight against fascism and its enduring allies, racism, colonialism, and sexism, she replied, "Freedom from unreal loyalties.... You must rid yourself of pride of nationality in the first place; also of religious pride and those unreal loyalties that spring from them."

Margo Jefferson, "Unreal Loyalties."

Skepticism is defined as questioning all beliefs and apparent facts in an open-minded, rational pursuit of truth, accepting nothing just on faith, authority, community, or majority opinion. Skepticism is not synonymous with cynicism, which is defined as contempt for standards of honesty or morality, especially in behavior that hypocritically exploits those standards. In other words, skepticism is valuable in questioning the sincerity of public figures who, for example, might claim to speak for belief in patriotism or religion, while cynically exploiting those beliefs, or one like Bennett who cashes in on writings like *The Book of Virtues* by spending his profits gambling millions and staying in VIP suites in Las Vegas casinos. CHEAP SHOT! AD HOMINEM! —conservatives will cry, but is it unreasonable to hold those who posture as guardians of public virtue accountable for practicing what they preach? Montaigne drily comments on "those venerable souls exalted by the ardor of devotion and religion to a constant and conscientious meditation on divine things, who...disdain to apply themselves to our beggarly, fleeting, and ambiguous comforts.... Between ourselves, these are things that I have always seen to be in remarkable agreement: supercelestial thoughts and subterranean conduct" (601). Montaigne's three volumes of essays conclude, "So it is no use for us to mount on stilts, for on stilts we must still walk with our own legs. And on the loftiest throne in the world we are still sitting on our own behind" (602). Similarly, nearly every year brings a new example of politicians or clergymen—alternately Republicans and Democrats—who advertise a self-righteous public image but who fall victim to Montaigne's axiom of "supercelestial thoughts and subterranean conduct."

THE BOOK OF DISSENTING VIRTUES

In *Why We Fight* and *America*, Bennett gives short shrift to the rich American heritage of dissent, epitomized in Thoreau's "Civil Disobedience": "Why does it [government] not cherish its wise minority?...Why does it not encourage its citizens to be on the alert to point out its faults?....Why does it always crucify Christ, and excommunicate Copernicus and Luther, and pronounce Washington and Franklin rebels?" (*Walden and Other Writings* 644).

In a *Newsweek* column titled "The Voices of Dissent," following 9/11, David Gates wrote: "Most writers are dissenters by nature—and dissent, by definition, implies an orthodoxy that's getting its way. The hell of it is, history often proves dissenting writers weren't crazy. Now, had Robert Lowell rather than Robert McNamara been LBJ's secretary of Defense...oh well." Gates went on to defend writers of fiction like Barbara Kingsolver, Arundhati Roy, Susan Sontag, and Alice Walker who spoke out against the American military response to 9/11:

> Sontag, the essayist and author of the National Book Award-winning "In America: A Novel," drew a bizarrely fierce reaction for a 473-word New Yorker piece. Her main point was that the government was talking down to us. "They consider their task to be...confidence-building and grief management. Politics, the politics of a democracy—which entails disagreement, which promotes candor—has been replaced by psychotherapy." For this, she was called a "traitor" and a "moral idiot [by William J. Bennett] on ABC's "Nightline."

Sontag's *New Yorker* article began, "The disconnect between last Tuesday's monstrous dose of reality and the self-righteous drivel and outright deceptions being peddled by public figures and TV commentators is startling, depressing. The voices licensed to follow the event seem to have joined together in a campaign to infantilize the public." She specified complex issues in American foreign policy pertinent to 9/11, then commented, "But the public is not being asked to bear much of the burden of reality. The unanimously applauded, self-congratulatory bromides of a Soviet Party Congress seemed contemptible. The unanimity of the sanctimonious, reality-concealing rhetoric spouted by American officials and media commentators in recent days seems, well, unworthy of a mature democracy" ("Talk" 24). Is this the language of moral idiocy, Mr. Bennett, or was your attack on Sontag precisely "self-righteous drivel" that whitewashed any element of fault in American foreign policy in the Middle East or elsewhere?

Bennett's *Why We Fight* was a slapdash effort thrown together without documentation or even an index, mainly recycling the tired conservative culture-war script and rhetorical tricks like attacking straw man opponents and cherry-picking quotations out of context from the usual leftist suspects like Chomsky. Bennett does make an effort toward substantive defense of American foreign policy in the Middle East prior to and in response to 9/11, and he laudably acknowledges, "What is truth on one side of the Pyrenees is error on the other, exclaimed the French philosopher Blaise Pascal in the seventeenth century...But relativity, [Peter] Berger reminds us, is not the same thing as relativism. Although we cannot assume that our values are universally shared, we need not conclude either that our deepest values lack universal validity or that *no* values are universally shared" (64). Well said, but not very applicable to any specific political or cultural dispute past or present, such as the examples he follows it with of defense of the American incursion in Afghanistan and alliance with Israel, which he supports with only glib, one-sided assertions with no substantive evidence or evaluation of contradictory evidence by opposing scholars and journalists. That is all too typical of the modus operandi of Bennett and his associates, who may have the credentials to meet liberal or left scholars and journalists on the same field of intellectual disputation but who choose instead to play to the public and media with infantilizing sound bites and manichean oversimplifications.

The Book of Religious Skepticism

Bennett and other conservative Christians proclaim that the American founders were devout Christians and advocates of free enterprise, and they claim that the Republican Party champions a return to their values; but these claims are debatable and often either ignorant or dishonest. I submit that the Puritans and founders of the republic would be considered dangerous radicals, even subversives, by today's Republicans. In *America*, Bennett cites Puritan leader John Winthrop's foundational 1635 sermon on the ship Arbella, "A Model of Christian Charity," with its exhortation to the Massachusetts Bay Colony to be "a city on a hill" of Christian virtue. But he does not cite Winthrop's actual model of charity:

> For this end, we must be knit together in this work as one man. We must entertain each other in brotherly affection, we must be willing to abridge ourselves of our superfluities, for the supply of other's necessities. We must uphold a familiar commerce with each other in all meekness, gentleness, patience and liberality. We must delight in each other, make other's condition our own, rejoice together, mourn

together, labor and suffer together, always having before our eyes our commission and community in the work, our community as members of the same body.... But if our hearts shall turn away, so that we will not obey, but shall be seduced, and worship other gods, our pleasures and profits, and serve them; it is propounded unto us this day, we shall surely perish out of the good land whither we pass over this vast sea to possess it. (*Winthrop Papers* 18–19).

What's all this about abridging our luxuries to care for others' necessities, about laboring and suffering together for the common good of the community? Let's face it, Mr. Bennett, John Winthrop was a socialist if not a communist, and all the New Testament passages he cites for support suggest that Jesus Christ was too. Do you and today's Republican leaders sacrifice your pleasures and profits to care for the needy, or advocate government tax policies toward these ends? Did you abridge your superfluities when you were gambling millions or amassing your portly physique? Are meekness, gentleness, and humility words that you would use to describe yourself, George Bush, Richard or Lynne Cheney, Rush Limbaugh, Bill O'Reilly, Ann Coulter, Michelle Bachman, or Glenn Beck? In one of his last speeches as president, Ronald Reagan cited Winthrop, but said that he pictured Winthrop's city on the hill as "a city with free ports that hummed with commerce" ("Farewell"). Mr. Bennett, will you admit that your revered president Reagan was either lying or deluded?

As for religion in the revolutionary period, Hector St.-John Crèvecoeur's "What Is An American" (1782) approvingly observed that the rise of free enterprise was directly proportionate to the decline of religious zeal, to the point of general "religious indifference": "How does it concern the welfare of the country, or of the province at large, what this man's religious sentiments are, or really whether he has any at all?" (*Letters* 66). Jefferson similarly wrote, "The legitimate powers of government extend to such acts only as are injurious to others. But it does me no injury for my neighbor to say there are twenty gods, or no god. It neither picks my pocket nor breaks my leg" (Jefferson, *Writings* 285). Ben Franklin waffled a great deal on religion, but his *Autobiography* clearly states that after an orthodox Christian youth, he "soon became a thorough deist" (Franklin, *Writings* 1359). In a deathbed letter to Reverend Ezra Stiles, he expressed doubts about the divinity of Christ or justice in an afterlife, concluding nonchalantly, "I expect soon an opportunity to know the truth" (Franklin, *Writings* 1179–80). There was no waffling or ambiguity in Thomas Paine's *The Age of Reason*: "I do not believe in the creed professed by the Jewish church, by the Roman church, by the Turkish church, by the Protestant church, nor by any church I know of. My mind is my own church.... All national institutions of churches, whether Jewish, Christian, or Turkish, appear to me no other than human inventions set up to terrify and enslave mankind, and monopolize power and profit" (Paine, *Collected Writings* 660).

Certainly the evidence is mixed on the religion of the founders, "The Declaration of Independence," and the Constitution, and there is ample room for informed disagreement. (Bennett's *America* is disappointingly superficial on the subject.) However, the torrent of polemics from the Christian right in America contains a disgraceful quotient of untruths, half-truths, omissions, quotations out of context or wholly fabricated, as in the influential book and Web empire of David Barton, author of *The Separation Myth*, which any self-respecting Christian intellectual should disown.[1] Worse yet is Bennett's hero Rush Limbaugh, who extols greed, demonizes the poor, and flaunts his sybaritic lifestyle while manipulating the ignorance of his Christian followers with assurances in his books like, "Don't believe the conventional wisdom of our day that claims [the Founding Fathers] were anything but orthodox, Bible-believing Christians" (*See* 82). My favorite Limbaugh howler on religion reads: "Is it possible that supply-side economics could have existed before the 1980s? Yes. Read the story of Joseph and Pharoah in Genesis 41. Following Joseph's suggestion (Gen 41:34), Pharoah reduced the tax on Egyptians to 20% during the 'seven years of plenty' and the 'Earth brought forth in heaps' (Gen 41:47)" (*See* 80). One has to be impressed with Rush's gall in figuring that his legion of religious conservative followers were so gullible they'd swallow this lie about one of the best-known passages in the Bible. Joseph's advice, of course, had nothing to do with taxes, but with the government laying up 20 percent of crops during the years of plenty, to consume during lean years—a rather socialistic imposition on free enterprise, we might think. Mr. Bennett, how do passages like this make you feel about your blurb for Limbaugh's first book?: "Full of verve, humor, and insight. Everyone knows Rush Limbaugh is a national phenomenon. But he is more than that; he is a national resource."

The Book of Anticapitalist Virtues

One constant conservative talking point is that vociferous criticism of American capitalism began with the "adversary culture" in the twentieth century and especially the 1960s. But I am sure Bennett and the others know that, with a few exceptions like Alexander Hamilton or inconsistencies like those of the transcendentalists, most American intellectuals and artists—like those in other countries—have typically detested corporate capitalism and the business ethos of philistines, Robber Barons, and Mencken's booboisie. As lefty lyricist E. Y. Harburg put it in his exuberantly socialistic *Finian's Rainbow* in 1947, Adam and Eve

> Begat the babbits of the bourgeoisie,
> Who begat the misbegotten GOP. (103)

Finian's "When the Idle Poor Become the Idle Rich" also proclaims that on that day, "You won't know your banker from your *but*ler." (84)[2]

If conservatives wanted to mount a serious critique of anticapitalism, it would need to go much farther back in American history, say to Winthrop's "Model of Christian Charity," and dig much deeper than cheap shots at the sixties counterculture and tenured radicals. When pressed on economic history, conservatives reply, well, the first Puritans may have been socialists, but their model didn't take roots and was replaced by that of free enterprise and private property, as advocated by the eighteenth-century founders. Not exactly. When writers like Jefferson, Franklin, and Crèvecoeur praised free enterprise, they meant individual farms or trades, not the modern usage of corporate enterprise free from government regulation. When they lauded "industry," they meant individual industriousness, not corporate industries. Thus Crèvecoeur emphasized in "What Is An American," "Here there are...no great manufacturers employing thousands, no great refinements of luxury.... We are all animated with the spirit of an industry which is unfettered and unrestrained, because each person works for himself" (*Letters* 40–41). And by private property, they meant ownership of one's own house, farm, or trade, not private ownership through stocks and bonds of giant corporations that exert overpowering influence over government—one of the most insidious deceptions in modern public discourse, underlying court decisions like Citizens United equating corporations with individuals.

In fact, Jefferson wrote in 1816, "I hope we shall crush in its infancy the aristocracy of our monied corporations which dare already to challenge our government to a trial of strength, and bid defiance to the laws of our country" ("To George Logan"). As recounted by Thom Hartmann in his book anatomizing the rise of corporate dominance, *Unequal Protection,* Jefferson kept pushing for a law, written into the Constitution as an amendment, which would prevent companies from growing so large that they could dominate entire industries or have the power to influence the government. However, while the people continued to favor strict restraints, by the time of the Civil War, corporate fiefdoms like the railroads were growing with industrialization, and the war itself fueled these new empires with rich government war contracts. But in *America,* Bennett says little about the history of corporate concentration of wealth or power over government, and while he does discuss some of the grosser cases of corruption, he tends to single out those that can be rationalized because of their long-term benefits to the nation.

Emerson charged in "The American Scholar," "Young men of the fairest promise, who begin life upon our shores, inflated by the mountain winds, shined upon by the fairest stars of God, find the earth below not in unison with these, —but are hindered from action by the disgust with which the principles of business is managed inspire, and turn drudges, or die of disgust—some suicides" (*Selections* 79). (Cf. Melville's "Bartleby the Scrivener: A Tale of Wall Street."). Thoreau seconded the motion in "Life Without Principle": "I think that there is nothing, not even crime, more opposed to poetry, to philosophy, ay, to life itself, than this incessant business....The ways by which you may get money almost without exception lead downward....Do not hire a man who does your work for money, but him who does it for love of it" (*Walden and Other Writings* 712–14). To be sure, other passages in Emerson, Thoreau, and Whitman contradict these, and these contradictions are fruitful conflicts to teach.

THE BOOK OF CULTURAL RELATIVISM: CIVILIZING THE SAVAGES

One of the most influential works in the European Renaissance, Michel de Montaigne's essay "Of Cannibals" (1580) was based on reports of cannibal tribes in Brazil: "I think there is nothing barbarous and savage in that nation, from what I have been told, except that each man calls barbarism whatever is not his own practice; for indeed it seems we have no other test of truth and reason than the example and pattern of the opinions and customs of the country we live in" (152). Montaigne went on to compare reported instances of barbarism among the cannibals to no less barbaric practices in contemporary Christian Europe, preeminently the bloodbaths between Catholics and Protestants in France and England,

Montaigne's theme was picked up 146 years later by Jonathan Swift in Book IV of *Gulliver's Travels*, which, describes English and European conquest of distant lands "by Divine Right": "Ships are sent with the first opportunity; the natives driven out or destroyed, their princes tortured to discover their gold; a free license given to all acts of inhumanity and lust; the earth reeking with the blood of its inhabitants; and this execrable crew of butchers employed in so pious an expedition is a *modern colony* sent to convert and civilize an idolatrous and barbaric people" (*Gulliver's* 237). Similarly, in Voltaire's *Candide*, while traveling in a Dutch colony in Latin America, Candide meets a black slave missing a leg and a hand. When asked how he came to this condition, he replies, "If we catch a finger in the sugar mill where we work, they cut off our hand; if we try to run away, they cut off our leg: I have undergone both these experiences. This is the price of the sugar you eat in Europe.... The Dutch witch doctors who converted me tell me every Sunday that we are all sons of Adam, black and white alike. I am no genealogist, but if those preachers are right, we must all be remote cousins; and you must admit no one could treat his own flesh and blood in a more horrible fashion" (*Candide* 72–73).

Another variation on this theme is found in a little-known, Swiftian satire by Benjamin Franklin, "Remarks Concerning the Savages of North America," written in 1784, which deflates the ethnocentrism of white Christians' sense of moral superiority over Native Americans during the colonial period. In one of Franklin's anecdotes, "A Swedish Minister, having assembled the chiefs of the Susquehanah Indians, made a Sermon to them, acquainting them with the principal historical Facts on which our Religion is founded; such as the Fall of our first parents by eating an Apple, the coming of Christ to repair the Mischief, his Miracles and Suffering, &c. When he had finished, an Indian Orator stood up to thank him. 'What you have told us,' says he, 'is all very good. It is indeed bad to eat Apples. It is better to make them all into Cider.'" The Indian then tells some of his tribe's beliefs. "The good Missionary, disgusted with this idle Tale, said, 'What I delivered to you were sacred Truths; but what you tell me is mere Fable, Fiction, and Falsehood.' The Indian, offended, reply'd 'My brother, it seems your Friends have not done you Justice in your Education; they have not well instructed you in the Rules of common Civility. You saw that we, who understand and practice those Rules, believ'd all your stories; why do you refuse to believe ours?'" (*Writings* 971–72.) Notice Franklin's reduction of the central faiths of Christianity to one sketchy sentence, ending blithely in "et cetera." A final anecdote in "Remarks" recounts a discussion between two native Americans about why they are excluded from the Christians' Sunday church services; their conclusion is that the meetings must be about how to cheat them on the price of beaver skins. Pseudosophisticated relativism, Mr. Bennett?

Herman Melville's 1856 story, "Benito Cereno" recounts the history of a mutiny on a Spanish slave ship, through the eyes of Delano, the Protestant captain of an American ship that eventually rescues the surviving crew and captures the mutinous slaves. In a key sequence, Delano boards the slave ship in response to a distress signal, and finds its captain, Benito Cereno, surrounded by ostensibly loving slaves, particularly Babo, Cereno's valet, who is shaving him. Delano does not realize until after the mutiny has been revealed that Babo, the leader of the mutiny, is holding the razor to Cereno's throat ready to kill him if he reveals the truth. Delano meditates, "There is something in the negro which, in a peculiar way, fits him for avocations about one's person. Most negroes are natural valets and hair-dressers....And above all is the great gift of good humor. Not the mere grin or laugh is here meant. These were unsuitable. But a certain easy cheerfulness, harmonious in every glance and gesture; as though God had set the negro to some pleasant tune" (*Billy Budd and Other Tales* 184). After the truth has finally been revealed, Delano and Cereno can only recoil in horror at the deceitfulness and treachery of the slaves as well as of "the negro" as a race.

It is a prototypical example of canon revision that up until the 1960s most Melville scholarship, including Newton Arvin's then-definitive critical biography, interpreted Delano's viewpoint and attitudes as those of Melville himself. It was only with the heightened consciousness in the sixties of the history of white, Christian delusions of moral superiority (in works like Baldwin's *The Fire Next Time*, below) that critical opinion shifted to an ironic reading of the story. In that reading it becomes apparent that Melville, who was not only an abolitionist and believer in equality of the races but an artist whose profound sense of ambiguity and irony anticipated literary modernism, intended readers to view Delano as a fool blinded by the culturally conditioned assumptions of his time from the truth: that whites were the treacherous race in perpetrating slavery, while the mutinous blacks were courageously fighting for the same freedom always extolled by whites in our nation's founding.

Twain worked a similar twist on slavery and criminality in *Pudd'nhead Wilson*, in which the murderer and thief Tom Driscoll is 31/32 parts white, the offspring of white masters raping their slaves, who has passed as a privileged white until his capture and trial reveals his black blood, which is assumed by the white community to explain his criminal nature. In a soliloquy that Twain squeamishly cut from the published version, Tom reflects that his criminal "blood" is that of the primal crime of whites' enslavement of blacks: "That which was base was the *white blood* in him debased by the brutalizing effects of a long-drawn heredity of slave-owning" (191).

In *A Room of One's Own*, Virginia Woolf wrote:

> Life for both sexes...is arduous, difficult, perpetual struggle. It calls for gigantic courage and strength. More than anything, perhaps, creatures of illusion as we are, it calls for confidence in oneself. Without self-confidence we are as babes in the cradle. And how can we generate this imponderable quality, which is yet so invaluable, most quickly? By thinking that other people are inferior to oneself. By feeling that one has some innate superiority—it may be wealth, or rank, a straight nose, or the portrait of a grandfather by Romney—for there is no end to the pathetic devices of the human imagination—over other people. Hence the enormous importance to a patriarch who has to conquer, who has to rule, of feeling that great numbers of people, half the human race indeed, are by nature inferior to himself....Women have served all these centuries as looking-glasses possessing the magic and delicious power of reflecting the figure of man at twice its natural size....That serves to explain in part the necessity that women so often are to men. And it serves to explain how restless they are under her criticism; how impossible it is for her to say to them this book is bad, this picture is feeble, or whatever it may be, without giving far more pain and rousing far more anger than a man would do who gave the same criticism. For if she begins to tell the truth, the figure in the looking-glass shrinks; his fitness for life is diminished. How is he to go on giving judgements, civilizing natives, making laws, writing books, dressing up and speechifying at banquets, unless he can see himself at breakfast and dinner at least twice the size he really is? (34–36)

Woolf's "civilizing savages" in the last sentence, probably a conscious allusion to Swift's "this execrable crew of butchers employed in so pious an expedition is a *modern colony* sent to convert and civilize an idolatrous and barbaric people," is a metonymy for the entire history of the British Empire and European-American colonialism, as well as the tacit role in them of the patriarchal, white ethnocentrism satirized in the rest of her paragraph.

In one of Mark Twain's many spins on this trope, he observes in "The Lowest Animal," a Swftian satire on the "descent" of humans from the higher animals:

> Man is the only Patriot. He sets himself apart in his own country, under his own flag, and sneers at the other nations, and keeps multifarious uniformed assassins on hand at heavy expense to grab slices of other people's countries.... Man is the Religious Animal. He is the only Religious Animal. He is the only animal that has the True Religion—several of them. He is the only animal that loves his neighbor as himself, and cuts his throat if his theology isn't straight. He has made a graveyard of the globe in trying his honest best to smooth his brother's path to happiness and heaven. (*Letters* 225–27)

The "civilizing savages" motif returned with a vengeance in Baldwin's 1963 *The Fire Next Time*, which was occasioned by the rise of the Nation of Islam, attracting American blacks who turned against Christianity and became Muslims. In an extensive survey of the causes for this turn (which Baldwin himself ultimately rejects, in spite of his own, ongoing disillusionment with Christianity), he charges:

> Neither civilized reason nor Christian love would cause any of those [white] people to treat you as they presumably wanted to be treated.... The Negro's experience of the white world cannot possibly create in him any respect for the standards by which the white world claims to live.... In spite of the Puritan-Yankee equation of virtue with well-being, Negroes had excellent reasons for doubting that money was made or kept by any very striking adherence to the Christian virtues; it certainly did not work that way for black Christians. In any case, white people, who had robbed black people of their liberty and who profited by this theft every hour that they lived, had no moral ground on which to stand.... And those moral virtues preached but not practiced by the white world were merely another means of holding Negroes in subjection. (*Fire* 21–23)

Baldwin later adds, relating black rebellion in America to anticolonialist and anti-Judeo-Christian—especially Islamic—movements around the world since World War II:

> Thus, in the realm of morals the role of Christianity has been, at best, ambivalent. Even leaving out of account the remarkable arrogance that assumed that the ways and morals of others were inferior to those of Christians, and that they therefore had every right, and could use any means, to change them, the collision between cultures—and the

schizophrenia in the mind of Christendom—had rendered the domain of morals as chartless as the sea once was, and as treacherous as the sea still is. It is not too much to say that whoever wishes to be a truly moral human being (and let us not ask whether or not this is possible) must first divorce himself from the all the prohibitions, crimes, and hypocrisies of the Christian church. (46–47)

In the concluding section of *The Fire,* Baldwin rejects hatred and violent revenge as means for ending the long legacy of colonialism and racism, and he appeals for mutual understanding; however, he insists that whites, Christians, and the West must make amends for their crimes and illusions of moral superiority before those they have oppressed can be expected to believe in their good faith. He ironically returns to embrace a secular version of Christian love as compassion and self-sacrifice. The imagery he uses here of whites' self-image in relation to blacks, Europeans' in relation to the Third World, is that of overcoming infantile narcissism, in the metaphor of a mirror like Woolf's in which men habitually view women "as looking-glasses possessing the magic and delicious power of reflecting the figure of man at twice its natural size."

> A vast amount of the energy that goes into what we call the Negro problem is produced by the white man's profound desire not to be judged by those who are not white, not to be seen as he is, and at the same time a vast amount of the white anguish is rooted in the white man's equally profound need to be seen as he is, to be released from the tyranny of his mirror. All of us know, whether or not we are able to admit it, that death by drowning is all that awaits one there. It is for this reason that love is so desperately sought and so cunningly avoided. Love takes off the masks that we fear we cannot live without and know we cannot live within. (95)

Postcolonialist writers like Frantz Fanon, Jean-Paul Sartre, and Jean Gênet (in his play *The Blacks*) similarly used mirror and mask metaphors in the existentialist conception of the colonized as the objectified Other obediently reflecting back the inflated self-esteem of the colonizer-subject.

THE BOOK OF BAWDY VIRTUES

Oh yes, she [the town librarian] advocates dirty books—Chaucer, Rabelaize [*sic*], *Balz*-ac.

Meredith Willson, *The Music Man*

Cultural history in the version of Bennett, Lynne Cheney, ACTA, and many other conservatives, expurgates vast realms of human experience and cultural history that are not only skeptical and irreverent but unabashedly earthy, erotic, and ribald. In 1956, poet and literary critic Louis Untermeyer edited an anthology titled *A Treasury of Ribaldry*, which is still in print and which I have used as a textbook. Bawdy humor fills the Greek and Roman classics of literature and art, as well as Chaucer, Boccaccio, Villon, Rabelais, Montaigne ("On Some Verses of Virgil," a witty compendium of sexual lore through the ages and a celebration of sexuality against prudery), Shakespeare (see Eric Partridge's *Shakespeare's Bawdy*), Donne ("To His Mistress Going to Bed"), Marvell ("To His Coy Mistress"), the Earl of Rochester, Molière, Swift, Voltaire, Fielding, Balzac, Flaubert, Mark Twain, Joyce, Colette, Henry Miller, and Anaïs Nin. Most that survives in this tradition, unfortunately, has been written by men and much of it is embarrassingly masculinist, but we do more recently have female, feminist takes on bawdry like Erica Jong's *Fear of Flying* and the discovery of repressed erotica by earlier writers like Edith Wharton.

Swift wrote a series of poems satirizing the sentimentality in the tradition of courtly love, pastoral poetry, and romanticism in general. The characters have names derived from the literature of pastoral romance about bucolic shepherds and shepherdesses. One, "The Lady's Dressing Room," begins,

> Five hours (and who can do it less in?)
> By haughty Celia spent in dressing;
> The goddess from her chamber issues,
> Array'd in lace, brocades and tissues.

The rest of the poem goes behind the scenes to survey the array of artifice, clutter, soiled underwear, and stench left behind in the production of Celia's divine appearance. "A Beautiful Young Nymph Going to Bed" reverses the process as the lady removes all the artificial apparatus of "the beauty myth" and is reduced to an unglamorous human body. In "Strephon and Chloe," naïve young newlyweds expect romantic bliss in the bridal chamber—until Chloe has to use the chamber pot, shocking Strephon into crying:

> Ye Gods! What sound is this?
> Can Chloe, heavenly Chloe, - - ?

However, he soon reaches for the chamber pot too, and "let fly a rouser in her face." Strephon, Chloe, and the other naives in these poems quickly come to accept pissing, shitting, and farting as natural and unremarkable. (Conservatives who take offense at such language are directed to Nixon's White House tapes or the private exchange, caught on-mike, between George Bush and Dick Cheney calling a *New York Times* reporter a "major-league asshole.") The skeptical moral:

> Adieu to ravishing delights,
> High raptures and romantic flights....
> How great a change! How quickly made!
> They learn to call a spade a spade.
> They soon from all constraint are freed;
> Can see each other do their need.

These poems have always been troublesome for Swift scholars because of the fixation on filth and stench, which are skewed toward misogyny, though Swift ostensibly takes the woman's side:

> Authorities, both old and recent,
> Direct that women must be decent;
> And from the spouse each blemish hide,
> More than from all the world beside.
> Unjustly all our nymphs complain
> Their empire holds so short a reign;
> Is, after marriage, lost so soon,
> It hardly lasts the honey-moon.

The poems ultimately are affirmations of classical stoic virtue:

> Rash mortals, ere you take a wife,
> Contrive your pile to last for life;
> Since beauty scarce endures a day,
> and youth so swiftly glides away...
> On sense and wit your passion found,
> By decency cemented round;
> Let prudence with good nature strive,
> To keep esteem and love alive,
> Then come old age whene'er it will,
> Your friendship shall continue still;
> And thus a mutual gentle fire
> Shall never but with life expire. (*Poems*)

But wasn't Swift also a devout Christian and official of the Anglican Church? To be sure, though the epigraph he wrote for himself—"Gone where savage indignation can no longer lacerate his heart"—is a classic of skeptical ambiguity. Some critics suggest that the misanthropy in these poems, as well as in Book IV of *Gulliver's Travels*, reflects Swift's belief in the taint of original sin on humanity, which can only be erased by belief in Christian redemption. The poems can also be read in the same tradition as Anne Bradstreet's "The Flesh and the Spirit" and Samuel Johnson's "The Vanity of Worldly Things," condemning superficial, physical attractions as a distraction from spiritual priorities, in a similar manner to the modern leftist critique of the worship of the physical and "the beauty myth" in mass culture. So why not just teach the conflicts between all these opposing strains in Swift and so many great writers? Bennett and Cheney would probably be outraged at the idea of teaching these poems in high school or college English, but my students love them and generate some thoughtful discussions out of them.

Mark Twain, pigeonholed as a children's writer and twinkly eyed humorist in what he in fact derided as the goody-goody culture, wrote Swiftian satires suppressed in his lifetime, like "Some Thought on the Science of Onanism," *The Mysterious Stranger*, and *Letters from the Earth*, the latter being one of the most devastating attacks on religious belief and the Bible ever written. After a catalogue of all the physical outrages inflicted on the human body and all the horrors that humans have inflicted on each other through history, the extraterrestrial narrator observes that Christians attribute the origin of these evils to an all-powerful, benevolent God, and concludes:

> Having thus made the Creator responsible for all those pains and diseases and miseries above enumerated, and which he could have prevented, the gifted Christian blandly calls him Our Father!....It is as I tell you. He equips the Creator with every trait that goes to the making of a fiend, and then arrives at the conclusion that a fiend and a father are the same thing! Yet he would deny that a malevolent lunatic and a Sunday school superintendent are essentially the same. What do you think of the human mind? I mean, in case you think there is a human mind? (*Letters* 29–30)

As for sexuality, *Letters* notes, "The human being, like the immortals, naturally places sexual intercourse far and away above all other joys—yet he has left it out of his heaven!....From youth to middle age all men and all women prize copulation above all other pleasures combined, yet it is actually as I have said; it is not in their heaven; prayer takes its place" (10). Among Twain's catalogue of the ways the alleged Creator bungled in the production of humans is the discrepancy between female and male sexual capacity (a theme indebted to Montaigne's "On Some Verses of Virgil," with which Twain was familiar):

> After fifty, his performance is of poor quality, the intervals between are wide, and its satisfactions of no great value to either party; whereas his great-grandmother is as good as new. There is nothing wrong with her plant. Her candlestick is as firm as ever, whereas his candle is increasingly softened and weakened by the weather of age, as the years go by, until at last it can no longer stand, and is mournfully laid to rest in the hope of a blessed resurrection which is never to come. (40)

American popular culture (as opposed to corporate-produced mass culture) has its own great traditions of irreverence and bawdiness, in genres like folk music ("Four Nights Drunk"), jazz (the very word was a synonym for the sexual verb), country ("Pistol Packin' Mama"), the blues (Bessie Smith's "Kitchen Man," Brownie McGhee and Sonny Terry's "My Baby Done Changed the Lock on Her Door") ("That key you got, Sonny Terry, don't fit no more"), vaudeville, burlesque, and Hollywood film prior to Production Code prudery in the late 1930s (which consigned married couples to twin beds and banned words like "pregnant" and "bosom"). Uncle Dave Macon, the banjo virtuoso of the Grand Ole Opry in the 1930s, wrote "The Wreck of the Tennessee Gravy Train" about a state financial scandal ("The engineer blew the whistle, the brakeman rang the bell/The conductor hollered 'All aboard,' and the banks all went to hell"). He wrote lines of earthy wit like the description of a bearded man: "Look at that hair all around his mouth/Like he swallowed a mule and left the tale a-hangin' out," and of irreverence like: "I know a man who's a 'vangelist; his tabernacle's always full;/People come from miles around just to hear him shoot the bull." One Macon song was titled "The Old Man's Drunk Again," but others testified "The Bible's True" and "Jordan Is a Hard Road to Travel."

Broadway musicals in the first half of the twentieth century were frequented by a cosmopolitan, thoroughly secular audience, and many shows, epitomized by *Finian's Rainbow*, thumbed their nose at religious, patriotic, sexual, racial, and class pieties. In George and Ira Gershwin's 1927 show *Strike Up the Band*, a satire on faux-patriotism, political opportunism, and mercenary motives in war, the little-known verse to the famous title song begins:

> We're in a bigger, better war for your patriotic pastime.
> We don't know what we're fighting for, but we didn't know the last time.

Cole Porter's 1948 *Kiss Me Kate*, a wickedly literate spin on Shakespeare's *The Taming of the Shrew*, includes a jaunty soft-show number called "Brush Up Your Shakespeare," with lines like,

> If she says your behavior is heinous,
> Kick her right in the Coriolanus.

I am willing to bet that Bennett, Allan Bloom, Norman Podhoretz in his bad boy early years, and many ostensibly pious conservative leaders have been fully familiar with and enjoyed works in this tradition, though they might try to protect the unsophisticated masses from them. This is one version of the "noble lie," neoconservative mentor Leo Strauss's formula for ruling elites to feed pabulum to the masses with lip service to religion, patriotism, and moral rectitude—virtues to be preached but not practiced by the elites.

I do not want to be misunderstood as approving of the flood of sexual vulgarity and obscenity in recent American pop culture, an equal-and-opposite extreme from earlier decades of prudery; however, I condemn it on different grounds from those of conservatives. First, it serves the primary purpose of corporate profits, in the mode of appealing to the lowest common denominator of taste. Second, it is an offense to the classical sense of proportion in its excesses and failure to draw the line between healthy earthiness and debased nastiness. Lenny Bruce used obscenity creatively in social satire and dramatic dialogue; HBO's *Deadwood* incorporated it in Shakespearean poetic dialogue and *The Wire* in naturalistic depiction of inner-city argot. *Deadwood*'s brutal depiction of the degradation of prostitutes was the opposite of prurient—an antidote to the images in Production-Code-Hollywood Westerns of mythical "dance-hall girls." But many recent TV comedy and talk shows, films, and songs have just escalated the obscenity, vulgarity, and sexual quotient as a substitute for wit or serious artistic intent. Hollywood and TV have a deplorably higher tolerance level for violence than for bawdiness, and less often with redeeming artistic merit, though there are borderline cases like Quentin

Tarantino's *Pulp Fiction* (which I personally hated) and Vince Gilligan's *Breaking Bad* (which I loved). We should certainly teach our students to debate such critical distinctions as an essential part of cultural studies courses.

American mass culture's long-established higher tolerance level for violence than for sexuality became a political flash point during the Vietnam War in the sixties, when "Make Love, Not War" was chanted by dissidents of the New Left and counterculture. That view had recently been advanced in influential scholarly works celebrating eros over thanatos, like Norman O. Brown's *Life Against Death* and Herbert Marcuse's *Eros and Civilization*. Marcuse's pamphlet *An Essay on Liberation* in 1969 emblemized the case I have made throughout this chapter and book against American conservatives' double standards and skewed priorities:

> This society is obscene in producing and indecently exposing a stifling abundance of wares while depriving its victims abroad of the necessities of life; obscene in stuffing itself and its garbage cans while poisoning and burning the scarce foodstuffs in the fields of its aggression; obscene in the words and smiles of its politicians and entertainers; in its prayers, in its ignorance, and in the wisdom of its kept intellectuals.
>
> Obscenity is a moral concept in the verbal arsenal of the Establishment, which abuses the term by applying it, not to expressions of its own morality, but to those of another. Obscenity is not the picture of a naked woman who exposes her pubic hair but that of a fully clad general who exposes his medals in a war of aggression; obscene is not the ritual of the Hippies but the declaration of a high dignitary of the Church that war is necessary for peace. (8)

One of the songs that comes to my mind more and more frequently of late, and which I will leave here as my valedictory (with an apology for its phallocentrism), was sung by the Weavers, led by Pete Seeger, one of the great artistic rebels of our time, who at this writing was past 90 with ample get up and go:

> How do I know my youth is all spent?
> My get up and go has got up and went.
> But in spite of it all, I'm able to grin,
> And think of the places my get up has been.

Conclusion

AN APPEAL TO CONSERVATIVE READERS

And so my case rests in favor of a leftist bias in higher education and media. I make the same appeal to conservative readers that Lynne Cheney made to liberal readers of *Telling the Truth*: "Try to show I am mistaken if you wish, but do so with sound evidence and sound reasoning. Invective and accusation will merely serve as evidence of the low status into which truth has fallen in our time" (6). In other words, abide by my "Ground Rules for Polemicists," and call me out when I have broken them, but "try scrupulously to establish an accurate proportion and sense of reciprocity." Conservatives will protest, "But you have piled on a couple hundred pages of one-sided arguments and evidence, and it would take that many pages to refute them all. No one has that kind of time." Quite right, and it is precisely my point that conservatives attempt to propagate similar saturation in all the arenas of public discourse that they dominate. QED.

Since it is virtually impossible for any of us to escape the ESBYODS Principle—"Everyone shits, but your own doesn't stink" —the only remedy would seem to be to devise arenas in which the one-sided viewpoints on opposing sides can be brought to the table of negotiation, refereed in the manner of management-labor arbitration or a South African–style "truth and reconciliation commission." As noted in chapter 10 above, William J. Bennett calls for "a thorough and honest study of our history...with a genuine inquiry into fact and a genuine openness to debate. I, for one, am hardly in doubt as to the outcome." Very well, bring it on. Since conservative foundations and think tanks (such as those that have sponsored Bennett's various projects), media, and academic organizations like NAS, ACTA, and ISI lay claim to superior arguments and evidence, shouldn't they leap at the opportunity to sponsor extended, face-to-face debates with liberals and leftists? How about the format of a yearlong colloquium at a university humanities center or a private think tank, televised by C-SPAN or PBS? How about FOX News and MSNBC collaborating on an ongoing series of one- or two-hour debates on these issues between polemicists on the right and left, with requirement of documentary support, a moderator who keeps them from evading direct responses, and open question periods from informed partisans on both sides?

As I suggested in my introduction, a neutral starting point for dialogues like these might be identifying the major realms of power and interest groups in contemporary America, to the agreement of those on all sides, followed by exposition of the opposing bodies of evidence and lines of argument in these realms—then finally, debate on them within the boundaries of something like my "Ground Rules for Polemicists." This process can lead, at the very least, toward agreement between opponents on what they disagree about and reduction of their talking past each other with differing definitions, slanted language, and stacking the deck through selectivity in subjects. Any such endeavor obviously depends on willingness by those on both sides to engage in good faith dialogue. If those on one side are unwilling, that would seem to be smoking-gun evidence discrediting their position.

In any such dialogue or debate, conservatives would be expected to lay on all their evidence about leftist PC in politics, media, and education, but also to place it in proportion to a body of evidence on the other side like that I have amassed here. Whatever the conservatives' best shots may be, then, they would need at the very least to be formulated as a response to definitive arguments on the left like Gary Dorrien's:

> The moral corruption and narcissism that neoconservatives condemned in American society...owed more to commercial imperatives than to the failures of some fictionally autonomous "culture."...It was primarily under the pressure of the business civilization they celebrated...that the communities of memory that once sustained these values were being eviscerated.

Conservative cultural critics cherry-pick instances of overt leftist bias out of the whole flood of American public discourse, while ignoring all of the more pervasive and invasive biases of "the business civilization." Thus conservatives generally refuse to consider that at least some mass media and public education (at the K-12 and especially collegiate level) might have a responsibility to provide an explicit corrective to all the cognitive restrictions inflicted by "commercial imperatives." If conservatives will at least acknowledge this responsibility, then we can, finally, proceed to "a genuine inquiry" into how teachers and journalists can fulfill it while avoiding the very real dangers of political correctness.

Once again, I might be wrong about anything or everything I have said in this book, and I welcome reasonable correction. All I ask is that conservatives who take me to task acknowledge the same about themselves and their allies.

NOTES

1 Conservatism as the Unmarked Norm

1. In an interview with Matthew Continetti in the *Weekly Standard*, billionaire David Koch is quoted on Obama:
   > He's the most radical president we've ever had as a nation, he said, "and has done more damage to the free enterprise system and long-term prosperity than any president we've ever had." David suggested the president's radicalism was tied to his upbringing. "His father was a hard core economic socialist in Kenya," he said. "Obama didn't really interact with his father face-to-face very much, but was apparently from what I read a great admirer of his father's points of view. So he had sort of anti-business, anti-free enterprise influences affecting him almost all his life."
2. When I recently asked the Greek-born owner of a restaurant in Knoxville, in his sixties, what he thought about the economic crisis in Greece, he started ranting that the communists and socialists have been destroying the country for the last 40 years, and that the last government that knew what it was doing was the fascistic military dictatorship of the sixties. Few conservatives in American public life want to acknowledge this perennial tendency in conservative thought.

2 Restricted-Code Conservatism

1. I delineated components of critical-thinking instruction and incorporated them into critical pedagogy in "Postmodern Pluralism" and *Reading and Writing for Civic Literacy* (54–77).
2. I would also be remiss not to affirm that East Tennessee has a rich tradition of progressive activism for civil rights, labor, world peace, environmentalism, women's, gay, and immigrant rights. For an excellent recent survey, see *Transforming Places: Lessons from Appalachia*, edited by Stephen L Fisher and Barbara Ellen Smith. Much of this activism has been connected to the Highlander Research and Education Center, near Knoxville, which since 1932 has been a national beacon for the best of left populism (and which was long subjected to red-baiting harassment from the right). Highlander was a major staging area for the civil rights movement in the fifties and sixties. See John M. Glen, *Highlander: No Ordinary School*.

3. The following section needs to be qualified by acknowledging that TV's constant degeneration toward infantalization and shortening of attention span has been partially countered by the invention in the past decade of elaborated-code, "long-form" serial dramas, uninterrupted by commercials, mainly on subscription channels. HBO began the trend with *The Sopranos*, followed by *The Wire*, *Deadwood*, and *Game of Thrones*. Their success trickled down, first to AMC, a cable channel with commercials (but otherwise respecting artistic quality in these dramas), in *Mad Men* and – best of all – *Breaking Bad*, then eventually to some network dramas, again with commercials. Many viewers by now have learned to evade the commercials by watching these programs on DVD, On Demand, or DVRs. This new genre thumbed its nose at commercial TV's restricted-code conventions by deliberately cultivating extended plot lines and character development, along with thematic, narrative, visual, or oral complexities (e.g., the cryptic black street argot in *The Wire*, the dialogue in *Deadwood* combining nonstop obscenity with elevated diction and Shakespearean poetic meter). These features demanded multiple viewings – all to the good cognitively. (At the extreme, *Game of Thrones* seemed perversely designed to overwhelm viewers with an excess of characters and plot lines and the thwarting of dramatic expectations, as when a whole family who were the most sympathetic characters were abruptly killed off in mid-plot.) The only, predictable, downside of these dramas was that their audience was mainly limited to an upscale, college-educated one acclimated to cognitive complexity.
4. When Sinatra became an idol of the "bobby-soxers" in 1944, he was already close to 30, a veteran of the great swing bands, and a singer of extraordinary skill and taste (qualities that got dissipated in his later career) who appealed equally to musically sophisticated adults. In a signal event of postwar culture, Mitch Miller, a classical oboist who played in the New York Philharmonic under Toscanini and contributed memorable solos to Sinatra's best records at Columbia, became Columbia's artistic director in the fifties, when as recounted by Sinatra biographer Roy Hemming, "the average age of record buyers dropped to the increasingly affluent postwar teens and sub-teens" ("Sinatra Standards" 36). Miller's introduction of the era of pop schlock novelty tunes and "Sing Along With Mitch" provoked Sinatra to lead a walkout of leading artists from Columbia to the newly formed Capitol Records.

3 Socialism as a Cognitive Alternative

1. In saying that even social democracy is excluded from the American agenda, I do not mean to dismiss varieties of socialism farther to the left, including Marxism and communism, which also deserve a place on the agenda if only in the interest of free speech. Terry Eagleton's *Why Marx Was Right* cogently updates Marxist critiques of social democracy, in the

course of a nuanced contemporary defense of Marxist history, political economy, and cultural studies against all the common lines of argument claiming to refute them. Eagleton also responds to recent claims that Marxism has been superseded by postmodernist theory, identity politics, or the neoliberal, "world is flat" celebrations of the global economy by the likes of Thomas Friedman. Several mainstream journalists have made a similar case that globalization has largely confirmed Marx's prediction of nation-states being eclipsed by the worldwide concentration of capital.
2. Other post-2008 reaffirmations of democratic socialism or social democracy include Geoghegan, Wolff, Lundberg, and Alperovitz.

4 The Conservative Attack Machine: "Admit Nothing, Deny Everything, Launch Counterattack"

1. David Horowitz wrote a review of Lind's book, predictably dismissing it as a "mean-spirited little tract," "the kind of crackpot conspiracy theory [Lind] ostentatiously derides," "a pathetic rant," and a "reprehensible, gutter-sniping book" (*Left Illusions* 282–87). Thus do conservatives uphold restraint and civility against leftist abusers of them. Still, Horowitz does make some substantive arguments suggesting that Lind overgeneralizes and exaggerates about the conservative intelligentsia. Now, if Horowitz would only apply the same standard to his own and other conservatives' sweeping generalizations and exaggerations about leftists. This is a good illustration of a corollary to "A Semantic Calculator" and the ESBYODS Principle, that each side tends to perceive the other as monolithic while emphasizing the internal diversity in its own ranks.
2. On the other hand, Abramoff's book might be studied in comparison with *Lynched!: The Shocking Story of How the Political Establishment Manufactured a Scandal to Have Republican Super-Lobbyist Jack Abramoff Removed from Power*, self-published by Susan Bradford, a Fox News producer, which appeared in 2010 before Abramoff's own book and that exonerates him of charges that he admits guilt to in his book.
3. In his book Abramoff seems to have only momentary misgivings about how his professions of orthodox Jewish piety square with his involvements in the gambling industry, involvements that have become a motif among other pious Republicans like William J. Bennett (a VIP high roller in Vegas and Atlantic City) and Newt Gingrich, who was bankrolled in his 2012 presidential bid by billionaire casino magnate Sheldon Adelson; Adelson later that year also contributed heavily to Mitt Romney and Paul Ryan. Gingrich was silent about Adelson's lucrative concession with Communist China to extend his Las Vegas empire to Macao. In 2013, the *New York Times* reported that Adelson's company "has

informed the Securities and Exchange Commission that it likely violated a federal law against bribing foreign officials.... The former president of Adelson's Macao operations...also accused the company of turning a blind eye toward Chinese organized crime figures operating in its casinos" (Schwirtz). Bennett, Gingrich, and Adelson likewise were silent on the association of Las Vegas and Atlantic City casinos with prostitution, nude shows (Lenny Bruce proposed that the marquees for all the Vegas pseudo-high-class spectacles should simply read, "Tits and Ass"), and, at least in earlier periods, organized crime. One of Abramoff's partners in a fraudulent gambling-ship business was bumped off gangland-style in 2001.

5 Right-Wing Deconstruction: Mimicry and False Equivalencies

1. Neither Frank (who twice refers to "the Koch-backed FreedomWorks"), Continetti, nor Jane Mayer in her article discussed here, is clear on the relation of the Kochs to FreedomWorks, whose codirectors Dick Armey and Matt Kibbe, published *Give Us Liberty: A Tea Party Manifesto* in 2010. Apparently FreedomWorks was created in 2004 as a result of an internal split in the Kochs' Citizens for a Sound Economy, which Armey had cochaired and Kibbe worked for. According to *Wikipedia*, in 2004 the Kochs started Americans for Prosperity, while "Citizens for a Sound Economy merged with Empower America in 2004 and was renamed FreedomWorks, with Dick Armey, Jack Kemp and C. Boyden Gray serving as co-chairmen, Bill Bennett focusing on school choice as a Senior Fellow, and Matt Kibbe as President and CEO."http://en.wikipedia.org/wiki/Empower_America – cite_note-3.So the Kochs appear to have no direct connection to FreedomWorks, although its funders include Verizon, AT&T, Philip Morris, and the Scaife foundations (*Wikipedia*). Armey is a former corporate lobbyist and Kibbe edited a free market economics journal at George Mason, as well as being an analyst for the US Chamber of Commerce and the Republican National Committee.
2. In a farcical episode, a liberal prankster called Walker's office claiming to be David Koch. Walker not only took the call but spent some 20 minutes chatting about their common union-busting agenda with the imposter, who recorded the conversation. As Continetti reports, the Kochs reacted with outrage against this fraud while failing to acknowledge Walker's inadvertent confirmation of complicity with Koch. Conservatives might say that liberals have a double standard in laughing off this episode while getting outraged over Andrew Breitbart's pranks, but no harm was done to anyone here, while Breitbart single-handedly brought about the demise of ACORN and the firing of Shirley Sherrod and two instructors at the University of Missouri-Kansas City.

3. Michael Tomasky's "Something New On the Mall" in October 2009 reported on further instances of "astroturf" organizing of Tea Party activities by Citizens for Prosperity and FreedomWorks.
4. This asymmetry of forces and motives on the left and right has been most prominent in scientific issues. See *Merchants of Doubt: How a Handful of Scientists Obscured the Truth on Issues from Tobacco Smoke to Global Warming*, by Naomi Oreskes and Erik M. Conway, as well as Banning's "When Poststructural Theory," which documents Frank Luntz's role in global warming denial through right-wing deconstruction of scientific research, and the financing of the usual think tank suspects by lobbies like those of the Kochs, the Petroleum Institute, and Exxon-Mobil.

6 From *Partisan Review* to *Fox News*: Neoconservatives as Defenders of Intellectual Standards

1. For histories of the New York Intellectuals, see Dorman; Howe; Wald.
2. In Horowitz's scholarly mode, he gave a speech at the 2009 MLA convention (with a bodyguard at his side), at the invitation of President Gerald Graff in the interests of teaching the political conflicts. During the question period, I asked Horowitz to comment on his failure to correct Robertson's ravings in their appearances as a team. He only shrugged his shoulders and said, "I was promoting my book."
3. I have analyzed Bloom at length in "Political Correctness Left and Right" and "Thumbs Up."
4. Bloom's account of this episode at Cornell claims that the faculty and administrators gave in to them cravenly. He says the provost showed "a mixture of cowardice and moralism because he did not want trouble"—from the protestors. "His president had frequently cited Kerr's dismissal at the University of California as the great danger. Kerr had not known how to conciliate the students" (*Closing* 316) Bloom's account here stood the truth on its head. Campus protestors in the sixties at Berkeley and elsewhere were stunned when they found out how quickly administrators like Clark Kerr and professors like Nathan Glazer with liberal reputations lurched to the right when their business as usual and personal authority were challenged. In 1964 Kerr first refused to negotiate the Free Speech Movement's demands and suspended its student leaders, then when some thousand students staged a nonviolent sit-in at the administration building, he set the precedent for calling the riot squad onto a campus to make mass arrests, many violently conducted—a precedent that would culminate in 1971 with police killing students at Kent State and Jackson State universities. Yet when Reagan ran for governor in 1966 on a platform of cracking down on "the Berkeley riots," which sold well in Reagan's Southern California base, he made Kerr a scapegoat precisely as a liberal

"conciliator" and as soon as he was elected, pressured the corporate-conservative Board of Regents to fire Kerr for being too soft on protest. My experiences at the time indicated that presidents and faculty administrators caved in less often to students than to conservative officials like Reagan and later President Nixon and the FBI (with their covert campaign against antiwar protesters and Nixon's "these bums on campus," which led to Watergate).Mark Kitchell's great documentary *Berkeley in the Sixties* vividly recaptured these events. Mario Savio's brilliant speeches as a leader of the Free Speech Movement framed it as a reaction against the conservative bureaucratization of American society, in which educational administrators had become integrated as technocrats dedicated to serving "the Utopia of sterilized, automated contentment" (332 in Savio's speeches collected by Robert Cohen in *Freedom's Orator*). Glazer's *Remembering the Answers* presented a generally evenhanded case for his disagreements with the Berkeley movement, in the wake of which he left there for Harvard.

7 Conservative Scholarship: Seeing the Object as It Really Isn't

1. See Aufderheide; Diamond (*Facing, Roads*); Newfield and Strickland, Wiener ("Dollars"); Wilson (*Myth, Patriotic*).
2. Horowitz was equally equivocal in making frequent allegations of shoddy scholarship against left academics (albeit sometimes accurately) while not even making a pretense to scholarly accuracy in his own work, claiming that he was just a popular journalist; most of his recent books have no or skimpy documentation, and he admitted that he didn't even take responsibility for the accuracy of information posted by his employees or contributors in his multiple websites. (Jaschik, "Retractions from David Horowitz.") Ironically, his most-fully documented books were two of them that he wrote when he was a leftist in the sixties, *Empire and Revolution* and *The Free World Colossus*. His chapter "The Intellectual Class War" in *The Art of Political War* was one of the more cogent attempts I have seen to refute liberal and left lines of arguments like those I present here, though it too lacked documentation; I included it in *Reading and Writing for Civic Literacy*, juxtaposed to a leftist counterpart, with study guides aimed to discern their strong and weak points (389–90). Horowitz's website, Discover the Networks, does attempt extensively to document bias on the left on about the same scale as my book does, although with uneven accuracy as noted above.
3. For a critique of *Defending Civilization*, see Wilson's *Patriotic Correctness*, 9–10.
4. I am grateful to the staff of the SAT guide for helping to locate these passages in their voluminous, unindexed book.

10 The Radical Humanistic Canon

1. For example, Barton includes deism in a list of Christian denominations on page 24, with specific reference to Franklin, without defining the term or quoting what Franklin says about it in the *Autobiography* or his other expressions of skepticism toward Chrisianity. Barton also argues that the "founding fathers" intended the First Amendment only to protect the practice of religion from government, not also to protect individuals from government imposition of religion. (The main object of his criticism is the 1962 Supreme Court decision declaring officially sponsored and organized prayer in public schools unconstitutional.) Barton quotes Jefferson's 1802 letter to the Danville Baptist Association, the best-known statement of the notion of a wall of separation between church and state, as saying, "'I contemplate with sovereign reverence that act of the whole American people which declared that their legislature should "make no law respecting an establishment of religion, or prohibiting the free exercise thereof," thus building a wall of separation between church and state'" (*Myth* 41). However, Barton leaves out the first part of the same sentence: "Believing with you that religion is a matter which lies solely between man and his God, that he owes account to none other for his faith or his worship, that the legislative powers of government reach actions only, and not opinions" (Jefferson, *Writings* 510).
2. *Finian's Rainbow* was one of the last gasps of Popular Front culture, with some foreshadowing of impending McCarthyism in lines like, "If this isn't love, it's Red propaganda."

Works Cited

Abramoff, Jack. *Capitol Punishment.* New York: WND Books, 2011.
Abrams, Elliott. *Undue Process: A Story of How Political Differences Are Turned into Crimes.* New York: Free P, 1992.
Ackerman, John, and David Coogan, eds. *The Public Work of Rhetoric: Citizen Scholars and Civic Engagement.* Columbia: U of South Carolina P, 2010.
Adorno, Theodor W. "Television and the Patterns of Mass Culture." Ed. Bernard Rosenberg and David Manning White. *Mass Culture: The Popular Arts in America.* New York: Free P, 1957. 474–78.
Allison, Tom. "Beck Pushes False Claims about Sunstein, OIRA." *Media Matters* 17 May 2010. Web.
Alperovitz, Gar. *America beyond Capitalism.* New York: John Wiley & Sons, 2004. Rev. Ed., New York: Dollars and Sense, 2011.
Alterman, Eric. *What Liberal Media?* New York: Basic, 2003.
American Council of Trustees and Alumni. "Mission." *goacta.org.* No date. Web.
Annas, Pamela, and Robert Rosen, eds. *Literature and Society.* Englewood Cliffs: Prentice Hall, 1990.
Armey, Richard, and Matt Kibbe. *Give Us Liberty: A Tea Party Manifesto.* New York: Morrow, 2010.
Aronowitz, Stanley. *The Knowledge Factory: Dismantling the Corporate University and Creating True Higher Learning.* Boston: Beacon, 2001.
———. *The Politics of Identity: Class, Culture, Social Movements.* London: Routledge, 1992.
Aronowitz, Stanley, and Henry A. Giroux. *Postmodern Education: Politics, Culture, and Social Criticism.* Minneapolis: U of Minnesota P, 1991.
Atlas, James. *Bellow: A Biography.* New York: Modern Library, 2000.
Aufderheide, Patricia, ed. *Beyond PC: Toward a Politics of Understanding.* St. Paul: Greywolf, 1992.
Aune, James Arnt. *Selling the Free Market: The Rhetoric of Economic Correctness.* New York: Guilford, 2001.
Bady, Aaron, and Mike Konczal. "From Master Plan to No Plan: The Slow Death of Public Higher Education." *Dissent* 59.4 (Fall 2012): 10–16.
Baldwin, James. *The Fire Next Time.* New York: Dial 1963.
Balint, Benjamin. *Running Commentary.* New York: Public Affairs, 2010.

Banning, Marlia. "When Poststructural Theory and Contemporary Politics Collide: The Vexed Case of Global Warming." *Communication and Critical/Cultural Studies* 6:3 (September 2009): 285–304.

Barer, Marshall, and Mary Rodgers. *Once Upon a Mattress*. Cast recording. Columbia, 1959.

Barnouw, Erik. *The Sponsor: Notes on a Modern Potentate*. Oxford: Oxford UP, 1978.

Barton, David. *The Separation Myth*. Plano: Wallbuilder P, 1991.

Bell, Daniel. *The Cultural Contradictions of Capitalism*. New York: Basic, 1978.

Bellow, Saul. *Ravelstein*. New York: Viking, 2000.

Bennett, William J. *America: The Last Best Hope*, Volume 1. New York: Nelson Current, 2002.

———, ed. *The Book of Virtues*. New York: Simon, 1993.

———. *The De-Valuing of America: The Fight for Our Culture and Our Children*. New York: Simon, 1992.

———. "Faced with Evil on a Grand Scale, Nothing Is Relative." *Los Angeles Times* 1 Oct. 2001: B12.

———. *Why We Fight: Moral Clarity in the War on Terrorism*. New York: Doubleday, 2002.

Bernstein, Basil. *Class, Codes, and Control: Theoretical Studies toward a Sociology of Language*. New York: Schocken Books, 1975.

Biemiller, Lawrence. "Over 20 Years, State Support for Public Higher Education Fell More than 25%." *Chronicle of Higher Education* 9 Apr. 2012.

Biskind, Peter. "The Politics of Power in *On the Waterfront*." *Film Quarterly* 29.1 (Fall 1975): 26. Reprinted in Lazere, *American Media*, 184–200.

Bloom, Allan. *The Closing of the American Mind*. New York: Simon, 1987.

———. *Giants and Dwarfs*. New York: Simon, 1990.

Blumenthal, Sidney. *The Rise of the Counter-Establishment*. New York: Times Books, 1986.

Bogdanor, Paul. "Chomsky's War Against Israel." Collier and Horowitz, 87–116.

Borchgrave, Arnaud de, and Robert Moss. *The Spike*. New York: Crown, 1980.

Bradford. Susan. *Lynched!: The Shocking Story of How the Political Establishment Manufactured a Scandal to Have Republican Super-Lobbyist Jack Abramoff Removed from Power*. New York: Susan Bradford, 2010.

Brock, David. *Blinded by the Right: The Conscience of an Ex-Conservative*. New York: Crown, 2002.

———. "Confessions of A Right-Wing Hit Man." *Esquire*, July 1997: 52.

———. *The Real Anita Hill*. New York: Free P, 1993.

———. *The Republican Noise Machine*. New York: Crown, 2004.

Camus, Albert. *Resistance, Rebellion, and Death*. Trans. Justin O'Brien. New York: Knopf, 1960.

Cassino, Daniel. "Some News Leaves People Knowing Less." *PublicMind. fdu.edu* 21 Nov. 2011. Web.
Cauchon, Rich. "Tuition Burden Falls by a Third." *USA Today* 28 June 2004. Web.
Chait, Jonathan. "The Koch Brothers' Self-Exposé." *New Republic* 28 Mar. 2011. Web.
Chace, William M. "The Decline of the English Department." *American Scholar* Autumn 2009. Web.
Cheney, Lynne V. *Telling the Truth: A Report on the State of the Humanities in Higher Education.* Washington: National Endowment for the Humanities, 1992.
———. *Telling the Truth: Why Our Culture and Our Country Have Stopped Making Sense—and What We Can Do about It.* New York: Simon, 1995.
Clarren, Rebecca. "Paradise Lost." *Ms.* Spring 2006. Web.
Cloud, John. "The Right's New Wing." *Time* 22 Aug. 2004. Web.
Cohen, Robert. *Freedom's Orator: Mario Savio and the Radical Legacy of the 1960s.* New York: Oxford UP, 2009.
Cohn, Werner. "Chomsky and Holocaust Denial." Collier and Horowitz, 117–58.
Colby, Anne, and Thomas Ehrlich. "From Ideology to Inquiry," *Inside Higher Education* 2 June 2006. Web.
College Board SAT. *The Official SAT Study Guide: For the New SAT.* New York: College Board, 2005.
Collier, Peter, and David Horowitz, eds. *The Anti-Chomsky Reader.* San Francisco: Encounter, 2004.
Common Dreams Staff. "Prolonged Attack on Public Education and Unions Leaves Teaching Profession Woeful" *Common Dreams* 8 Mar. 2012. Web.
"Confessions of a Tobacco Lobbyist." *60 Minutes*, Mar. 19, 1995. Burrell's transcripts.
Conason, Joe. *Big Lies: The Right-Wing Propaganda Machine and How It Distorts the Truth.* New York: St. Martin's, 2003.
Continetti, Matthew. "The Paranoid Style in Liberal Politics: The Left's Obsession with the Koch Brothers." *Weekly Standard* 4 Apr. 2011. Web.
Council for National Policy. Member Biographies. John T. Teny Dolan. n.d. Web.
Crèvecoeur, Hector St.-John. *Letters from an American Farmer.* Ed. Susan Manning. New York: Oxford UP, 1997.
Crick, Bernard. *George Orwell: A Life.* London: Secker and Warburg Ltd., 1980.
Crossen, Cynthia. "Kahlo, Trotsky, and Kingsolver." *Wall Street Journal* 30 Oct. 2009. Web.
———. *Tainted Truth: The Manipulation of Fact in America.* New York: Simon & Schuster, 1994.

Curran, James, et al. "Media System, Public Knowledge, and Democracy." *European Journal of Communication* 24.1 (Mar. 2009): 5–26. Web.

Davis, Lennard J., and M. Bella Mirabella, eds. *Left Politics and the Literary Profession*. New York: Columbia UP, 1990.

Dean, John W. *Conservatives without Conscience*. New York: Viking, 2006.

Decter, Midge. *An Old Wife's Tale*. New York: ReganBooks, 2001.

———. "Ronald Reagan & the Culture War." *Commentary* Mar. 1991. Web.

DeForest, Elizabeth. "Ohio Bill Would Mandate Diverse Opinions." *Associated Press* 13 Feb. 2005. Web.

Dershowitz, Alan. *The Case for Peace*. New York: Wiley, 2006.

Diamond, Sarah. *Facing the Wrath: Confronting the Right in Dangerous Times*. Monroe, Maine: Common Courage P. 1996.

———. *Roads to Dominion: Right-Wing Movements and Political Power in the United States*. New York: Guilford P, 1995.

Dorfman, Ariel. *The Empire's Old Clothes*. New York: Pantheon, 1983.

Dorfman, Ariel, and Armand Mattelart. *How to Read Donald Duck: Imperialist Ideology in the Disney Comics*. New York: International General, 1975.

Dorman, Joseph. *Arguing the World: The New York Intellectuals in Their Own Words*. New York: Free P, 2000.

Dorrien, Gary. *Imperial Designs: Neoconservatism and the New Pax Americana*. New York: Routledge, 2004.

———. *The Neoconservative Mind*. Philadelphia: Temple UP, 1994.

Dostoyevsky, Fyodor. *The Brothers Karamazov*. Trans. Constance Garnett. New York: Modern Library, 1950.

Dowie, Mark. *American Foundations: An Investigative History*. Cambridge: MIT P, 2001.

Eagleton, Terry. "What Is the Worth of Social Democracy?" *Harper's* Oct. 2010: 77–80.

———. *Why Marx Was Right*. New Haven: Yale UP, 2010.

Easton, Nina. *Gang of Five: Leaders at the Center of the Conservative Crusade*. New York: Simon, 2000.

Ehrenreich, Barbara. *Fear of Falling*. New York: Pantheon, 1989.

"Elliott Abrams." *Wikipedia*. 7 Mar. 2013. Web.

Ellis, John: *Literature Lost: Social Agendas and the Corruption of the Humanities*. New Haven: Yale UP, 1997.

Emerson, Ralph Waldo. *Selections from Ralph Waldo Emerson*. Ed. Stephen E. Whicher. Boston: Houghtons, 1960.

Empson, William. *Some Versions of Pastoral*. New York: New Directions, 1960.

Erlanger, Steven. "What's a Socialist?" *New York Times* 7 Dec. 2010. Web.

Fang, Lee. "Blogger from Koch's Law Firm Defends Koch." *Think Progress* 3 Mar. 2011. Web.

Fanon, Frantz. *The Wretched of the Earth*. Trans. Constance Farrington. New York: Evergreen, 1968.

Felski, Rita. *Literature after Feminism*. Chicago: U of Chicago P, 2003.
Ferguson, Andrew. "The Book that Drove Them Crazy." *Weekly Standard* 9 Apr. 2012. Web.
———. "What Does Newt Know?" *New York Times Magazine* 3 July 2011: 18–21.
Fisher, Stephen, and Barbara Ellen Smith, eds. *Transforming Places: Lessons from Appalachia*. Urbana: U of Illinois P, 2012.
Foner, Phillip. *Mark Twain Social Critic*. New York: International Publishers, 1958.
Fones-Wolf, Elizabeth. *Selling Free Enterprise*. Urbana: U of Illinois P, 1994.
Fox-Genovese, Elizabeth. "American Culture and New Literary Studies." *American Quarterly* 42:1 (1990): 15–29.
———. "The Claims of a Common Culture: Gender, Race, Class, and the Canon." *Salmagundi* 72 (Fall 1986): 131–43.
Frank, Thomas. *One Market under God: Extreme Capitalism, Market Populism, and the End of Economic Democracy*. New York: Doubleday, 2000.
———. *Pity the Billionaire*. New York: Metropolitan, 2012.
———. *What's the Matter with Kansas?* New York: Metropolitan, 2004.
———. *The Wrecking Crew: How Conservatives Rule*. New York: Metropolitan, 2008.
Franklin, Benjamin. *Writings*. New York: Library of America, 1985.
"FreedomWorks." *Wikipedia*. Web.
Gates, David. "The Voices of Dissent." *Newsweek* 19 Nov. 2001. Web.
Gelernter, David. "A World without Public Schools." *Weekly Standard* 4 June 2007. 29–35.
Geoghegan, Thomas. *Were You Born on the Wrong Continent?* New York: New P, 2010.
Gerbner, George, et al. "Charting the Mainstream: Television's Contributions to Political Orientations," Lazere, *American Media*, 441–64.
Gershwin, Ira. *Strike Up the Band*. Studio cast recording, 1990. Electra. CD.
Gibbs, Nancy. "Living: How America Has Run Out of Time." *Time* 24 Apr. 1989: 58–60.
Giroux, Henry A. *Breaking in to the Movies: Film and the Culture of Politics*. London: Blackwell, 2002.
———. *The Mouse that Roared: Disney and the End of Innocence*. Lanham: Rowman and Littlefield, 1999.
———. *Public Spheres and Private Places*. Lanham: Rowman & Littlefield, 2001.
———. *Stealing Innocence: Corporate Culture's War on Children*. New York: St. Martin's, 2001.
———. *Youth in Revolt: Reclaiming a Democratic Future*. Boulder: Paradigm, 2013.
Giroux, Henry A., and Roger I. Simon. *Popular Culture, Schooling & Everyday Life*. Granby: Bergin & Garvey, 1989.

Giroux, Susan Searls. "The Age of Irony?" *Journal of Advanced Composition* 22:4 (Fall 2002): 960–76.
Gitlin, Todd. *Media Unlimited: How the Torrent of Images and Sounds Overwhelms Our Lives.* New York: Metropolitan, 2001.
Glazer, Nathan. "Neoconservative from the Start." *Public Interest* Spring 2005: 12–18.
———. "On Being De-Radicalized." *Commentary* Oct. 1970. Web.
———. *Remembering the Answers. Essays on the American Student Revolt.* New York: Basic, 1970.
———. *We Are All Multiculturalists Now.* Cambridge: Harvard UP, 1997.
Glen, John M. *Highlander: No Ordinary School.* Knoxville: U of Tennessee P, 1996.
Goldberg, Jonah. "The Rich Aren't Made of Money." *Los Angeles Times* 13 Nov. 2007. Web.
Goldstein, Richard. "The War for the American Mind." *Village Voice* 8 June 1982: 1.
Graff, Gerald. *Beyond the Culture Wars: How Teaching the Conflicts Can Revitalize American Education.* New York: Norton, 1992.
———. *Clueless in Academe.* New Haven: Yale UP, 2003.
Greenwald, Robert. *Outfoxed.* New York: Brave New Films, 2004.
Grossberg, Lawrence. *We Gotta Get Out of This Place: Popular Conservatism and Postmodern Culture.* London: Routledge, 1992.
Guess, Andy. "What If Higher Ed Funds Don't Help Economy?" *Inside Higher Education* 22 June 2007. Web.
Halloran, Michael. "Rhetoric in the American College Curriculum: The Decline of Public Discourse." *PRE/TEXT* 3 (1982): 245–69.
Harburg, E. Y., and Fred Saidy. *Finian's Rainbow.* New York: Berkley Medallion, 1968.
Harrington, Carly. "Study Shows UT's Impact." *Knoxville News Sentinel* 18 May 2010: B1.
Hart, Peter. "Is Glenn Beck Working for Reuters?" *FAIR Blog* 13 Oct. 2011.
Hartmann, Thom. *Unequal Protection: The Rise of Corporate Dominance and the Theft of Human Rights.* New York: Rodale, 2004.
Hayward, Steven F. "Fill 'er Up," *Weekly Standard* 26 Apr. 2010. Web.
———. "How to Think about Oil Spills: The Perils of Over-Reaction." *Weekly Standard* 21 June 2010. Web.
Heilbrunn, Jacob. *They Knew They Were Right: The Rise of the Neocons.* New York: Doubleday, 2008.
Heller, Joseph. *Catch-22.* New York: Dell, 1961.
Hemming, Roy. "Sinatra Standards." *Frank Sinatra: The Best of the Columbia Years 1943–52.* Columbia, 1995. Text: 25–37.
Hinderacker, John. "Think Ignorance Swings and Misses." *Powerline* 3 Mar. 2011. Web.
Hodson, Gordon, and Michael Bussari, "Bright Minds and Dark Attitudes: Lower Cognitive Ability Predicts Greater Prejudice Through Right-Wing

Ideology and Low Intergroup Contact." *Psychological Science* 23 (Feb. 2012): 187–95.
Horowitz, David. *The Art of Political War, and Other Radical Pursuits*. Dallas: Spence, 2000.
———. "The Campus Blacklist." *Frontpagemag.com* 18 Apr. 2003. Web.
———. *How to Beat the Democrats*. Dallas: Spence, 2002.
———. *Left Illusions: An Intellectual Odyssey*. Edited, with an Introduction, by Jamie Glazov. Dallas: Spence, 2003.
———. *The Professors: The 101 Most Dangerous Academics in America*. Washington: Regnery, 2006.
Howe, Irving. "The New York Intellectuals." *World of Our Fathers*. New York: Harcourt, Brace, Jovanovich, 1976. 598–607.
Hundley, Kris. "Billionaire's Role in Hiring Decisions at Florida State University Raises Questions." *Tampa Bay Times* 9 May 2011. Web.
Huxley, Aldous. *Brave New World and Brave New World Revisited*. New York: Harper, 1960.
Independent Socialist Club. *The Regents*. Berkeley: Independent Socialist Club, 1965.
Jacobson, Jennifer. "What Makes David Run." *Chronicle of Higher Education* 6 May 2006: A9.
Jameson, Fredric. *The Ideologies of Theory, vol. 2*. Minneapolis: U of Minnesota P, 1988.
———. *Late Marxism*. London: Verso, 1990.
———. *Signatures of the Visible*. London: Routledge, 1990.
Jaschik, Scott. "Retractions from David Horowitz." *Inside Higher Education* Feb. 10, 2008. Web.
Jefferson, Margo. "Unreal Loyalties." *New York Times Book Review* 13 Apr. 2003: 31.
Jefferson, Thomas. "Letter to George Logan." *The Works of Thomas Jefferson*, Vol. 12. Federal Edition. New York and London: G. P. Putnam's Sons, 1904–5. Accessed from http://oll.libertyfund.org/title/808/88352.
———. *Writings*. Ed. Merrill D. Peterson. New York: Library of America, 1984.
Jong, Erica. *Fear of Flying*. New York: Holt Rinehart & Winston, 1973.
Judt, Tony. *Ill Fares the Land*. London: Penguin, 2010.
Kahn, Seth, and JongHwa Lee, eds. *Activism and Rhetoric: Theories and Contexts for Political Engagement*. New York: Routledge, 2011.
Kaiser, Robert G, and Ira Chinoy. "Scaife: Funding Father of the Right." *Washington Post* 2 May 1991: A1.
Kampf, Louis. "The Scandal of Literary Scholarship." *The Dissenting Academy*. Ed. Theodor Roszak. New York: Vintage, 1968.
Kampf, Louis, and Paul Lauter, eds. *The Politics of Literature: Dissenting Essays on the Teaching of English*. New York: Vintage, 1973.
Katz, Stan. "Can We Afford State Colleges?" *Chronicle of Higher Education* 3 Apr. 2010. Web.

Kimball, Roger. "Fredric Jameson's Laments." *New Criterion* 9.10 (June 1991): 9–16.

———. *Tenured Radicals: How Politics Has Corrupted Our Higher Education.* New York: Harper & Row, 1990.

Kirkpatrick, Jeanne J. "Dictatorships and Double Standards." *Commentary* Nov. 1979. Web.

Kozol, Jonathan. *Savage Inequalities.* New York: Crown, 1991.

Kristol, Irving. "American Conservatism 1945–1995." *Public Interest* 121 (Fall 1995): 80–91.

———. "Conservatives' Greatest Enemy May Be the GOP." *Wall Street Journal* 20 Feb. 1990: A24.

———. *Neoconservatism: The Autobiography of an Idea.* New York: Free P, 1995.

———. "On Economic Education." *Wall Street Journal* 18 Feb. 1976: 20.

———. "The Political Dilemma of American Jews." *Commentary* July 1984. Web.

———.. *Reflections of a Neoconservative.* New York: Basic Books, 1983.

Krugman, Paul. "Ignorance Is Strength." *New York Times* 8 Mar. 2012. Web.

Kull, Steven, et al. "Misperceptions, the Media, and the Iraq War." Program on International Public Attitudes. University of Maryland. 2 Oct. 2003. Web.

Lakoff, George. *Don't Think of an Elephant. Know Your Values and Frame the Debate.* White River Junction: Chelsea Green Publishing, 2004.

———. *Thinking Points: Communicating Our American Values and Vision.* New York: Farrar, 2006.

"Language: A Key Mechanism of Control." *Extra!* 1 Feb. 1995. Web.

Lasch. *The Agony of the American Left.* New York: Random House, 1968.

———. *The Culture of Narcissism.* New York: Norton, 1978.

Laster, Jill. "$700,000 Pay for Leader of Civic-Literacy Research Group Raises Eyebrows." *Chronicle of Higher Education* 11 Apr. 2010. Web.

Lauter, Paul. *Canons and Contexts.* New York: Oxford UP, 1991.

———, et al. *Heath Anthology of American Literature.* New York: Heath, 1990.

Lazere, Donald. "American Criticism of the Sartre-Camus Dispute: A Chapter in the Cultural Cold War." *The Philosophy of Jean-Paul Sartre.* Ed. Paul Arthur Schilpp. Library of Living Philosophers, La Salle, IL: Open Court 1981. 108–21.

———. ed. *American Media and Mass Culture: Left Perspectives.* Berkeley: U of California P, 1987.

———. "Comment and Response." *College English* 61 (1998): 83–88.

———. "Conservatives Have an Upside-Down View of What Constitutes Bias in Academe." *Chronicle of Higher Education* 9 Nov. 1989: A52.

———. "Forum" exchange with Herbert London, *Profession* 90 (1990): 76–78.

---. "Ground Rules for Polemicists: The Case of Lynne Cheney's Truths." *College English* 59 (1997): 661–85.

---. "Higher Education: Golden Goose or Dead Duck?" *Chronicle of Higher Education* 14 Apr. 2011. Web.

---. "Is Rush Limbaugh a Racist?" *Chronicle of Higher Eduction* 22 Oct. 2009. Web.

---. "Literary Revisionism, Partisan Politics, and the Press." *Profession* 89 (1989): 49–54.

---. "Neoconservatism as Orthodoxy." *American Quarterly* 47, 2 (1995): 361–68.

---. "*Partisan Review*, Our Culture and Our Country." *College English* 67 (2005): 296–308.

---. "Patriotism, Partisanship, and the Conscience of Conservative Scholars." *Journal of Advanced Composition* 23 (2003): 641–48.

---. "Political Correctness Left and Right." *College English* 54 (1992): 333–42.

---. *Reading and Writing for Civic Literacy: The Critical Citizen's Guide to Argumentative Rhetoric.* Boulder: Paradigm, 2006.

---. *The Retreat from Political Literacy in Rhetcomp Studies.* Forthcoming.

---. "Thumbs Up on Hirsch, Thumbs Down on Bloom." *Pedagogy* 9 (2009): 501–08.

---. "Why is the National Association of Scholars Saying Such Awful Things about Critical Thinking?" *RAIL* 29 Dec. 2011. railct.org. Web.

Leibovich, Mark. "Being Glenn Beck." *New York Times Magazine* 3 Oct. 2010: 35–57.

Lewis, Oscar. *Five Families: Mexican Case Studies in the Culture of Poverty.* New York: Basic, 1959.

Limbaugh, Rush. *See, I Told You So.* New York: Pocket Books (paperback), 1994.

---. *The Way Things Ought to Be.* New York: Pocket Books (paperback), 1993.

Lind, Michael. *Up from Conservatism: Why the Right Is Wrong about America.* New York: Free P, 1996.

Loewen, James. *Lies My Teacher Told Me.* New York: New P, 1995.

"The Long March of Newt Gingrich." *Frontline.* PBS.org 16 Jan. 1996. Web.

Lowry, Rich. "Where's the Misery?" *National Review* 29 June 2004. Web.

Lundberg, Claire. "Trapped by European-Style Socialism—And I Love It." *Slate* 2 Nov. 2012. Web.

Luntz, Frank I. "The Language of Healthcare 2009." *Physicians for a National Health Program* 7 May 2009. Web.

Macon, Uncle Dave. *Uncle Dave Macon.* Record, Book, and Music Sales, 1963. LP.

Maggs, John. "Grover at the Gate." *National Journal* 10 Oct. 2003. Web.

Mann, James. *Rise of the Vulcans: The History of Bush's War Cabinet.* New York: Viking, 2004.

Marcuse, Herbert. *An Essay on Liberation.* Boston: Beacon, 1969.

———. *One-Dimensional Man.* Boston: Beacon, 1964.

———. "Repressive Tolerance." *A Critique of Pure Tolerance.* Ed. Robert Paul Wolff, Barrington Moore, and Herbert Marcuse. Boston: Beacon, 1969.

Marklein, Mary Beth. "Flag Is Raised on Admissions." *USA Today* 25 Oct. 2006. Web.

Martin, Jerry, and Anne D. Neal. *Defending Civilization: How Our Universities Are Failing America and What Can Be Done about It.* Washington: American Council of Trustees and Alumni, Revised and Expanded, February 2002.

Mattson, Kevin. "A Student Bill of Rights." *Nation* 4 Apr. 2005. Web

Max, D. T. "With Friends Like Saul Bellow." *New York Times Magazine* 16 Apr. 2000. Web.

Mayer, Jane. "Covert Operations." *New Yorker* 30 Aug. 2010. Web.

———. "Is Senator Ted Cruz Our New McCarthy?" *New Yorker* 22 Feb. 2013. Web.

———."The Money Man." *New Yorker* 18 Oct. 2004. Web.

Mayer, Jane, and Jill Abramson. *Strange Justice: The Selling of Justice Clarence Thomas.* Boston: Houghton, 1994

McChesney, Robert. *The Problem of the Media. U.S. Communication Politics in the 21st Century.* New York: Monthly Review P, 2004.

McChesney, Robert, and John Nichols. *The Death and Life of American Journalism.* New York: Nation Books, 2010.

McGhee, Brownie, and Sonny Terry. *Folk at Newport Vol 2. last.fm* 2010. Web.

Melville, Herman. *Billy Budd and Other Tales.* Ed. Frederick Baron Freeman. New York: New American Library, 1961.

Menand, Louis. "Faith, Hope, and Clarity." *New Yorker* 16 Sept. 2002. Web.

Michaels, Walter Benn. *The Trouble with Diversity.* New York: Metropolitan, 2006.

Mindich, David. *Tuned Out: Why Americans Under 40 Don't Follow the News.* New York: Oxford UP, 2005.

Minding the Campus. *mindingthecampuscom* n.d. Web.

Monbiot, George. "The Right's Stupidity Spreads, Enabled by A Too Polite Left." *Guardian/UT* 7 Feb. 2012. Web.

Montaigne, Michel de. *Selected Essays.* Trans. William Hazlitt. Ed. Blanchard Bates. New York: Modern Library, 1949.

Montopoli, Brian. "Just 53% Say Capitalism Is Preferable to Socialism." *CBSNews.com* 9 Apr. 2009. Web.

Mooney, Chris. *The Republican Brain: The Science of Why They Deny Science—and Reality.* New York: Wiley, 2012.

Morse, J. Mitchell. *The Irrelevant English Teacher*. Philadelphia: Temple UP, 1972.
Moyers, Bill, and Michael Winship. "Ralph Reed in the Marianas Trenches." *Common Dreams* 1 Sept. 2012. Web
National Association of Scholars. *nas.org*. Web.
Navasky, Victor S. *A Matter of Opinion*. New York: Farrar, 2005.
Newfield, Christopher. *Unmaking the Public University*. Cambridge: Harvard UP, 2011.
Newfield, Christopher, and Ron Strickland. eds. *After Political Correctness*. Boulder: Westview, 1995.
Newport, Frank. "Socialism Viewed Favorably by 36% of Americans." *Gallup Politics* 4 Feb. 2010. Web.
Nobile, Philip. *Intellectual Skywriting*. New York: Charterhouse, 1974.
Norquist, Grover. "Winner Takes All." *American Spectator* Apr. 1999, 66–67.
O'Malley, Susan Gush, Robert C. Rosen, and Leonard Vogt, eds. *Politics of Education: Essays from Radical Teacher*, Albany: SUNY P, 1990.
Ohmann, Richard. "Doublespeak and Ideology in Ads: A Kit for Teachers," Lazere, *American Media*, 106–15.
———. *English in America: A Radical View of the Profession*. New York: Oxford UP, 1977.
———. "The MLA and the Politics of Inadvertence." *PMLA* 83.4 (Sept. 1968). Web.
———. *Politics of Letters*. Middletown: Wesleyan UP, 1987.
Oreskes, Naomi, and Erick M. Conway. *Merchants of Doubt: How a Handful of Scientists Obscured the Truth on Issues from Tobacco Smoke to Global Warming*. New York: Bloomsbury, 2010.
Orwell, George. *Animal Farm*. New York: Harcourt Brace Jovanovich, 1948.
———. *1984*. New York: Signet, 1961.
Osborne, David. "Newt Gingrich: Shining Knight of the Republican Right." *Mother Jones* Nov. 1984. Web.
"Our Country, Our Culture." Special issue of *Partisan Review* 69.4 (2002).
Paine, Thomas. *Collected Writings*. New York: Library of America, 1995.
Partridge, Eric. *Shakespeare's Bawdy*. New York: Plume, 1960.
Perez, Emma. "Why We Need Ethnic Studies." Department of Ethnic Studies, University of Colorado, Boulder, 28 Apr. 2005. archived.wardchurchill.net/40_b_ethnic_studies_open_letter.pdf.
Perry, William. *Forms of Intellectual and Ethical Development in the College Years*. New York: Holt Rinehart & Winston, 1970.
Piaget, Jean. *The Language and Thought of the Child*. New York: New American Library, 1955.
Pinsker, Sanford. "Comment on Donald Lazere, "Ground Rules for Polemicists." *College English* 61 (1998): 83–88.

———. "Cooling the Polemics of the Culture Warriors." *Chronicle of Higher Education* 3 May 1996: A56.
Podhoretz, John. *Hell of a Ride: Backstage at the White House Follies 1989–93.* New York: Simon, 1993.
Podhoretz, Norman. "Appeasement by Any Other Name." *Commentary* July 1983: 33–38.
———. *The Bloody Crossroads: Where Literature and Politics Meet.* New York: Simon, 1986.
———. *Breaking Ranks: A Political Memoir.* New York: Harper & Row, 1979.
———. "In Defense of Sarah Palin." *Wall Street Journal* 29 Mar. 2010. Web.
———. *Making It.* New York: Random House, 1967.
———. *My Love Affair with America.* New York: Free P, 2000.
———. "My Negro Problem—and Ours." *Commentary* Feb.1963. Web.
———."New Hypocrisies." *Commentary* Dec. 1970: 5–6.
Porter, Cole. *Kiss Me, Kate.* Broadway cast recording. Columbia, 1950. LP.
Powell, Lewis. "Confidential Memorandum: Attack on American Free Enterprise System." U.S. Chamber of Commerce 23 Aug. 1971. Web.
Putnam, Robert. *Bowling Alone: The Collapse and Revival of American Community.* New York: Simon, 2000.
Rank, Hugh. *Persuasion Analysis.* Park Forest: Counter-Propaganda Press, 1988.
Readings, Bill. *The University in Ruins.* Cambridge: Harvard UP, 1997.
Reagan, Ronald. "Farewell Address to the Nation." Oval Office, 11 Jan. 1989. Web.
Reed, Adolph. "Majoring in Debt." *Progressive* Jan. 2004. Web.
Republican Party of Texas. *Republican Party Platform, 2012.* Web.
Sacks, Peter. *Tearing Down the Gates: Confronting the Class Divide in American Education.* Berkeley: U of California P, 2007.
Safire, William. *Before the Fall.* New York: Doubleday, 1975.
Saulny, Susan. "Cain Says 'We Need a Leader, Not a Reader.'" *New York Times* 17 Nov. 2011. Web.
Saunders, Francis. *The Cultural Cold War: The CIA and the World of Arts and Letters.* New York: New P, 1999.
Scheuer, Jeffrey. *The Sound-Bite Society: How Television Helps the Right and Hurts the Left.* New York: Routledge, 2001.
Schrag, Peter. *Paradise Lost: California's Experience: America's Future.* New York: New P, 1999.
Schrecker, Ellen. *The Lost Soul of Higher Education.* New York: New P, 2010.
Schwirtz, Michael. "In Filing, Casino Operator Admits Likely Violation of an Antibribery Law." *New York Times* 2 Mar 2013. Web.
Seeger, Pete. "Get Up and Go." New York: Melody Trails, 1964.
Sleeper, Jim. "Allan Bloom and the Conservative Mind." *New York Times* 4 Sept. 2005. Web.

Smith, Bessie. *The Complete Columbia Recordings*. Columbia, 2012. CD set.
Smith, Preston H. II, and Sharon Szymanski. "Why Political Scientists Should Support Free Higher Education." *Political Science and Politics* 36.4 (2003): 699–703.
Soley, Lawrence. *The Leasing of the University: The Corporate Takeover of Academia*. Boston: South End, 1995.
Somberg, Iris. "$36 Million from Soros Aids Groups That Support Occupy Wall Street." *Business and Media Institute* 13 Oct. 2011. Web.
Sontag, Susan. "The Talk of the Town." *New Yorker* 24 Sept. 2001. Web.
Soros, George. "My Philanthropy." *New York Review of Books*. 23 June 2011: 12–16.
Stauber, John, and Sheldon Rampton. *Toxic Sludge Is Good for You: Lies, Damn Lies and the Public Relations Industry*. Monroe, ME: Common Courage P, 1995.
Steinfels, Peter. *The Neoconservatives: The Men Who Are Changing American Politics*. New York: Simon, 1979.
Steinberg, Jacques. "Plan B: Skip College." *New York Times Week in Review* 15 May 2010. Web.
Suskind, Ron. "Faith, Certainty, and the Administration of George W. Bush." *New York Times Magazine* 17 Oct. 2004. Web.
Swift, Jonathan. *Gulliver's Travels and Other Writings*. Ed. Louis A. Landa. Boston: Houghton, 1990.
———. *Poems of Jonathan Swift*. Ed. Harold Williams. London: Oxford UP, 1958. Web.
Tanenhaus, Sam. "The Raging Center." *New York Times Book Review* 25 Apr. 2010: 27.
Thoreau, Henry David. *Walden and Other Writings*. Ed. Brooks Atkinson. New York: Modern Library, 1950.
Thurber, James. "The Bear Who Let It Alone." *The Thurber Carnival*. New York: Harper, 1945. 253.
Tomasky, Michael. "Something New on the Mall." *New York Review* 22 Oct. 2009: 4–8.
Toobin, Jeffrey. "The Dirty Trickster." *New Yorker* 2 June 2008. Web.
Trilling, Diana. "Letter to the Editor," *The New Republic* 189.27 (31 Dec. 1983): 40.
Twain, Mark. *Letters from the Earth*. New York: Harper Perennial, 1962.
———. "The Mysterious Stranger." *Great Short Works of Mark Twain*. New York: Harper Perennial, 1967. 278–366.
———. *Pudd'nhead Wilson and Those Extraordinary Twins*. Norton Critical Edition. New York: Norton, 2004.
———. "Some Thought on the Science of Onanism." *Mark Twain: Collected Tales, Sketches, Speeches and Essays* 1852–1890. Ed. Louis J. Budd. New York: Library of America, 1992.
Untermeyer, Louis. *A Treasury of Ribaldry*. New York: Hanover House, 1956.
Vedder, Richard. *Going Broke by Degree: Why College Costs So Much*. Washington: American Enterprise Institute, 2004.

———. "The Real Costs of Federal Aid to Higher Education." *Heritage Lectures, Heritage Foundation* 12 Jan. 2007. Web.

———. "Universities in America: Reply to a Critic." *Chronicle of Higher Education* 19 Apr. 2011. Web.

———. "Why Does College Cost So Much?" *Wall Street Journal* 23 Aug. 2005. Web.

Vedder, Richard, and Matthrew Denhart. "Michigan Higher Education: Facts and Fictions." *Mackinac Center for Public Policy* 20 June 2007. Web.

Vogel, Kenneth. "The Kochs Fight Back." *Politico* 2 Feb. 2011. Web.

Voltaire. *Candide*. Trans. Lowell Bair. New York: Bantam, 1959.

Wald, Alan M. *The New York Intellectuals*. Durham: U of North Carolina P, 1986.

Warshow, Robert. *The Immediate Experience*. Enlarged Edition. Cambridge: Harvard UP, 2001. Original edition, Garden City: Doubleday, 1962.

Washburn, Jennifer. *University Inc.: The Corporate Corruption of Higher Education*. New York: Basic, 2005.

Westin, Drew. *The Political Brain*. New York: Public Affairs, 2007.

Whitman, Walt. *Complete Poetry and Selected Prose*. Ed. James E. Miller, Jr. Boston: Houghton, 1959.

Wiener, Jon. "Dollars for Neocon Scholars." *Professors, Politics and Pop*. London and New York: Verso, 1991. 99–103.

———. "Professors Paid by Qaddafi: Providing Positive Public Relations." *Nation* 3 June 2011. Web.

Will, George. "Literary Politics." *Newsweek* 22 Apr. 1991. Web.

Willis, Oliver. "Beck Renews Witch Hunt." *Media Matters* 27 May 2010. Web.

Willson, Meredith. *The Music Man*. Broadway cast recording. Capitol, 1959. LP.

Wilson, John K. *The Myth of Political Correctness*. Durham: Duke UP, 1995.

———. *Patriotic Correctness: Academic Freedom and Its Enemies*. Boulder: Paradigm, 2008.

Winthrop, John. *The Winthrop Papers*. Vol. 1, *1645–1649*. Ed. Allyn B. Forbes. Boston: Massachusetts Historical Society, 1947.

Woessner, Matthew. "Rethinking the Plight of Conservatives in Higher Education." *Academe* 98 (Jan.–Feb. 2012): 22–8.

Wolff, Richard. *Democracy at Work: A Cure for Capitalism*. Chicago: Haymarket, 2012.

Wood, Peter. "Civics Lessons." *Chronicle of Higher Education* 26 Jan. 2012. Web.

———. "The Curriculum of Forgetting." *Chronicle of Higher Education* 21 Nov. 2011. Web.

———. "Gay Marriage." *Chronicle of Higher Education* 11 May, 2012. Web.

———. "Politics, Education, and More Politics: The NAS's New Report on the University of California." *Chronicle of Higher Education* 4 Apr. 2012. Web.

Woolf, Virginia. *A Room of One's Own*. New York: Harcourt, 1989. First edition, New York: Harcourt, 1929.

Zywicki, Todd. "On Charles and David Koch." *Volokh Conspiracy* 31 Aug. 2010. Web.

INDEX

Note: Locators followed by 'n' refer to notes.

9/11, 39, 44, 67, 91, 127, 135, 153, 184, 210, 215–16
1984 (Orwell), 38, 48, 55, 68, 84–5, 95, 123
60 Minutes, 25

Abramoff, Jack, 26, 82, 85–93, 97, 146, 239n. 2–3
Abrams, Elliot, 125–6, 132, 149
Abrams, Rachel, 135
Abramson, Jill, 136
ACORN, 23, 26, 49, 97, 117, 240n. 2
ActivistCash, 116
Adams, John, 32
Adbusters, 9–10, 115
Adelson, Sheldon, 239n. 3
Adorno, Theodor, 137, 164
Afghanistan, 86, 91, 135, 153–4, 210, 216
Agnew, Spiro, 76–7
Ailes, Roger, 82, 110, 114
Alinsky, Saul, 97–8
Al-Qaeda, 44, 91, 128, 178
Alterman, Eric, 1, 79–80
American Civil Liberties Union, 147–8
American Council of Trustees and Alumni (ACTA), 148, 151–3, 155, 211, 226, 233
American Enterprise Institute, 62, 78–80, 101, 160, 194
American Foundations (Dowie), 112

American Legislative Exchange Council (ALEC), 106
Americans for Prosperity (AFP), 10, 88, 97–8, 104, 108, 112, 114, 116, 240n. 1
Animal Farm (Orwell), 38, 48, 95
Armey, Dick, 10, 97, 100, 102, 240n. 1
Arnold, Matthew, 17, 160
Aronowitz, Stanley, 33, 70, 196
Arvin, Newton, 222
Aspen Institute, 113, 144
Association for Informal Logic and Critical Thinking (AILACT), 155
Atwater, Lee, 82

Bachmann, Michele, 94, 217
Balch, Stephen, 148–9
Baldwin, James, 222, 224–5
Balint, Benjamin, 123, 134
Banfield, Edward, 128, 132
Banning, Marlia, 100, 241n. 4
Barber, Benjamin, 24
Baroody, William, 80, 101, 118
Bartlett, Bruce, 46, 129
Barton, David, 218, 243n. 1
Beatty, Warren, 70
Beck, Glenn, 10, 18–19, 82, 100, 103, 114, 132, 154, 217
Bell Curve, The (Herrnstein and Murray), 194
Bell, Daniel, 27, 123–4, 128–9, 132
Bell, Pearl K., 123

Index

Bellow, Adam, 96
Bellow, Saul, 138–40
Bennett, William J., 68, 72, 102, 132, 138, 144, 151, 153–4, 194, 201, 205, 210–12, 214–20, 222, 226, 228, 230, 233, 239–40n. 3
Berkeley Free Speech Movement, 52–3, 121–2
Bernstein, Basil, 37–8, 40, 47
Bernstein, David, 106
Bernstein, Richard, 62
Best Years of Our Lives, The, 69
Bircher, John, 104
Biskind, Peter, 70
Blinded by the Right (Brock), 2, 80, 93
Bloom, Allan, 24, 30, 96, 99–100, 136–40, 144, 152, 194, 230, 241n. 3
Blumenthal, Sidney, 1, 129
Bogdanor, Paul, 157
Bolton, John, 151
Bork, Robert, 124, 144, 151
Boskin, Michael, 55
Bozell, Brent, 61, 114
Bradford, William, 32
Brave New World (Huxley), 47, 68
Breaking Ranks (Podhoretz), 23, 121–2, 133
British Petroleum (BP) oil spill, 78
Brock, David, 1–2, 80–2, 93, 96, 102, 114, 124
Brooks, David, 62–3, 134, 151
Buchanan, Pat, 19
Buckley, William F., 80, 127, 132
Burke, Edmund, 19
Burnham, James, 95, 123
Bush, George H.W., 55, 125–6, 134, 136, 177, 180
Bush, George W., 62, 82–3, 87, 92, 109, 126, 134–5, 138, 148, 153, 177, 179–80, 194, 196, 217, 227
Business and Media Institute (BMI), 115, 118

Cain, Herman, 46, 100, 104, 114, 154
"Campus Blacklist, The" (Horowitz), 2
Camus, Albert, 123, 167, 211
Carnegie, Andrew, 101, 109
Carnegie Commission, 62
Carnegie, Dale, 137
Carter, Jimmy, 110
Cato Institute, 79, 101, 105–7, 110, 112, 114, 117, 146
Cauchon, Rich, 192–3, 198
Center for American Freedom, 111–12
Center for American Progress, 77, 111, 146
Chace, William M., 202–3
Chait, Jonathan, 112
Chaplin, Charlie, 29, 31
Cheney, Dick, 135, 227
Cheney, Lynne, 72, 75–6, 82, 102, 124, 144, 151, 160–2, 165–7, 176, 206, 211, 217, 226, 228, 233
Chevron, 62–3
Chomsky, Noam, 153, 157–8, 212, 216
Christian Coalition, 90, 127
Churchill, Ward, 15, 147–8
Citizens for a Sound Economy (CSE), 97–8
Citizens United case, 20–1, 219
Clinton, Bill, 46, 77, 81, 102–3, 108, 114, 129, 135, 180
Closing of the American Mind, The (Bloom), 24, 96, 136, 152, 194
CNN, 51
Cohn, Werner, 157–8
Colby, Anne, 99
Cold War, 55, 69–70, 91, 93, 95, 120, 123, 127, 130–1, 135, 184
College Republicans (CR), 83, 85–7, 146
Collier, Peter, 157

Index

Commentary magazine, 68, 120–5, 127, 134–6, 140, 149, 156, 159
Common Cause, 112, 115
Conason, Joe, 1
Congress for Cultural Freedom, 95
Continetti, Matthew, 94, 97–8, 106–13, 237n. 1, 240n. 1–2
Coors family, 81, 101
Cornell University, 139, 241n. 4
corporate underwriting, 62
Coulter, Ann, 54, 82, 132, 151, 217
Council for National Policy, 84
Crawford, Victor, 25–7, 174
Crèvecoeur, Hector St. John, 217, 219
Crick, Bernard, 123
Crossen, Cynthia, 67, 161
Cruz, Arturo, 149
Cruz, Ted, 18–19
C-SPAN, 28, 43, 77–8, 147, 162, 234
Curran, James, 59
Current TV, 102

Dean, John, 92–3, 149
Decter, Midge, 93, 120, 122, 125–6, 131, 134–5, 149
DeLay, Tom, 82, 88–90, 93, 148
Dershowitz, Alan, 158
Dolan, Terry, 84
Dorrien, Gary, 130, 133–5, 141, 234
Dostoyevsky, Fyodor, 52–3
doublethink, 18, 22, 84, 95, 161, 183
Douglass, Frederick, 32
Douthat, Ross, 46, 62, 151
Dowie, Mark, 112–13
Drudge, Matt, 10
D'Souza, Dinesh, 96, 144
Dyson, Michael Eric, 102

Easton, Nina, 85–6, 91, 136
Economic Education Trust, 106
Egan, Mark, 9

Ehrlich, Thomas, 99
elaborated code (EC), 37
Ellis, John, 144, 151, 163–5
El Salvador, 91–2, 124–5, 184
Emerson, Ralph Waldo, 17, 67, 220
Empson, William, 1, 213
End of Ideology, The (Bell), 128
Environmental Protection Agency (EPA), 108–9
Epstein, Joseph, 120
Erlanger, Steven, 58–9
Escape from Freedom (Fromm), 137, 164

Fairness and Accuracy in Media (FAIR), 9, 61, 78, 111
Falwell, Jerry, 127
Fang, Lee, 107
Finn, Chester, 102
Foner, Philip S., 68
Ford Foundation, 9, 101, 107, 116
Ford, Gerald, 122, 144
Fox-Genovese, Elizabeth, 71–2
Fox News, 9–10, 28, 39–40, 49, 71–2, 82, 97, 102, 110, 113–14, 134, 139, 143, 160, 239n. 2
Frank, Thomas, 85–6, 89–91, 96–7, 104, 130, 205, 240n. 1
Frankfurt School, 33–4, 47, 69, 137, 163–4
Franklin, Benjamin, 32, 215, 217, 219, 221–2, 243n. 1
Freddie Mac, 100
FreedomWorks, 10, 97, 108, 112, 115–16, 240n. 1, 241n. 3
Freire, Paulo, 33
Friedman, Milton, 64, 194, 205
Friedman, Thomas, 239n. 1
Fromm, Erich, 137, 164
Frontline, 63, 83
Frum, David, 46

Gang of Five (Easton), 85
Gates, Bill, 104
Gates, David, 2115

Gates Foundation, 9
Gates, Henry Louis, 148
Gates, Jeff, 65
Gates, Preston, 87
Gates, Skip, 147–8
Gelernter, David, 156–7
G.I. Bill, 189, 203
Gilman, Charlotte Perkins, 67–8
Gingrich, Newt, 75, 82–3, 88, 93, 100, 102, 151, 161, 239–40n. 3
Giroux, Henry, 33, 70
Giroux, Susan Searls, 33, 65
Gitlin, Todd, 48–9
Glazer, Nathan, 56, 120, 128–9, 132, 241–2n. 4
Glazov, Jamie, 75
Glickes, Erwin, 96
Goldberg, Bernard, 43, 54, 61
Goldberg, Jonah, 55
Goldfarb, Michael, 111–12
Goldsmith, Oliver, 32
Goldstein, Richard, 126
Gorman, Phil, 138
Gouldner, Alvin, 173
Graff, Gerald, 33–4, 163, 174, 21, 241n. 2
Gramm, Phil, 102
Greenpeace, 105
Greenwald, Robert, 110

Habitat for Humanity, 23
Harburg, E.Y., 219
Hartford, Huntington, 23
Hartmann, Thom, 20, 220
Hayek, Friedrich, 19
Hayes, Chris, 28
Hayward, Stephen F., 78–9
Heilbrunn, Jacob, 24, 135, 138–9
Heller, Joseph, 209–10
Herbert, Bob, 62
Heritage Foundation, 62, 79–80, 91, 96, 101, 194–5, 197, 201–3
Herzberg, Hendrik, 110
Hill, Anita, 2, 81, 96, 105, 136

Hinteraker, John, 107
Hoover, Herbert, 47
Hoover, Margaret, 9–10
Horkheimer, Max, 164
Horowitz, David, 2, 35, 45, 54, 75, 82, 84, 95, 99, 114, 128, 132, 143, 146–8, 157, 174, 206, 239n. 1, 241n. 2, 242n. 2
Horton, Willy, 82
Hurricane Katrina, 127
Huxley, Aldous, 47–8, 51, 68, 130

Iannone, Carol, 123–4, 144, 155, 160
Ill Fares the Land (Judt), 32, 56, 205
Inconvenient Truth, An, 78
International Freedom Foundation, 91
Iran-Contra scandal, 81, 125
Iraq, 39–40, 62, 86, 92, 104, 135, 138, 154, 184, 210
Islam, 38, 44, 57, 91–2, 135, 224
Israel, 19, 126–7, 130, 135, 157–8, 216

Jameson, Fredric, 162–4
Jarvis, Howard, 47
Jefferson, Margo, 214
Jefferson, Thomas, 53, 213, 217, 219–20, 243n. 1
Johnson, Lyndon B., 128
Johnson, Samuel, 228
Jones, Thomas, 139
Jones, Van, 97, 103
Judt, Tony, 32, 56, 205

Kampf, Louis, 69
Kazan, Elia, 70
Kennedy family, 135
Kerry, John, 48, 114
Keyes, Alan, 132
Kibbe, Matt, 97, 240n. 1
Kimball, Roger, 138, 144, 162–4
Kingsolver, Barbara, 67, 215
Kirkpatrick, Jean, 124, 149

Knoxville, Tennessee, 42–4
Koch, Charles and David
   attack campaigns and, 81, 98
   Continetti and, 94, 97–8, 107–12
   criticism of, 105–6
   defense of, 106–8
   FreedomWorks and, 240n. 1
   Mayer and, 98, 105–10, 113–14
   NCI and, 109–10
   on Obama, 237n. 1
   political influence, 58, 79, 100–101, 104–18
   Tea Party and, 10–11, 49, 100
   Volokh and, 106–7
   Walker and, 58, 240n. 2
Kozody, Neil, 123, 134
Kozol, Jonathan, 201
Kramer, Hilton, 120, 127, 163
Kristol, Irving, 24, 46, 50, 56, 76, 80, 95–6, 101–2, 110, 119–20, 122, 124, 127–38, 144, 149, 151
Kristol, William, 102, 110, 124, 132, 134–5, 138
K Street Project, 88–9
Krugman, 62, 189
Kucinich, Dennis, 187

Lakoff, George, 78
Larssen, Stieg, 57
Lasch, Christopher, 69
Ledeen, Michael, 149
Lehrer, Jim, 63
Lerman, Robert, 204
Libby, Lewis "Scooter," 135
Limbaugh, Rush, 9–10, 82, 84, 94, 100, 114, 132, 151, 217–18
Lind, Michael, 80, 95, 127, 206, 239n. 1
Loewen, James, 153, 212
London, Jack, 67
London, Herbert, 16, 148–9
Lowry, Rich, 190–3, 198, 201, 204
Luntz, Frank, 78, 82, 103, 241n. 4

Maher, Bill, 42, 48
Making It (Podhoretz), 23–4, 132
Mandela, Nelson, 91
Manhattan Institute, 79, 132, 148, 152, 155
Mann, James, 135
Marcuse, Herbert, 17, 51, 137, 164, 231
Mariana Islands, 87, 89, 97
Marxism, 15, 17, 30, 33, 44, 55, 64, 68–72, 86, 95, 162–4, 238–9n. 1
Mattson, Kevin, 147
Max, D. T., 139–40
Mayer, Jane, 98, 101, 105–10, 113–14, 116, 136, 240n. 1
McCain, John, 111
McCarthyism, 67, 107, 243n. 2
McChesney, Robert, 50, 62
McConnell, Mitch, 77
McGrath, Charles, 62
McKibben, Bill, 115
McNamara, Robert, 215
Meacham, Jon, 63
Media Matters, 61, 103, 112
Media Research Center, 61, 114, 116
Medicare, 21, 58, 177, 182
Medved, Michael, 54
Melville, Herman, 67, 220, 222
Merkin, Daphne, 123
Michaels, Walter Benn, 71
Miller, Judith, 62
Miller, Mitch, 238n. 4
Mindich, David, 39
Mitchell, John, 82
Montaigne, Michel de, 77, 213–14, 220–1, 226, 229
Moon, Sun Myung, 81, 102, 134
Mooney, Chris, 39
Moore, Michael, 44, 59
Morse, J. Mitchell, 213
Mother Jones, 28, 83, 102, 111
MoveOn.org, 9, 77, 112, 115
Moyers, Bill, 63, 90

Moynihan, Daniel Patrick, 64, 128–9, 132
MSNBC, 28, 48, 59–60, 102, 111, 234
Mumper, Larry, 99
Murdoch, Rupert, 45, 57, 81, 100–102, 110–11, 114, 134

Nader, Ralph, 15, 85
Nation, 57, 60, 101–2, 111
National Association of Scholars (NAS), 16, 54, 68, 124, 145, 148–52, 154–5, 163–4, 233
National Cancer Institute (NCI), 109–10
National Council of Teachers of English (NCTE), 145
National Endowment for the Humanities (NEH), 160
National Public Radio (NPR), 61–3, 110
National Security Council (NSA), 126
Navasky, Victor, 101
New Criterion, 127, 138, 163
New Criticism, 31–2
Newhouse, S. I., 110
New Republic, 112, 120
Newsmax, 114
Nichols, John, 62
Nichols, Michelle, 9
Nixon, Richard, 35, 64, 76–7, 79, 81–2, 93, 129, 227, 242n. 4
Norquist, Grover, 85–9, 91, 93, 132, 143, 146, 205
Nye, Joseph, 24

Obama, Barack, 17, 18, 20, 43, 46, 48, 77, 96, 98, 102–3, 105, 110–11, 119, 129, 148, 180, 187, 190, 237n. 1
Obamacare, 43
Occupy Wall Street (OWS), 9–10, 42, 44, 59–60, 105, 114–16, 118

O'Donnell, Lawrence, 111
Office of Information and Regulatory Affairs (OIRA), 103
Ohmann, Richard, 26, 32, 212
Olbermann, Keith, 42
Olin Foundation, 79, 96, 101, 114, 116, 118, 137–8, 144, 149, 151
Ong, Walter J., 37
Open Society Foundation, 9, 101, 112, 114–16
O'Reilly, Bill, 9–10, 82–3, 114, 151, 217
Orion Strategies, 111
Orman, Suze, 62
Orwell, George, 11, 22, 38, 48, 68, 84–5, 94, 95, 113, 123, 126, 161, 163–4
Osborne, David, 83
Outfoxed, 110
Ozick, Cynthia, 159

Pacifica Radio, 57, 61
Paine, Thomas, 217–18
Palin, Sarah, 94, 111, 119, 132, 154
Perry, William, 171
Phillips Foundation, 111
Phillips, Tim, 98
Phillips, William, 159
Pinsker, Sanford, 152, 162
Plame, Valerie, 135
Podesta, John, 102
Podhoretz, Norman, 23–4, 50, 119–27, 131–6, 140, 151, 230
political correctness, 1, 11, 15–17, 54, 76, 81, 87, 119, 121, 127, 143, 153, 160–2, 165–6, 203–5, 212, 234–5
Powell, Lewis F., 79, 95, 129
power groups, 4
Powerline blog, 107
Public Broadcasting Service (PBS), 61–3, 83, 110, 151, 234
Public Interest, 56, 128, 129–30, 134

Public Interest Research Groups (PIRGs), 85–6
Putnam, Robert, 48–9

Qaddafi, Moammar, 24
Quayle, Dan, 110, 124, 134–5

Rank, Hugh, 5
Ravelstein (Bellow), 138–40
Reagan, Ronald, 46, 57–8, 65, 87, 91, 122, 124–5, 130, 133–4, 136, 138, 149, 177–80, 185, 194, 197, 203, 206, 217, 241–2n. 4
Reed, Adolph, 187–94, 198
Reed, Ralph, 146
Reich, Robert, 102–3
Remnick, David, 110
restricted code (RC), 37–8
Reuters, 9–10, 115
Rich, Frank, 62
right-wing deconstruction, 76, 82–3, 95–118
Rise of the Counter-Establishment, The (Blumenthal), 129
Robertson, Pat, 127–8, 147, 241n. 2
Rove, Karl, 82–3, 86, 93, 148
Rumsfeld, Donald, 124, 135
Ruskin, John, 17

Salmon, Felix, 10
Sanders, Bernie, 55, 187
Santorum, Rick, 88, 154, 165, 189
Sartre, Jean-Paul, 123, 225
Savimbi, Jonas, 91–2
Scaife Foundation, 79, 116, 146–9, 240n. 1
Scaife, Richard Mellon, 81, 101, 114
Scheuer, Jeffrey, 48
Scheunemann, Randy, 111
Schultz, Ed, 102
Semantic Calculator, 5–7, 10, 85, 108, 110, 239n. 1

Service Employees International Union (SEIU), 115–16, 118
Sharpton, Al, 48
Shaw, Peter, 100
Shields, Mark, 63
Simon, William, 81, 101, 137, 144, 149
Smith, Adam, 19
Smith, Preston H., 188
Smith-Richardson foundation, 149, 151
Social Security, 21, 58, 177, 182–3
Sokal, Alan, 167
Soley, Lawrence, 196
Somberg, Iris, 114–17
Somin, Ilya, 106
Soros, George, 9–11, 44, 77, 94, 98, 101, 104–6, 109, 111–18
Stahl, Leslie, 25
Steinberg, Jacques, 204
Steinfels, Peter, 129
Stiles, Ezra, 217
Stone, Roger, 82
Strauss, Leo, 19, 46, 99, 138, 140, 230
Strauss-Kahn, Dominique, 59
Sullivan, Andrew, 46
Sunstein, Cass, 102–3
Suskind, Ron, 82
Swift Boat controversy, 48
Swift, Jonathan, 1, 95, 213, 221, 223, 226–8

Tainted Truth (Crossen), 161
talk radio, 28, 48, 50, 81, 114, 132, 202
Talking Points Memo blog, 111
Tanenhaus, Sam, 46, 62, 203
Tea Party, 110, 112, 114–16, 119, 132, 139, 143, 240n. 1, 241n. 3
  Koch brothers and, 10, 14, 104–5, 108
  mimicry and, 97–8
  populism and, 97, 100
  rise of, 97

Telling the Truth (Cheney), 75–6, 82, 144, 160–2, 165–6, 176, 233
terrorism, 7, 17, 43–4, 70, 91, 153, 178, 184
Thatcher, Margaret, 57–8, 138
They Knew They Were Right (Heilbrunn), 24, 135, 138
Think Progress blog, 107, 111
Thomas, Clarence, 2, 81, 105, 110, 136
Thoreau, Henry David, 29, 67, 214, 220
Thurber, James, 121
Tides Center, 9, 115–16
Tomlinson, Kenneth, 63
Toqueville, Alexis de, 69
Trilling, Diana, 120
Trotsky, Leon, 67, 69, 96, 120
Trouble with Diversity, The (Michaels), 71
Twain, Mark, 67–8, 211, 223–4, 226, 228–9

Up from Conservatism (Lind), 80, 127, 206

Vedder, Richard, 193–208
Venable, Peggy, 108
Volokh Conspiracy, 106–7

Walker, Scott, 58, 106, 240n. 2
Wall Street Journal, 41, 67, 91, 110, 119, 130, 138, 145, 161, 173, 195, 197, 205

Warren, Elizabeth, 103
Warshow, Robert, 68–70
Watergate scandal, 76, 79, 81, 92, 129, 242n. 4
Weekly Standard, 41, 78, 94, 97, 107, 110–11, 126, 134–6, 140, 156, 173
Wellstone, Paul, 55
West, Allen, 18–19
West, Cornel, 147–8
Westin, Drew, 39
What Liberal Media (Alterman), 79
Whitman, Walt, 67, 209, 220
Why We Fight (Bennett), 153, 210–12, 214–16
Will, George, 160
Williams, Walter, 114
Wilson, James Q., 128, 132
Wilson, Joe, 135
Wilson, John K., 166
Wincroft, Michael, 90
Winthrop, John, 32, 216–17, 219
Woessner, Matthew S., 104
Wolfowitz, Paul, 135, 138–9
Wood, Peter, 145, 148–50, 154–6, 164–6
Woolf, Virginia, 214, 223, 225
Wrecking Crew, The (Frank), 85, 89–91, 130, 205

Zinn, Howard, 153, 212
Zywicki, Todd, 107, 109

GPSR Compliance

The European Union's (EU) General Product Safety Regulation (GPSR) is a set of rules that requires consumer products to be safe and our obligations to ensure this.

If you have any concerns about our products, you can contact us on

ProductSafety@springernature.com

In case Publisher is established outside the EU, the EU authorized representative is:

Springer Nature Customer Service Center GmbH
Europaplatz 3
69115 Heidelberg, Germany

www.ingramcontent.com/pod-product-compliance
Lightning Source LLC
LaVergne TN
LVHW051914060526
838200LV00004B/145